Fifth Edition

NorthStar 3

Listening & Speaking

Authors:	Helen Solórzano
	Jennifer P. L. Schmidt
Series Editors:	Frances Boyd
	Carol Numrich

NorthStar: Listening & Speaking Level 3, Fifth Edition

Pearson Education, 221 River St, Hoboken, NJ 07030

Staff credits: The people who made up the *NorthStar: Listening & Speaking Level 3, Fifth Edition* team, representing content creation, design, manufacturing, marketing, multimedia, project management, publishing, rights management, and testing, are Pietro Alongi, Stephanie Callahan, Gina DiLillo, Tracey Cataldo, Dave Dickey, Warren Fishbach, Sarah Hand, Lucy Hart, Gosia Jaros-White, Stefan Machura, Linda Moser, Dana Pinter, Karen Quinn, Katarzyna Starzynska - Kosciuszko, Paula Van Ells, Claire Van Poperin, Joseph Vella, Peter West, Autumn Westphal, Natalia Zaremba, and Marcin Zimny.

Project consultant: Debbie Sistino
Text composition: ElectraGraphics, Inc.
Development editing: Sarah Wales-McGrath
Cover design: Studio Montage

Library of Congress Cataloging-in-Publication Data

A Catalog record for the print edition is available from the Library of Congress.

Printed in the United States of America

ISBN-13: 978-0-13-522703-9 (Student Book with Digital Resources)
ISBN-10: 0-13-522703-8 (Student Book with Digital Resources)

ISBN-13: 978-0-13-522695-7 (Student Book with MyEnglishLab Online Workbook and Resources)
ISBN-10: 0-13-522695-3 (Student Book with MyEnglishLab Online Workbook and Resources)

11 2022

CONTENTS

WELCOME TO NORTHSTAR

A Letter from the Series Editors

We welcome you to the 5th edition of *NorthStar Listening & Speaking Level 3*.

Engaging content, integrated skills, and critical thinking continue to be the touchstones of the series. For more than 20 years *NorthStar* has engaged and motivated students through contemporary, authentic topics. Our online component builds on the last edition by offering new and updated activities.

Since its first edition, *NorthStar* has been rigorous in its approach to critical thinking by systematically engaging students in tasks and activities that prepare them to move into high-level academic courses. The cognitive domains of Bloom's taxonomy provide the foundation for the critical thinking activities. Students develop the skills of analysis and evaluation and the ability to synthesize and summarize information from multiple sources. The capstone of each unit, the final writing or speaking task, supports students in the application of all academic, critical thinking, and language skills that are the focus of unit.

The new edition introduces additional academic skills for 21st century success: note-taking and presentation skills. There is also a focus on learning outcomes based on the Global Scale of English (GSE), an emphasis on the application of skills, and a new visual design. These refinements are our response to research in the field of language learning in addition to feedback from educators who have taught from our previous editions.

NorthStar has pioneered and perfected the blending of academic content and academic skills in an English Language series. Read on for a comprehensive overview of this new edition. As you and your students explore *NorthStar*, we wish you a great journey.

Carol Numrich and Frances Boyd, the editors

New for the FIFTH EDITION

New and Updated Themes

The new edition features one new theme per level (i.e., one new unit per book), with updated content and skills throughout the series. Current and thought-provoking topics presented in a variety of genres promote intellectual stimulation. The real-world-inspired content engages students, links them to language use outside the classroom, and encourages personal expression and critical thinking.

Learning Outcomes and Assessments

All unit skills, vocabulary, and grammar points are connected to GSE objectives to ensure effective progression of learning throughout the series. Learning outcomes are present at the opening and closing of each unit to clearly mark what is covered in the unit and encourage both pre- and post-unit self-reflection. A variety of assessment tools, including online diagnostic, formative, and summative assessments and a flexible gradebook aligned with clearly identified unit learning outcomes, allow teachers to individualize instruction and track student progress.

Note-Taking as a Skill in Every Unit

Grounded in the foundations of the Cornell Method of note-taking, the new note-taking practice is structured to allow students to reflect on and organize their notes, focusing on the most important points. Students are instructed, throughout the unit, on the most effective way to apply their notes to a classroom task, as well as encouraged to analyze and reflect on their growing note-taking skills.

Explicit Skill Instruction and Fully-Integrated Practice

Concise presentations and targeted practice in print and online prepare students for academic success. Language skills are highlighted in each unit, providing students with multiple, systematic exposures to language forms and structures in a variety of contexts. Academic and language skills in each unit are applied clearly and deliberately in the culminating writing or presentation task.

Scaffolded Critical Thinking

Activities within the unit are structured to follow the stages of Bloom's taxonomy from *remember* to *create*. The use of APPLY throughout the unit highlights culminating activities that allow students to use the skills being practiced in a free and authentic manner. Sections that are focused on developing critical thinking are marked with 🔍 to highlight their critical focus.

Explicit Focus on the Academic Word List

AWL words are highlighted at the end of the unit and in a master list at the end of the book.

The Pearson Practice English App

The **Pearson Practice English App** allows students on the go to complete vocabulary and grammar activities, listen to audio, and watch video.

ExamView

ExamView Test Generator allows teachers to customize assessments by reordering or editing existing questions, selecting test items from a bank, or writing new questions.

MyEnglishLab

New and revised online supplementary practice maps to the updates in the student book for this edition.

THE NORTHSTAR UNIT

1 FOCUS ON THE TOPIC

Each unit begins with an eye-catching unit opener spread that draws students into the topic. The learning outcomes are written in simple, student-friendly language to allow for self-assessment. Focus on the Topic questions connect to the unit theme and get students to think critically by making inferences and predicting the content of the unit.

UNIT **1**

A Test of Endurance

1 FOCUS ON THE TOPIC

1. Endurance is the ability to do something difficult or stressful over a long period of time. Look at the photo. What is the man doing? Does this require endurance? Why or why not?

2. What other sports require endurance? Why do people choose to participate in these kinds of sports?

LEARNING OUTCOMES

> Infer implied meaning from context
> Take notes on main ideas
> Recognize and understand signal words

> Use reflexive and reciprocal pronouns
> Pronounce expressions with *other*
> Ask for and express opinions

Go to **MyEnglishLab** to check what you know.

2 UNIT 1

A Test of Endurance **3**

MyEnglishLab

The "Check What You Know" pre-unit diagnostic checklist provides a short self-assessment based on each unit's GSE-aligned learning outcomes to support the students in building an awareness of their own skill levels and to enable teachers to target instruction to their students' specific needs.

2 FOCUS ON LISTENING

A vocabulary exercise introduces words that appear in the listenings, encourages students to guess the meanings of the words from context, and connects to the theme presented in the final speaking task.

Go to MyEnglishLab lines indicate when additional practice is available online.

Note-taking practice on main ideas and details appears in every unit.

Two contrasting listenings on a contemporary topic are presented in every unit.

Use Your Notes boxes remind students to use their notes to complete exercises that support language, academic skills, production and critical thinking.

Every unit focuses on noting main ideas and details and features an additional note-taking skill applicable to the listenings. Activities are designed to support students in successfully completing the final speaking tasks.

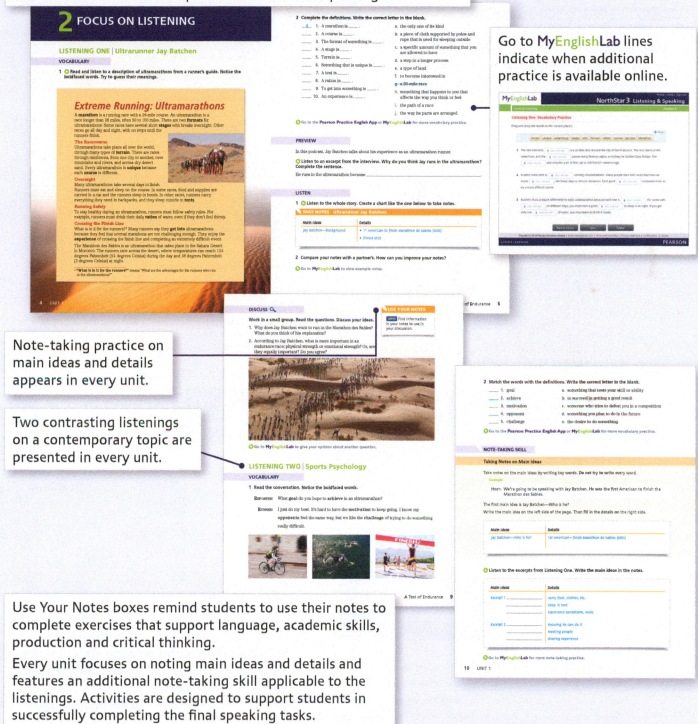

EXPLICIT SKILL INSTRUCTION AND PRACTICE

Step-by-step instructions and practice guide students to move beyond the literal meaning of the listenings. 🔍 highlights activities that help build critical thinking skills.

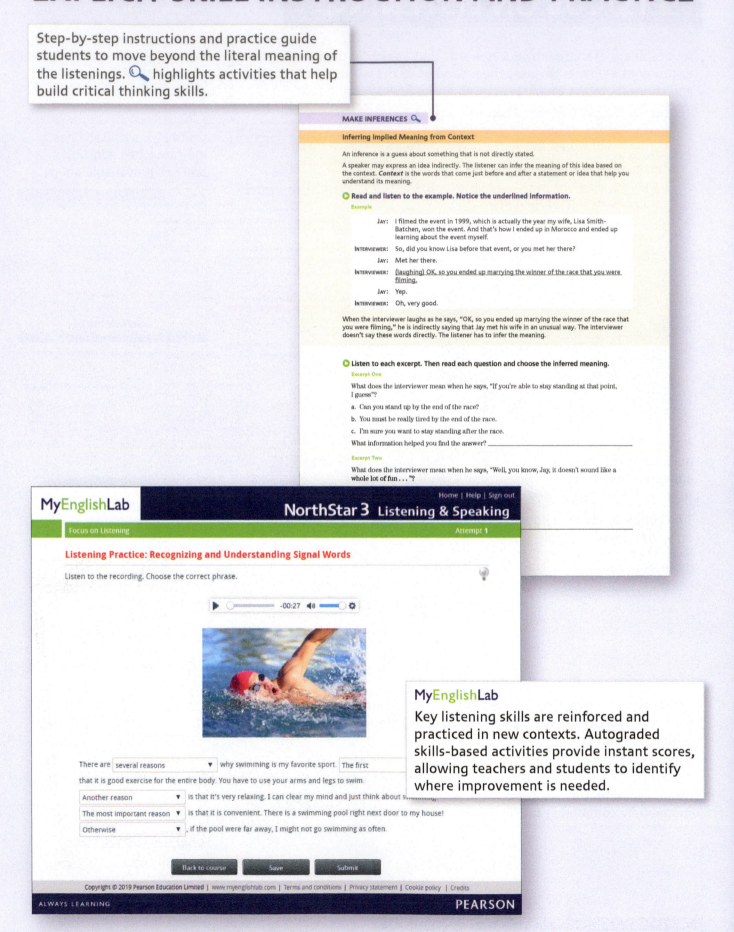

MAKE INFERENCES 🔍

Inferring Implied Meaning from Context

An inference is a guess about something that is not directly stated.

A speaker may express an idea indirectly. The listener can infer the meaning of this idea based on the context. *Context* is the words that come just before and after a statement or idea that help you understand its meaning.

▶ **Read and listen to the example. Notice the underlined information.**

Example

JAY: I filmed the event in 1999, which is actually the year my wife, Lisa Smith-Batchen, won the event. And that's how I ended up in Morocco and ended up learning about the event myself.

INTERVIEWER: So, did you know Lisa before that event, or you met her there?

JAY: Met her there.

INTERVIEWER: (laughing) OK, so you ended up marrying the winner of the race that you were filming.

JAY: Yep.

INTERVIEWER: Oh, very good.

When the interviewer laughs as he says, "OK, so you ended up marrying the winner of the race that you were filming," he is indirectly saying that Jay met his wife in an unusual way. The interviewer doesn't say these words directly. The listener has to infer the meaning.

▶ **Listen to each excerpt. Then read each question and choose the inferred meaning.**

Excerpt One

What does the interviewer mean when he says, "If you're able to stay standing at that point, I guess"?

a. Can you stand up by the end of the race?

b. You must be really tired by the end of the race.

c. I'm sure you want to stay standing after the race.

What information helped you find the answer? _____

Excerpt Two

What does the interviewer mean when he says, "Well, you know, Jay, it doesn't sound like a whole lot of fun . . . "?

MyEnglishLab

Home | Help | Sign out

NorthStar 3 Listening & Speaking

Focus on Listening

Attempt **1**

Listening Practice: Recognizing and Understanding Signal Words

Listen to the recording. Choose the correct phrase.

▶ ───────── -00:27 🔊 ▬▬▬● ⚙

There are [several reasons ▼] why swimming is my favorite sport. [The first] that it is good exercise for the entire body. You have to use your arms and legs to swim.

[Another reason ▼] is that it's very relaxing. I can clear my mind and just think about swimming.

[The most important reason ▼] is that it is convenient. There is a swimming pool right next door to my house!

[Otherwise ▼], if the pool were far away, I might not go swimming as often.

[Back to course] [Save] [Submit]

Copyright © 2019 Pearson Education Limited | www.myenglishlab.com | Terms and conditions | Privacy statement | Cookie policy | Credits

ALWAYS LEARNING

PEARSON

MyEnglishLab

Key listening skills are reinforced and practiced in new contexts. Autograded skills-based activities provide instant scores, allowing teachers and students to identify where improvement is needed.

Productive vocabulary targeted in the unit is reviewed, expanded upon, and used creatively.

Grammar presentations focus on skills that are used in the listenings and applied in the final speaking task. A concise grammar skills box serves as a reference point for students throughout the unit and beyond.

MyEnglishLab
Auto-graded vocabulary and grammar practice activities reinforce meaning, form, and function. Meaningful and instant feedback guides students to self-correct and provides students and teachers with essential information to monitor progress.

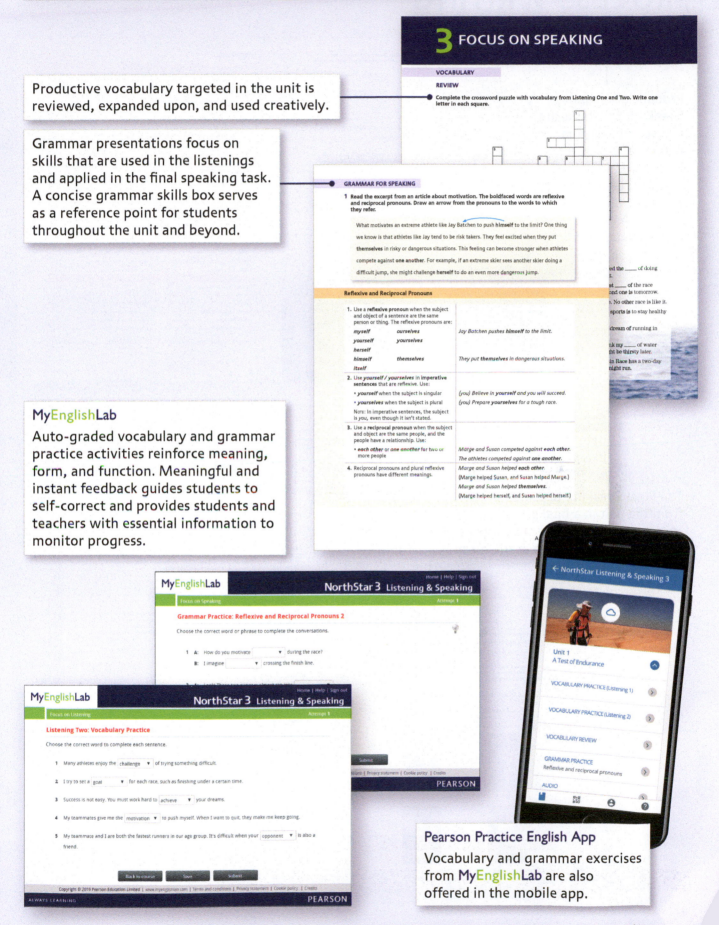

Pearson Practice English App
Vocabulary and grammar exercises from MyEnglishLab are also offered in the mobile app.

The NorthStar Uni

A TASK-BASED APPROACH TO PROCESS WRITING

Pronunciation and Speaking Skill tasks are focused on learning outcomes which are later used in the final speaking task, helping students develop their professional and academic public speaking skills.

APPLY calls out activities that get students to use new skills in a productive task.

The Final Speaking task incorporates themes and skills from the unit in a final productive task that engages students in a variety of public speaking genres, from interactive role-plays to academic presentations.

(Sample page 20–21)

2 Fill in the blanks with expressions from Exercise One. Check your answers with a partner's. Then practice reading the sentences to your partner. Join words together and pronounce the "th" in *other* carefully.

1. _____ my two roommates and I go for a long walk.

2. _____ we were walking in the park behind a very old couple.

3. They were holding hands and talking to _____ .

4. The woman slipped on _____ and fell.

5. _____ people were passing by, but they didn't do anything.

6. We ran to help them, and when we saw them, we realized we all knew _____ . They live in our building.

3 Work with a partner. Create five short conversations by drawing lines to match Student A's part with Student B's part. Then practice the conversations. The underlined words are idioms with *other*. Do you know what they mean?

Student A

1. Sharon's sons are at each other's throats all the time. She doesn't know what to do.

2. This has been one of the worst days of my life.

3. What's the difference between a rainproof tent and a rain-resistant tent?

4. The lecture was really hard. I don't think I understood anything the professor said.

5. The elderly couple that I helped in the park last week brought me a cake.

Student B

a. Nothing, as far as I'm concerned—six of one, half a dozen of another.

b. Me neither—the material went in one ear and out the other.

c. I guess it's true that one good turn deserves another.

d. She might not be able to do anything. My brother and I fought with each other until he went away to school.

e. Don't give up. Tomorrow's another day.

20   UNIT 1

SPEAKING SKILL

Asking for and Expressing Opinions

To keep a discussion going (and to make it interesting), it is important for everyone to share ideas. To do this, express your opinion, ask for other people's opinions, and agree or disagree with other people's opinions.

▶ Read and listen to the example. Notice the language used to ask for and express opinions.

Example

SUNG LEE: Look at that guy. **What do you think** he's doing?

AHMED: **It looks like** he's running forward and then backward. Maybe he's training for a race.

ELI: **I'm not sure.** See how slowly he's going? He can't be a racer.

AHMED: **You're right.** He is pretty slow. **I think** he's probably just doing that for fun.

To Ask for an Opinion

Use *What do you think (about) . . . ?* to ask for a general opinion.	*What do you think about extreme sports?*
Use *Do you think (that . . .) / Do you agree (with) . . . ?* to ask about specific points.	*Do you think extreme sports are dangerous?* *Do you agree (with Eli) that extreme sports are dangerous?*

To Express an Opinion

Use *I think* to sound stronger and more certain.	*I think Bridgit won the race.*
Use *I'm pretty sure* or *It seems like* to sound less certain and / or more polite.	*I'm pretty sure Bridgit won the race.* *It seems like Bridgit won the race.*

To Agree

To agree with someone, use:	
I think . . .	*I think Ron is the best runner.*
Yeah / Yes. . . . (I think) You're right.	*Yeah, he is. I think you're right.*
I agree (with name).	*I agree (with Michelle).*

To Disagree

To disagree with someone, use:

Indirect:	Direct:
I don't know.	*I don't think so.*
I'm not sure about that.	*I disagree (with name).*
I don't know. Jack is a great runner, too.	*I don't think so. Jack is better.*
I'm not sure about that. Jack is a great runner, too.	*I disagree (with Kyoko). Jack is better.*
Indirect disagreement sounds more polite.	Direct disagreement sounds stronger and can be less polite.

A Test of Endurance   21

(Sample page 22–23)

indirect and polite?" Underline the words and phrases that helped you decide.

Conversation 1

A: I think extreme sports are the most dangerous sports.

B: I don't think so. All sports can be dangerous.

C: You're right. I think that athletes hurt themselves in all sports, not just extreme sports.

Conversation 2

A: I think extreme sports are the most dangerous sports.

B: I'm not sure about that. It seems to me that all sports can be dangerous.

C: Yeah. I'm pretty sure that athletes hurt themselves in all sports, not just extreme sports.

2 Work in a group of three. Look at the pictures of the athletes. Discuss how each athlete is feeling. Make sure everyone in the group gets to express an opinion. Under each picture write the adjective(s) that you think best describe(s) the athlete's feelings.

Example

STUDENT 1: In Picture A, I think the guy on the left is angry. Look at his face. Doesn't he look angry?

STUDENT 2: I don't know. See how he's looking at the ball? It just seems like he's trying to get it. What do you think, Maria?

STUDENT 3: I agree with Roberto. He looks angry to me.

A   *angry*   B

C   D

22   UNIT 1

---

3 APPLY Work with a new group of three. Compare the adjectives that you wrote with your first group. Do you agree with your classmates' lists of adjectives? Work together to choose the three best adjectives for each picture. Then share with the class.

▶ Go to **MyEnglishLab** for more skill practice and to check what you learned.

FINAL SPEAKING TASK: Group Discussion 🔍 APPLY

An **aphorism** is a short, wise, and inspiring expression that is easy to remember. It expresses an idea or belief in a new and interesting way. Athletes sometimes use aphorisms to help motivate themselves to keep going when they are training for, or participating in, a challenging athletic event. For example, some people put up posters with aphorisms on the walls of their homes or place them on their computers' screen savers so they can read them often and feel inspired.

In this activity, you will work in a group to discuss aphorisms about motivation, write one of your own, and explain its meaning.

PREPARE

Work in a small group. Read and discuss the aphorisms written by athletes.

- What are the athletes saying about themselves and their motivation for running? Explain.
- Which aphorism do you like best? Why?
- Athletes aren't the only people who use aphorisms to encourage motivation. Think of other situations in which aphorisms could be useful.

Quotes on Motivation

1. Motivation is what gets you started. Habit is what keeps you going.
   Jim Ryun (Olympic runner and politician)

2. When I run a long race, I get to meet some new people—including myself.
   Anonymous

3. The fear of not finishing is often greater than the fear of pain.
   Laurie Dexter (endurance runner and Anglican minister)

4. The heart controls the mind, and the mind controls the body.
   Jim Lampley (sportscaster)

5. Find the joy in the journey—the finish line will come soon enough.
   Anonymous

6. The glory of sport comes from dedication, determination, and desire.
   Jackie Joyner-Kersee (Olympic athlete)

A Test of Endurance   23

---

ix

: NorthStar Unit

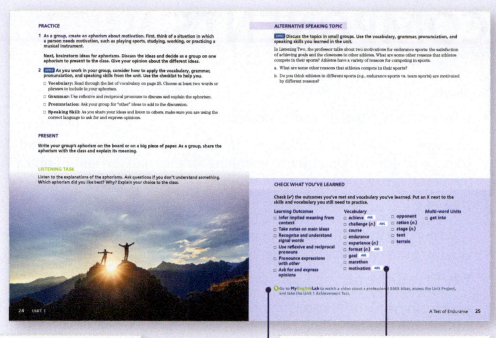

At the end of the unit, students are directed to MyEnglishLab to watch a video connected to the theme, access the Unit Project, and take the Unit Achievement Test.

Academic Word List words are highlighted with **AWL** at the end of the unit.

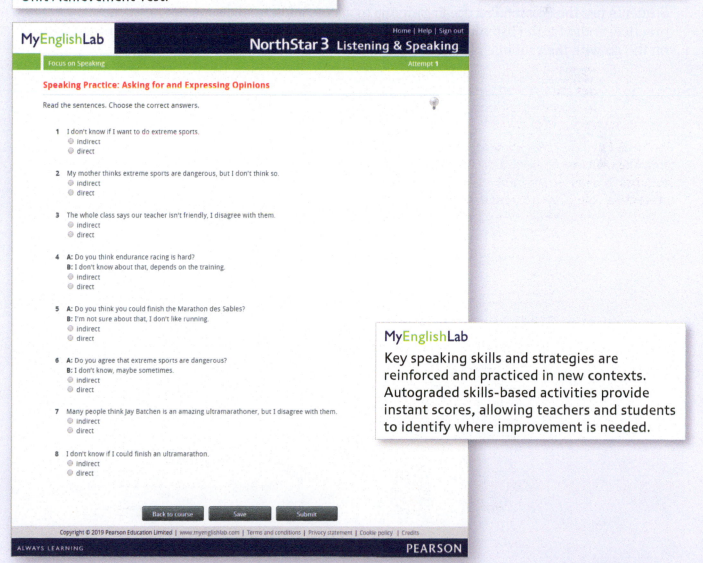

MyEnglishLab

Key speaking skills and strategies are reinforced and practiced in new contexts. Autograded skills-based activities provide instant scores, allowing teachers and students to identify where improvement is needed.

COMPONENTS

Students can access the following resources on the Pearson English Portal.

- **Classroom Audio and Videos**

  Classroom audio (the readings for the Reading & Writing strand and the listenings and exercises with audio for the Listening & Speaking strand) and the end-of-unit videos are available on the portal.

- **Etext**

  Offering maximum flexibility in order to meet the individual needs of each student, the digital version of the student book can be used across multiple platforms and devices.

- **MyEnglishLab**

  MyEnglishLab offers students access to additional practice online in the form of both auto-graded and teacher-graded activities. Auto-graded activities support and build on the academic and language skills presented and practiced in the student book. Teacher-graded activities include speaking and writing.

- **Pearson Practice English App**

  Students use the **Pearson Practice English App** to access additional grammar and vocabulary practice, audio for the listenings and readings from the student books, and the end-of-unit videos on the go with their mobile phone.

INNOVATIVE TEACHING TOOLS

With instant access to a wide range of online content and diagnostic tools, teachers can customize learning environments to meet the needs of every student. Digital resources, all available on the Pearson English Portal, include **MyEnglishLab** and ExamView.

Using MyEnglishLab, *NorthStar* teachers can

Deliver rich online content to engage and motivate students, including

- student audio to support listening and speaking skills, in addition to audio versions of all readings.
- engaging, authentic video clips tied to the unit themes.
- opportunities for written and recorded reactions to be submitted by students.

Use diagnostic reports to

- view student scores by unit, skill, and activity.
- monitor student progress on any activity or test as often as needed.
- analyze class data to determine steps for remediation and support.

Access Teacher Resources, including

- unit teaching notes and answer keys.
- downloadable diagnostic, achievement and placement tests, as well as unit checkpoints.
- printable resources including lesson planners, videoscripts, and video activities.
- classroom audio.

Using ExamView, teachers can customize Achievement Tests by

- reordering test questions.
- editing questions.
- selecting questions from a bank.
- writing their own questions.

SCOPE AND SEQUENCE

	1 A Test of Endurance Pages: 2–25 Listening 1: Ultrarunner Jay Batchen Listening 2: Sports Psychology	**2 Avoiding Identity Theft** Pages: 26–47 Listening 1: Lily's Story Listening 2: Public Service Announcements
Inference	Inferring implied meaning from context	Inferring emotion from intonation
Note-Taking	Taking notes on main ideas	Taking notes with lists
Listening	Recognizing and understanding signal words	Recognizing rhetorical questions
Grammar	Reflexive and reciprocal pronouns	Modals of advice
Pronunciation	Pronouncing expressions with *other*	Recognizing and pronouncing compound nouns
Speaking	Asking for and expressing opinions	Keeping a conversation going
Final Speaking Task	Group discussion: creating an aphorism	Role-play: identity theft
Video	A professional BMX biker	Identity theft

Assessments	Pre-Unit Diagnostic:
	   Check What You Know
	Checkpoint 1
	Checkpoint 2
	Unit Achievement Test
		Pre-Unit Diagnostic:
		   Check What You Know
		Checkpoint 1
		Checkpoint 2
		Unit Achievement Test

Unit Project	Research a sport, find a relevant picture, and share the information with the class.	Choose a topic related to either types of identify theft of methods for stealing information. Then research the topic or interview a victim of identity theft, and share the information with the class.

3 Why Explore Space?	4 Words That Persuade
Pages: 48–71 Listening 1: The Space Junk Problem Listening 2: The View from Space	Pages: 72–95 Listening 1: Corporate Euphemisms Listening 2: House Hunting
Inferring factual information from context	Inferring a speaker's purpose
Taking notes with abbreviations	Taking notes with columns
Recognizing and understanding pronoun references	Recognizing and understanding speaker emphasis
Present perfect and simple past	Superlative adjectives
Pronouncing -ed endings	Highlighting important information with word stress
Using eye contact in a presentation	Using appropriate volume and pacing in a presentation
Oral presentation: pros and cons of space exploration	Oral presentation: create and perform ads
Space	Language

Pre-Unit Diagnostic:
   Check What You Know
Checkpoint 1
Checkpoint 2
Unit Achievement Test
	Pre-Unit Diagnostic:
	   Check What You Know
	Checkpoint 1
	Checkpoint 2
	Unit Achievement Test

Research a space project, including its goals and plans to achieve those goals, and present the information to the class.	Analyze advertisements to understand the persuasive techniques used to sell products.

SCOPE AND SEQUENCE

	5 Follow Your Passion	6 Culture and Commerce
	Pages: 96–117 Listening 1: Changing Career Paths Listening 2: Finding Your Passion	Pages: 118–141 Listening 1: Tourist Attraction or Human Zoo? Listening 2: Town Hall Meeting in Cape Cod
Inference	Inferring feelings from context	Inferring opinion from word choice
Note-Taking	Taking notes on details	Taking notes with an outline
Listening	Recognizing and understanding reduced speech	Recognizing and understanding opinions
Grammar	Gerunds	*Will* and *if* clauses
Pronunciation	Using thought groups	Pronouncing the vowel /o/
Speaking	Using an introduction in a presentation	Making suggestions
Final Speaking Task	Oral presentation: my personal strengths, interests, and work preferences	Interactive poster presentation: a tourist attraction and its impacts
Video	Careers	Ecotourism

Assessments	Pre-Unit Diagnostic:
	    Check What You Know
	Checkpoint 1
	Checkpoint 2
	Unit Achievement Test
		Pre-Unit Diagnostic:
		    Check What You Know
		Checkpoint 1
		Checkpoint 2
		Unit Achievement Test

Unit Project	Interview a person about his / her current job, research to find more about the job, write a summary of the interview, and present all relevant findings to the class.	Research a service vacation, prepare a short report, then present it to the class.

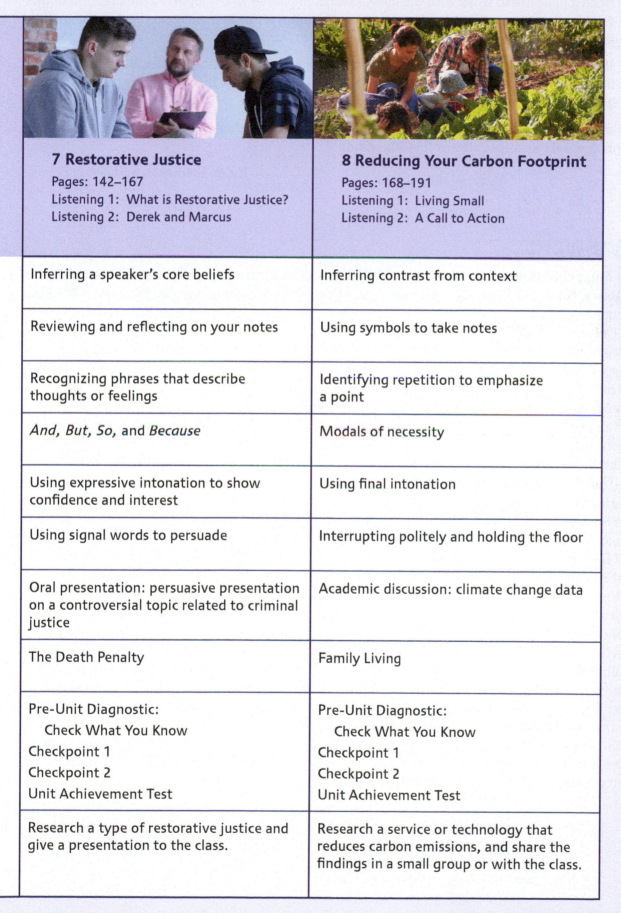

7 Restorative Justice	8 Reducing Your Carbon Footprint
Pages: 142–167 Listening 1: What is Restorative Justice? Listening 2: Derek and Marcus	Pages: 168–191 Listening 1: Living Small Listening 2: A Call to Action
Inferring a speaker's core beliefs	Inferring contrast from context
Reviewing and reflecting on your notes	Using symbols to take notes
Recognizing phrases that describe thoughts or feelings	Identifying repetition to emphasize a point
And, But, So, and *Because*	Modals of necessity
Using expressive intonation to show confidence and interest	Using final intonation
Using signal words to persuade	Interrupting politely and holding the floor
Oral presentation: persuasive presentation on a controversial topic related to criminal justice	Academic discussion: climate change data
The Death Penalty	Family Living

Pre-Unit Diagnostic:
   Check What You Know
Checkpoint 1
Checkpoint 2
Unit Achievement Test
	Pre-Unit Diagnostic:
	   Check What You Know
	Checkpoint 1
	Checkpoint 2
	Unit Achievement Test

Research a type of restorative justice and give a presentation to the class.	Research a service or technology that reduces carbon emissions, and share the findings in a small group or with the class.

ACKNOWLEDGMENTS

It has been a pleasure to work with the many dedicated people who supported the creation of this book. Special thanks go to Frances Boyd and Carol Numrich for their vision and guidance and to our editorial team for their feedback and support.

Many thanks to producers Tim Borquin, Erik Michielsen and Alison Grayson for their creative and thought-provoking audio pieces and to Jay Batchen, "Lily" and Julia Brown (Peters) for sharing their stories.

And finally, we thank our husbands, Roy Solórzano and David Schmidt, for their patience and support throughout the writing of this 5th edition.

Helen Solórzano and Jenny Schmidt

REVIEWERS

Chris Antonellis, Boston University – CELOP; Gail August, Hostos; Aegina Barnes, York College; Kim Bayer, Hunter College; Mine Bellikli, Atilim University; Allison Blechman, Embassy CES; Paul Blomquist, Kaplan; Helena Botros, FLS; James Branchick, FLS; Chris Bruffee, Embassy CES; Joyce Cain University of California at Fullerton; Nese Cakli, Duzce University; Molly Cheny, University of Washington; María Cordani Tourinho Dantas, Colégio Rainha De Paz; Jason Davis, ASC English; Lindsay Donigan, Fullerton College; Mila Dragushanskaya, ASA College; Bina Dugan, BCCC; Sibel Ece Izmir, Atilim University; Érica Ferrer, Universidad del Norte; María Irma Gallegos Peláez, Universidad del Valle de México; Vera Figueira, UC Irvine; Rachel Fernandez, UC Irvine; Jeff Gano, ASA College; Emily Ellis, UC Irvine; María Genovev a Chávez Bazán, Universidad del Valle de México; Juan Garcia, FLS; Heidi Gramlich, The New England School of English; Phillip Grayson, Kaplan; Rebecca Gross, The New England School of English; Rick Guadiana, FLS; Sebnem Guzel, Tobb University; Esra Hatipoglu, Ufuk University; Brian Henry, FLS; Josephine Horna, BCCC; Judy Hu, UC Irvine; Arthur Hui, Fullerton College; Zoe Isaacson, Hunter College; Kathy Johnson, Fullerton College; Marcelo Juica, Urban College of Boston; Tom Justice, North Shore Community College; Lisa Karakas, Berkeley College; Eva Kopernacki, Embassy CES; Drew Larimore, Kaplan; Heidi Lieb, BCCC; Patricia Martins, Ibeu; Cecilia Mora Espejo, Universidad del Valle de México; Oscar Navarro University of California at Fullerton; Eva Nemtson, ASA College; Kate Nyhan, The New England School of English; Julie Oni, FLS; Willard Osman, The New England School of English; Olga Pagieva, ASA College; Manish Patel, FLS; Paige Poole, Universidad del Norte; Claudia Rebello, Ibeu; Amy Renehan, University of Washington; Lourdes Rey, Universidad del Norte; Michelle Reynolds, FLS International Boston Commons; Mary Ritter, NYU; Ellen Rosen University of California at Fullerton; Dana Saito-Stehiberger, UC Irvine; Dariusz Saczuk, ASA College; Miryam Salimov, ASA College; Minerva Santos, Hostos; Sezer Sarioz, Saint Benoit PLS; Gail Schwartz, UC Irvine; Ebru Sinar, Tobb University; Beth Soll, NYU (Columbia); Christopher Stobart, Universidad del Norte; Guliz Uludag, Ufuk University; Debra Un, NYU; Hilal Unlusu, Saint Benoit PLS; María del Carmen Viruega Trejo, Universidad del Valle de México; Reda Vural, Atilim University; Douglas Waters, Universidad del Norte; Emily Wong, UC Irvine; Leyla Yucklik, Duzce University; Jorge Zepeda Porras, Universidad del Valle de México

LEARNING OUTCOMES

> Infer implied meaning from context
> Take notes on main ideas
> Recognize and understand signal words

> Use reflexive and reciprocal pronouns
> Pronounce expressions with *other*
> Ask for and express opinions

 Go to **MyEnglishLab** to check what you know.

A Test of Endurance

1 FOCUS ON THE TOPIC

1. Endurance is the ability to do something difficult or stressful over a long period of time. Look at the photo. What is the man doing? Does this require endurance? Why or why not?

2. What other sports require endurance? Why do people choose to participate in these kinds of sports?

LISTENING ONE | Ultrarunner Jay Batchen

VOCABULARY

1 ▶ **Read and listen to a description of ultramarathons from a runner's guide. Notice the boldfaced words. Try to guess their meanings.**

Extreme Running: Ultramarathons

A **marathon** is a running race with a 26-mile course. An ultramarathon is a race longer than 26 miles, often 50 to 100 miles. There are two **formats** for ultramarathons: Some races have several short **stages** with breaks overnight. Other races go all day and night, with no stops until the runners finish.

The Racecourse

Ultramarathons take place all over the world, through many types of **terrain**. There are races through rainforests, from one city to another, over mountains and rivers, and across dry desert sand. Every ultramarathon is **unique** because each **course** is different.

Overnight

Many ultramarathons take several days to finish. Runners must eat and sleep on the course. In some races, food and supplies are carried in a car and the runners sleep in hotels. In other races, runners carry everything they need in backpacks, and they sleep outside in **tents**.

Running Safely

To stay healthy during an ultramarathon, runners must follow safety rules. For example, runners must drink their daily **ration** of water, even if they don't feel thirsty.

Crossing the Finish Line

What is in it for the runners?[1] Many runners say they **get into** ultramarathons because they feel that normal marathons are not challenging enough. They enjoy the **experience** of crossing the finish line and completing an extremely difficult event.

The Marathon des Sables is an ultramarathon that takes place in the Sahara Desert in Morocco. The runners race across the desert, where temperatures can reach 125 degrees Fahrenheit (52 degrees Celsius) during the day and 38 degrees Fahrenheit (3 degrees Celsius) at night.

---

[1] **"What is in it for the runners?"** means "What are the advantages for the runners who run in the ultramarathons?"

2 Complete the definitions. Write the correct letter in the blank.

<u>g</u>   1. A marathon is _____ .

_____ 2. A course is _____ .

_____ 3. The format of something is _____ .

_____ 4. A stage is _____ .

_____ 5. Terrain is _____ .

_____ 6. Something that is unique is _____ .

_____ 7. A tent is _____ .

_____ 8. A ration is _____ .

_____ 9. To get into something is _____ .

_____ 10. An experience is _____ .

a. the only one of its kind

b. a piece of cloth supported by poles and rope that is used for sleeping outside

c. a specific amount of something that you are allowed to have

d. a step in a longer process

e. a type of land

f. to become interested in

g. ~~a 26-mile race~~

h. something that happens to you that affects the way you think or feel

i. the path of a race

j. the way its parts are arranged

➤ Go to the **Pearson Practice English App** or **MyEnglishLab** for more vocabulary practice.

PREVIEW

In this podcast, Jay Batchen talks about his experience as an ultramarathon runner.

▶ **Listen to an excerpt from the interview. Why do you think Jay runs in the ultramarathon? Complete the sentence.**

He runs in the ultramarathon because _____ .

LISTEN

1 ▶ **Listen to the whole story. Create a chart like the one below to take notes.**

TAKE NOTES Ultrarunner Jay Batchen	
Main Ideas	**Details**
Jay Batchen—background	• 1st American to finish Marathon de Sables (MDS) • filmed MDS

2 **Compare your notes with a partner's. How can you improve your notes?**

➤ Go to **MyEnglishLab** to view example notes.

MAIN IDEAS

All the statements contain some FALSE information. Use your notes to help you determine which information is false. Cross out the parts that are untrue and write corrections. Some statements can be corrected in more than one way.

an endurance runner

1. Jay Batchen is ~~a sports reporter~~.

   or

   Tim

   ~~Jay Batchen~~ is a sports reporter.

2. Jay Batchen ran in the Marathon des Sables in 1999.

3. During the 1999 race, Jay married his wife, Lisa.

4. The Marathon des Sables has one stage.

5. Runners have to carry water with them.

6. Runners sleep outside under the stars.

7. Jay feels that the race was a terrible experience.

DETAILS

1 ▶ **Listen again and add to your notes. Choose the correct answer to complete each statement. Use your notes to help you.**

1. In 1999, Jay Batchen was _____ the race for a TV cable channel called the Discovery Channel.

   a. doing research about

   b. filming

   c. reporting on

2. Jay Batchen's future wife, Lisa, _____ the race in 1999.

   a. watched

   b. didn't finish

   c. won

3. The racecourse _____ every year, but it is always about 150 miles long.

   a. changes

   b. gets more difficult

   c. moves to a different country

4. The first three stages are all about _____ .

   a. 10 miles long

   b. 20 miles long

   c. 26 miles long

5. The fourth stage is _____ .

    a. 20 miles

    b. 50 miles

    c. a full marathon

6. The fifth stage is _____ .

    a. 20 miles long

    b. 50 miles long

    c. a full marathon

7. Runners get _____ at checkpoints every few miles.

    a. a serving of food

    b. a ration of water

    c. medical help

8. Runners sleep in tents that are _____ .

    a. small and light

    b. crowded and uncomfortable

    c. warm and quiet

9. Jay Batchen says that he experienced _____ during the race.

    a. heat, cold, and sandstorms

    b. hunger and thirst

    c. injuries to his feet

10. Jay Batchen calls the race a "life experience" because he _____ .

    a. almost didn't finish the race

    b. shared the experience with other runners

    c. ran faster than the other runners

2 With a partner, take turns summarizing your notes. Then discuss how your notes and answer in Preview helped you understand the listening.

🅝 Go to **MyEnglishLab** for more listening practice.

Inferring Implied Meaning from Context

An inference is a guess about something that is not directly stated.

A speaker may express an idea indirectly. The listener can infer the meaning of this idea based on the context. **Context** is the words that come just before and after a statement or idea that help you understand its meaning.

▶ **Read and listen to the example. Notice the underlined information.**

Example

JAY:	I filmed the event in 1999, which is actually the year my wife, Lisa Smith-Batchen, won the event. And that's how I ended up in Morocco and ended up learning about the event myself.
INTERVIEWER:	So, did you know Lisa before that event, or you met her there?
JAY:	Met her there.
INTERVIEWER:	(laughing) OK, so you ended up marrying the winner of the race that you were filming.
JAY:	Yep.
INTERVIEWER:	Oh, very good.

When the interviewer laughs as he says, "OK, so you ended up marrying the winner of the race that you were filming," he is indirectly saying that Jay met his wife in an unusual way. The interviewer doesn't say these words directly. The listener has to infer the meaning.

▶ **Listen to each excerpt. Then read each question and choose the inferred meaning.**

Excerpt One

What does the interviewer mean when he says, "If you're able to stay standing at that point, I guess"?

a. Can you stand up by the end of the race?

b. You must be really tired by the end of the race.

c. I'm sure you want to stay standing after the race.

What information helped you find the answer? _____

Excerpt Two

What does the interviewer mean when he says, "Well, you know, Jay, it doesn't sound like a whole lot of fun . . . "?

a. Most people say they didn't have fun.

b. I understand why you enjoyed the race.

c. It seems to me that it was a very difficult experience.

What information helped you find the answer? _____

Work in a small group. Read the questions. Discuss your ideas.

1. Why does Jay Batchen want to run in the Marathon des Sables? What do you think of his explanation?

2. According to Jay Batchen, what is more important in an endurance race: physical strength or emotional strength? Or, are they equally important? Do you agree?

USE YOUR NOTES

APPLY Find information in your notes to use in your discussion.

🔼 Go to **MyEnglishLab** to give your opinion about another question.

LISTENING TWO | Sports Psychology

VOCABULARY

1 Read the conversation. Notice the boldfaced words.

REPORTER: What **goal** do you hope to **achieve** in an ultramarathon?

RUNNER: I just do my best. It's hard to have the **motivation** to keep going. I know my **opponents** feel the same way, but we like the **challenge** of trying to do something really difficult.

2 Match the words with the definitions. Write the correct letter in the blank.

_____ 1. goal

_____ 2. achieve

_____ 3. motivation

_____ 4. opponent

_____ 5. challenge

a. something that tests your skill or ability

b. to succeed in getting a good result

c. someone who tries to defeat you in a competition

d. something you plan to do in the future

e. the desire to do something

Go to the **Pearson Practice English App** or **MyEnglishLab** for more vocabulary practice.

NOTE-TAKING SKILL

Taking Notes on Main Ideas

Take notes on the main ideas by writing key words. Do not try to write every word.

Example

HOST: We're going to be speaking with Jay Batchen. He was the first American to finish the Marathon des Sables.

The first main idea is Jay Batchen—Who is he?

Write the main idea on the left side of the page. Then fill in the details on the right side.

Main Ideas	Details
Jay Batchen—Who is he?	1st American—finish Marathon de Sables (MDS)

Listen to the excerpts from Listening One. Write the main ideas in the notes.

Main Ideas	Details
Excerpt 1 _____	carry food, clothes, etc.
_____	sleep in tent
_____	experience sandstorm, rocks
Excerpt 2 _____	knowing he can do it
_____	meeting people
_____	sharing experience

Go to **MyEnglishLab** for more note-taking practice.

1 ▶ **Listen to an excerpt from a sports psychology lecture. The professor talks about the motivation of endurance athletes. Create a chart like the one below to take notes. Try to use key words to take notes on main ideas.**

TAKE NOTES Sports Psychology	
Main Ideas	**Details**

2 **Choose the correct answer to complete each statement. Use your notes to help you.**

1. Endurance athletes are often _____ .

   a. very healthy

   b. high achievers

   c. professional athletes

2. They focus on achieving personal goals, not _____ .

   a. finishing the event

   b. supporting other athletes

   c. winning the race

3. They choose goals that _____ .

   a. are easy to achieve

   b. they have achieved before

   c. are a difficult challenge

4. They usually feel the other athletes are _____ .

   a. friends who they can talk to

   b. opponents they want to beat

   c. partners in the experience

5. Endurance athletes are also motivated by _____ .

   a. the strong emotions they feel while racing

   b. the prizes they win at the end of a race

   c. the exercise they get while racing

USE YOUR NOTES

Compare your notes with a partner's. How can you improve your notes next time?

1 ▶ Listen to an excerpt from the sports psychology lecture. What will the professor discuss next? What words does the speaker use to signal that information?

Recognizing and Understanding Signal Words

Signal words tell the listener what to expect next. In a lecture, the speaker uses signal words to help the listener understand what the next idea will be.

▶ **Read and listen to the example. Notice the signal words.**

Example

PROFESSOR: Well, looking at the research, *there are a couple points* that seem especially important.

The signal words tell the listener what to expect: The speaker will talk about two important points about an athlete's motivation for getting into extreme sports.

2 ▶ Listen to the excerpts. What signal words does the speaker use? Choose the correct answer.

1. To introduce point #1: the personality of endurance athletes

    a. This first

    b. One of these

    c. The most important

    d. This one

2. To introduce a contrast: focus on winning the race versus focus on personal goals

    a. Otherwise

    b. However

    c. Sometimes

    d. Instead

3. To introduce point #2: the relationship between athletes

    a. Another

    b. The next

    c. One more

    d. Finally

4. To introduce a result: the effects of the emotional high

    a. As a result

    b. Because of this

    c. Consequently

    d. So

↳ Go to **MyEnglishLab** for more skill practice.

ORGANIZE

Listening Two presents general ideas about the psychology of endurance athletes. Listening One presents an example of an endurance athlete. Read the quote from the professor and the question about Jay Batchen. Then answer the question.

USE YOUR NOTES

APPLY Review your notes from Listening One and Two. Use the information in your notes to complete the chart.

LISTENING TWO: Sports Psychology	LISTENING ONE: Ultrarunner Jay Batchen	ANSWERS TO QUESTIONS
"As a group these people tend to be high achievers. . . . They like difficult challenges and they aren't happy with goals that are easy to achieve."	1. What are some of the challenges that Jay Batchen faced?	_____ _____ _____ _____
"And when setting goals, most endurance athletes don't focus on winning the race. Instead, they have personal goals, like maybe just finishing the race is enough, or finishing with a better time than before."	2. What are Jay Batchen's personal goals?	_____ _____ _____ _____
"In general, endurance athletes don't see the other athletes in a race as opponents or people they're trying to beat. Instead, they see them as partners—partners in this unique adventure, doing something that no one else is doing."	3. How does Jay Batchen feel about the other athletes in his race?	_____ _____ _____ _____

SYNTHESIZE

Work with a partner. Do you think the professor of sports psychology would agree with the statements? Discuss your answers. Use examples from Organize to support your opinion.

1. Running in the Marathon des Sables was a difficult challenge for Jay Batchen.

2. Jay Batchen was motivated by his relationship with other athletes during the race.

3. Jay Batchen was motivated by the personal goal of winning the race.

🔺 Go to **MyEnglishLab** to check what you learned.

VOCABULARY

REVIEW

Complete the crossword puzzle with vocabulary from Listening One and Two. Write one letter in each square.

Across

2. My ____ is to compete in three races this year, but I don't know if I'll have time.

6. In the Polar Circle Run, the ____ is steep and covered with ice.

8. The New York City ____ is the largest running race in the world.

10. Jay Batchen had an important life ____ running in the Marathon des Sables.

12. I tried to beat my ____ , but he was faster and won the race.

13. The race ____ is the same length every year.

14. Many athletes ____ endurance sports because they want a challenge.

Down

1. The runners enjoyed the ____ of doing something difficult.

3. We finished the first ____ of the race today, and the second one is tomorrow.

4. This is a ____ race. No other race is like it.

5. My ____ for doing sports is to stay healthy and have fun.

7. I hope to ____ my dream of running in the Olympics.

9. I don't want to drink my ____ of water now because I might be thirsty later.

11. The Super Mountain Race has a two-day ____ with an overnight run.

EXPAND

1 **Read the conversation between a reporter and an ultra-long-distance swimmer. Notice the boldfaced words.**

REPORTER: How did it go out there?

SWIMMER: I'm OK, but it was a tough day. I fell behind the group about halfway, and that really **(1) threw me for a loop**.
I never felt the same after that.

REPORTER: How come?

SWIMMER: Well, sometimes I can **(2) be my own worst enemy**. I mean, I start thinking negative thoughts, and I don't swim well.

REPORTER: How did you keep yourself going after that?

SWIMMER: I **(3) set my heart on** finishing the race. I really wanted to do it. I got a good start, and I didn't want to **(4) blow my chance**.

REPORTER: So, after your problems today, what's your plan for tomorrow?

SWIMMER: Well, I want to enjoy myself more.

REPORTER: **(5) Easier said than done!**

SWIMMER: So true! But I know I **(6) have what it takes** to finish the race, so I just need to go out and try my best.

2 **Match the boldfaced words from Exercise One with the definitions. Write the correct number.**

_____ a. decided that I really wanted to do this

_____ b. miss my opportunity by making a mistake

_____ c. have the ability to be successful

_____ d. surprised and confused me

_____ e. behave in a way that causes problems later

_____ f. That's really difficult to do.

3 **Work with a partner. Read the conversation in Exercise One out loud. Then switch roles and read it out loud again. Try to express emotion in your voice.**

CREATE

APPLY Work with a partner. Think about an important goal you have in your life. It can be a goal in sports, school, work, or another area. Take turns asking and answering the questions. Use the words and phrases in the box and the words and vocabulary from Review and Expand in your answers.

be my own worst enemy	format	set (your) heart on
blow my chance	motivation	throw (me) for a loop
easier said than done	opponent	unique
endurance		

Questions

1. What is your goal?

2. When did you set this goal?

3. What is your motivation for setting this goal?

4. How is your experience so far?

5. What challenges make it difficult to achieve your goal?

6. Do you have what it takes? Why or why not?

Example

STUDENT A: What is your goal?

STUDENT B: My goal is to be a news reporter.

STUDENT A: When did you set this goal?

STUDENT B: I set my heart on it in high school when I worked on the school newspaper. I really enjoyed the challenge.

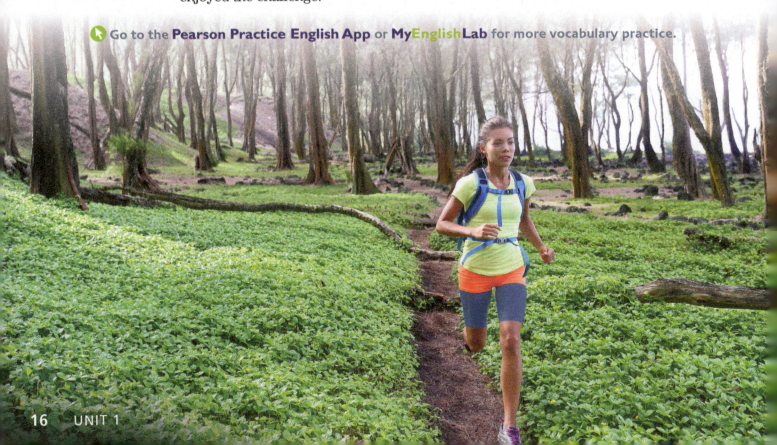

Go to the **Pearson Practice English App** or **MyEnglishLab** for more vocabulary practice.

GRAMMAR FOR SPEAKING

1 Read the excerpt from an article about motivation. The boldfaced words are reflexive and reciprocal pronouns. Draw an arrow from the pronouns to the words to which they refer.

What motivates an extreme athlete like Jay Batchen to push **himself** to the limit? One thing we know is that athletes like Jay tend to be risk takers. They feel excited when they put **themselves** in risky or dangerous situations. This feeling can become stronger when athletes compete against **one another**. For example, if an extreme skier sees another skier doing a difficult jump, she might challenge **herself** to do an even more dangerous jump.

Reflexive and Reciprocal Pronouns

1. Use a **reflexive pronoun** when the subject and object of a sentence are the same person or thing. The reflexive pronouns are: *myself* *ourselves* *yourself* *yourselves* *herself* *himself* *themselves* *itself*	*Jay Batchen pushes* **himself** *to the limit.* *They put* **themselves** *in dangerous situations.*
2. Use *yourself / yourselves* in **imperative sentences** that are reflexive. Use: • *yourself* when the subject is singular • *yourselves* when the subject is plural NOTE: In imperative sentences, the subject is *you,* even though it isn't stated.	*(you) Believe in* **yourself** *and you will succeed.* *(you) Prepare* **yourselves** *for a tough race.*
3. Use a **reciprocal pronoun** when the subject and object are the same people, and the people have a relationship. Use: • *each other* or *one another* for two or more people	*Marge and Susan competed against* **each other.** *The athletes competed against* **one another.**
4. Reciprocal pronouns and plural reflexive pronouns have different meanings.	*Marge and Susan helped* **each other.** (Marge helped Susan, and Susan helped Marge.) *Marge and Susan helped* **themselves.** (Marge helped herself, and Susan helped herself.)

2 Complete the conversation with the correct reflexive and reciprocal pronouns.

PIERRE: This is Pierre Blanc, reporting on the Extreme Alpine Bike Race in France. I'm talking to Tomas Bergetti, coach of cyclist Bridgit Jacobsen. Tomas, what does Bridgit do to prepare _____ for this race?
1.

TOMAS: Well, she pushes _____ pretty hard. She gets up at 4:00 A.M. every day to ride, and she only takes one day off a month!
2.

PIERRE: Wow! I know her brother Hans is on the same team. Do Bridgit and Hans help _____ with training?
3.

Cyclist Bridgit Jacobsen

TOMAS: Absolutely! And they're both part of a bigger team. All the athletes help _____ to set personal goals.
4.

PIERRE: You must be very proud of her big win in the race today!

TOMAS: Yes, the whole team is very happy. We're all going to reward _____ with a big dinner!
5.

PIERRE: That's great! One last question. What do you do to motivate Bridgit to keep going?

TOMAS: I always say, "Believe in _____ !" You have to have confidence if you want to win.
6.

3 Work with a partner. Imagine what Bridgit and her teammates do in these situations. Choose verbs from the box and use reflexive and reciprocal pronouns in your answers. Think of more than one answer for each situation.

be disappointed in	compete against	feel sorry for	push
blame	enjoy	imagine	support
challenge	feel proud of	make / force	tell

Example

A: What does Bridgit do if she starts feeling tired at the end of a race?

B: She **imagines herself** crossing the finish line.

What does Bridgit do if . . .

1. she starts feeling tired at the end of a race?

2. she sleeps late and misses her morning training?

3. she goes to a party to celebrate winning a race?

4. she doesn't achieve her training goals?

5. she wins a race?

What do Bridgit and her teammates do / feel . . .

6. when they are racing together?

7. if their team wins?

8. if their team loses?

🏃 Go to the **Pearson Practice English App** or **MyEnglishLab** for more grammar practice. Check what you learned in **MyEnglishLab**.

PRONUNCIATION

Pronouncing Expressions with *Other*

In speech, the word *other* joins very closely to the word in front of it or the word that follows it. In *another*, the two words (*an* and *other*) are written together. In the expression *each other*, the two words are written separately but, when spoken, they are pronounced as if they were one word.

▶ **Read and listen to the example. Notice the boldfaced words.**

Example

A: **The other** night I was talking to my roommate about starting a regular exercise program. She wants to start, too.

B: You should do it together. You'll motivate **each other**.

A: I have **another** motivation—the clothes in my closet that don't fit anymore!

1. Join *other* to the word before it. Pronounce the two words as if they were one word. Say "eachother" (ea-cho-ther).

2. Pronounce the "th" in *other* with the tip of your tongue between your teeth. Try it.

3. When *the* precedes (comes before) *other*, it is pronounced /thē/ (the e sounds like the vowel in *tree*). Use *the* pronounced /thē/ to join to *other*. Try it: /thē/ *other*.

1 ▶ **Listen to the phrases and repeat them. Then choose three phrases and say them to a partner. Join the words together closely and don't forget to pronounce *th* (/ð/) correctly. Then take turns. Listen to your partner. Say the number of each phrase you hear.**

1. the other night (recently, at night)

2. the other day (recently)

3. something or other (an idiom for *something*)

4. one another

5. each other

6. some other

7. one thing or another

8. every other day (on alternate days: Monday, Wednesday, Friday, etc.)

2 Fill in the blanks with expressions from Exercise One. Check your answers with a partner's. Then practice reading the sentences to your partner. Join words together and pronounce the "th" in *other* carefully.

1. _____ _____ _____ my two roommates and I go for a long walk.

2. _____ _____ _____ we were walking in the park behind a very old couple.

3. They were holding hands and talking to _____ _____ .

4. The woman slipped on _____ _____ _____ and fell.

5. _____ _____ people were passing by, but they didn't do anything.

6. We ran to help them, and when we saw them, we realized we all knew _____ _____ . They live in our building.

3 Work with a partner. Create five short conversations by drawing lines to match Student A's part with Student B's part. Then practice the conversations. The underlined words are idioms with *other*. Do you know what they mean?

Student A	Student B
1. Sharon's sons are <u>at each other's throats</u> all the time. She doesn't know what to do.	a. Nothing, as far as I'm concerned—<u>six of one, half a dozen of another</u>.
2. This has been one of the worst days of my life.	b. Me neither—the material went <u>in one ear and out the other</u>.
3. What's the difference between a rainproof tent and a rain-resistant tent?	c. I guess it's true that <u>one good turn deserves another</u>.
4. The lecture was really hard. I don't think I understood anything the professor said.	d. She might not be able to do anything. My brother and I fought with each other until he went away to school.
5. The elderly couple that I helped in the park last week brought me a cake.	e. Don't give up. <u>Tomorrow's another day</u>.

Asking for and Expressing Opinions

To keep a discussion going (and to make it interesting), it is important for everyone to share ideas. To do this, express your opinion, ask for other people's opinions, and agree or disagree with other people's opinions.

▶ **Read and listen to the example. Notice the language used to ask for and express opinions.**

Example

SUNG LEE: Look at that guy. **What do you think** he's doing?

AHMED: **It looks like** he's running forward and then backward. Maybe he's training for a race.

ELI: **I'm not sure.** See how slowly he's going? He can't be a racer.

AHMED: **You're right.** He is pretty slow. **I think** he's probably just doing that for fun.

To Ask for an Opinion	
Use **What do you think (about)** . . . ? to ask for a general opinion.	**What do you think** about extreme sports?
Use **Do you think (that . . .) / Do you agree (with)** . . . ? to ask about specific points.	**Do you think** extreme sports are dangerous? **Do you agree** (with Eli) that extreme sports are dangerous?

To Express an Opinion	
Use **I think** to sound stronger and more certain.	**I think** Bridgit won the race.
Use **I'm pretty sure** or **It seems like** to sound less certain and / or more polite.	**I'm pretty sure** Bridgit won the race. **It seems like** Bridgit won the race.

To Agree	
To agree with someone, use:	
I think . . .	**I think** Ron is the best runner.
Yeah / Yes. . . . (I think) You're right.	**Yeah,** he is. I think **you're right.**
I agree (with name).	**I agree** (with Michelle).

To Disagree	
To disagree with someone, use:	
Indirect:	**Direct:**
I don't know.	**I don't think so.**
I'm not sure about that.	**I disagree** (with name).
I don't know. Jack is a great runner, too.	**I don't think so.** Jack is better.
I'm not sure about that. Jack is a great runner, too.	**I disagree** (with Kyoko). Jack is better.
Indirect disagreement sounds more polite.	Direct disagreement sounds stronger and can be less polite.

1 Work with a partner. Read both conversations and discuss the differences. Take notes to answer the following questions: "Which conversation is more direct? Which is more indirect and polite?" Underline the words and phrases that helped you decide.

Conversation 1

A: I think extreme sports are the most dangerous sports.

B: I don't think so. All sports can be dangerous.

C: You're right. I think that athletes hurt themselves in all sports, not just extreme sports.

Conversation 2

A: I think that extreme sports are the most dangerous sports.

B: I'm not sure about that. It seems to me that all sports can be dangerous.

C: Yeah. I'm pretty sure that athletes hurt themselves in all sports, not just extreme sports.

2 Work in a group of three. Look at the pictures of the athletes. Discuss how each athlete is feeling. Make sure everyone in the group gets to express an opinion. Under each picture write the adjective(s) that you think best describe(s) the athlete's feelings.

Example

STUDENT 1: In Picture A, I think the guy on the left is angry. Look at his face. Doesn't he look angry?

STUDENT 2: I don't know. See how he's looking at the ball? It just seems like he's trying to get it. What do you think, Maria?

STUDENT 3: I agree with Roberto. He looks angry to me.

A

angry

B

C

D

3 [APPLY] **Work with a new group of three. Compare the adjectives that you wrote with your first group. Do you agree with your classmates' lists of adjectives? Work together to choose the three best adjectives for each picture. Then share with the class.**

◎ Go to MyEnglishLab for more skill practice and to check what you learned.

FINAL SPEAKING TASK: Group Discussion 🔍 [APPLY]

An **aphorism** is a short, wise, and inspiring expression that is easy to remember. It expresses an idea or belief in a new and interesting way. Athletes sometimes use aphorisms to help motivate themselves to keep going when they are training for, or participating in, a challenging athletic event. For example, some people put up posters with aphorisms on the walls of their homes or place them on their computers' screen savers so they can read them often and feel inspired.

In this activity, you will work in a group to discuss aphorisms about motivation, write one of your own, and explain its meaning.

PREPARE

Work in a small group. Read and discuss the aphorisms written by athletes.

- What are the athletes saying about themselves and their motivation for running? Explain.
- Which aphorism do you like best? Why?
- Athletes aren't the only people who use aphorisms to encourage motivation. Think of other situations in which aphorisms could be useful.

Quotes on Motivation

1. Motivation is what gets you started. Habit is what keeps you going.
Jim Ryun (Olympic runner and politician)

2. When I run a long race, I get to meet some new people—including myself.
Anonymous

3. The fear of not finishing is often greater than the fear of pain.
Laurie Dexter (endurance runner and Anglican minister)

4. The heart controls the mind, and the mind controls the body.
Jim Lampley (sportscaster)

5. Find the joy in the journey—the finish line will come soon enough.
Anonymous

6. The glory of sport comes from dedication, determination, and desire.
Jackie Joyner-Kersee (Olympic athlete)

PRACTICE

1 As a group, create an aphorism about motivation. First, think of a situation in which a person needs motivation, such as playing sports, studying, working, or practicing a musical instrument.

Next, brainstorm ideas for aphorisms. Discuss the ideas and decide as a group on one aphorism to present to the class. Give your opinion about the different ideas.

2 **APPLY** As you work in your group, consider how to apply the vocabulary, grammar, pronunciation, and speaking skills from the unit. Use the checklist to help you.

☐ **Vocabulary:** Read through the list of vocabulary on page 25. Choose at least two words or phrases to include in your aphorism.

☐ **Grammar:** Use reflexive and reciprocal pronouns to discuss and explain the aphorism.

☐ **Pronunciation:** Ask your group for "other" ideas to add to the discussion.

☐ **Speaking Skill:** As you share your ideas and listen to others, make sure you are using the correct language to ask for and express opinions.

PRESENT

Write your group's aphorism on the board or on a big piece of paper. As a group, share the aphorism with the class and explain its meaning.

LISTENING TASK

Listen to the explanations of the aphorisms. Ask questions if you don't understand something. Which aphorism did you like best? Why? Explain your choice to the class.

APPLY **Discuss the topics in small groups. Use the vocabulary, grammar, pronunciation, and speaking skills you learned in the unit.**

In Listening Two, the professor talks about two motivations for endurance sports: the satisfaction of achieving goals and the closeness to other athletes. What are some other reasons that athletes compete in their sports? Athletes have a variety of reasons for competing in sports.

a. What are some other reasons that athletes compete in their sports?

b. Do you think athletes in different sports (e.g., endurance sports vs. team sports) are motivated by different reasons?

CHECK WHAT YOU'VE LEARNED

Check (✔) the outcomes you've met and vocabulary you've learned. Put an X next to the skills and vocabulary you still need to practice.

Learning Outcomes
- ☐ Infer implied meaning from context
- ☐ Take notes on main ideas
- ☐ Recognize and understand signal words
- ☐ Use reflexive and reciprocal pronouns
- ☐ Pronounce expressions with *other*
- ☐ Ask for and express opinions

Vocabulary
- ☐ achieve AWL
- ☐ challenge (*n.*) AWL
- ☐ course
- ☐ endurance
- ☐ experience (*n.*)
- ☐ format (*n.*) AWL
- ☐ goal AWL
- ☐ marathon
- ☐ motivation AWL
- ☐ opponent
- ☐ ration (*n.*)
- ☐ stage (*n.*)
- ☐ tent
- ☐ terrain

Multi-word Units
- ☐ get into

🔵 Go to **MyEnglishLab** to watch a video about a professional BMX biker, access the Unit Project, and take the Unit 1 Achievement Test.

LEARNING OUTCOMES

> Infer emotion from intonation
> Take notes with lists
> Recognize rhetorical questions

> Use modals of advice
> Recognize and pronounce compound nouns
> Keep a conversation going

Go to **MyEnglishLab** to check what you know.

Avoiding Identity Theft

1 FOCUS ON THE TOPIC

1. Identity theft happens when thieves steal personal information. Identity theft is the fastest-growing crime around the world. Thieves steal more than $200 billion from victims each year. Why do you think this crime is increasing?

2. What can you do to keep your personal information safe?

LISTENING ONE | Lily's Story

VOCABULARY

1 ▶ **Thieves can use the internet in many ways to steal people's identities. Read and listen to the magazine article about phishing. Notice the boldfaced words. Try to guess their meanings.**

Identity Theft Online: Phishing

A few months ago, Henry Park received an email message from his bank. The message said there was a problem with his account. It said to follow a link[1] to the bank's website. He went to a web page that asked him to **confirm** the information about his bank account by entering his bank card number and password. "I followed the instructions and got a message that everything was fine, so I forgot about it," Mr. Park said.

A few weeks later, Mr. Park received a credit card bill for almost $10,000. There were **charges** from a department store[2] for a flat-screen TV and a diamond ring. However, Mr. Park hadn't made any of these **purchases** and had never **authorized** anyone to use his credit card.

Mr. Park immediately called the bank to **file a complaint**. Then he found out that he was the **victim** of the fastest-growing type of online fraud:[3] phishing (pronounced "fishing").

How does phishing work?

Criminals pretend to work for real companies. They send email messages to thousands of people. They trick people into going to a fraudulent website (which looks like a real site) and giving out their personal information. Then the thieves use the information to commit identity theft. In Mr. Park's case, the thief used the information to open a credit card in Mr. Park's name.

The experience has made Mr. Park more aware of the dangers of phishing. "I feel **exposed** now, like someone will do this to me again. And I'm more **paranoid**. I don't trust email anymore."

Keep yourself safe from phishing

• Be careful about email messages and websites that ask for personal information. Don't give out information that a thief could use as **proof of identification**, such as a driver's license or passport number.

• If you think you have been a victim of phishing, **deal with** it right away by calling your bank and the police. Don't wait until you start getting bills.

---

[1] **link:** a highlighted word or phrase on an internet web page or in an email message that takes you to another web page

[2] **department store:** a large store that sells many different kinds of products

[3] **fraud:** the crime of misleading people in order to get money or goods

2 Match the words with the definitions. Write the correct letter in the blank.

_____ 1. confirm

_____ 2. charge

_____ 3. purchase

_____ 4. authorize

_____ 5. file a complaint

_____ 6. victim

_____ 7. exposed

_____ 8. paranoid

_____ 9. proof of identification

_____ 10. deal with

a. believing that you cannot trust other people

b. the amount on a bill that you have to pay for something

c. in danger of being harmed

d. to say or prove that something is true

e. something that has been bought

f. documents, or papers, that show who you are

g. to do what is necessary to solve a problem

h. to give permission for something

i. someone who has been hurt by someone or something

j. make a statement in writing that something bad or illegal happened

Go to the **Pearson Practice English App** or **MyEnglishLab** for more vocabulary practice.

Lily's wallet was stolen at a restaurant. The thief used her personal information to open credit cards in her name. In this story, Lily describes what happened next.

▶ **Listen to the excerpt from Lily's story. Choose the correct answer. Discuss your answer with the class.**

This is an excerpt from the _____ of the story.

a. beginning

b. middle

c. end

LISTEN

1 ▶ **Listen to the whole story. Create a chart like the one below to take notes.**

2 **Compare your notes with a partner's. How can you improve your notes?**

◥ TAKE NOTES Lily's Story	
Main Ideas	**Details**
Lily's situation	• wallet stolen
	• victim—ID theft

↻ Go to **MyEnglishLab** to view example notes.

Choose the correct answers. Use your notes to help you.

1. How did Lily find out that her identity had been stolen?

   a. A store called her.

   b. She got a bill in the mail.

   c. The police came to her house.

2. What happened after Lily found out about the identity theft?

   a. She got bills for purchases that she didn't make.

   b. She got phone calls from a lot of different stores.

   c. She got a letter from the police.

3. How did Lily deal with the bills she received?

   a. She went to the stores and complained to the manager.

   b. She wrote letters to the stores and explained what happened.

   c. She sent the bills back to the stores without paying them.

4. How did being a victim of identity theft affect Lily?

   a. She had to borrow money to pay the bills.

   b. She doesn't use credit cards anymore.

   c. She worries that it will happen again.

DETAILS

1 ▶ **Listen again and add to your notes. Then complete the summary of Lily's story. Circle the correct words. Use your notes to help you.**

Lily got a phone call from a **(1) jewelry / department** store saying that someone with her name had purchased a **(2) computer / diamond ring**. They wanted her to authorize the purchase. Lily knew there was something wrong because she was at **(3) home / work** all day. The woman on the phone said that Lily was probably a victim of identity theft. She told Lily to **(4) file a complaint / go to the police station**.

In the next week, Lily received almost **(5) four / forty** bills from different stores, totaling about **(6) $13,000 / $30,000** in charges. She felt exposed because the thief knew her **(7) name and address / bank account number**. She didn't know what to do.

(continued on next page)

To deal with the problem, she sent **(8) the police report / her proof of identification** to all the stores and confirmed that she had not made the purchases. She stopped getting new bills after about **(9) four / eight** months.

Lily worries about becoming a victim again. She thinks that **(10) getting a credit card is too easy / paying off a credit card bill is difficult** at most department stores. She thinks everyone should be worried about identity theft.

2 **With a partner, take turns summarizing your notes. Then discuss how your notes and your answer in Preview helped you understand the listening.**

Go to MyEnglishLab for more listening practice.

MAKE INFERENCES 🔍

Inferring Emotion from Intonation

Speakers may use *intonation*, rising and falling voice, to express their feelings. The listener can infer a speaker's emotion by paying attention to intonation.

▶ **Read and listen to the examples. What is Speaker B feeling in each example? Notice how the speaker uses different intonation to express different feelings.**

Example One

A: What did the thief steal from you?

B: Five thousand dollars. A diamond ring.

Example Two

A: Somebody who has your name has purchased a diamond ring for $5,000.

B: Five thousand dollars! A diamond ring!

In Example One, the statement has falling intonation. Speaker B is not expressing emotion. She is reporting that a ring was stolen.

In Example Two, the statement has rising-falling intonation. Speaker B is expressing surprise about the purchase of a ring.

▶ **Listen to the pairs of statements (Statement A and Statement B). Identify the feeling based on the intonation. Is the speaker reporting information or is the speaker surprised? Write A or B in the blank.**

1. "I'm going to get a bill for this."

   Reporting: Statement _____

   Surprised: Statement _____

2. "We have a problem."

   Reporting: Statement _____

   Surprised: Statement _____

3. "You don't need proof of identification."

   Reporting: Statement _____

   Surprised: Statement _____

USE YOUR NOTES

APPLY Find information in your notes to use in your discussion.

DISCUSS 🔍

Work in a small group. Discuss the questions.

1. After the phishing incident, Lily became more paranoid. What did she do?

2. After hearing Lily's story, do you feel more paranoid about identity theft? Explain.

3. What did Lily do to prevent identity theft? What can you do?

▶ **Go to MyEnglishLab to give your opinion about another question.**

LISTENING TWO | Public Service Announcements

1 Read the message from a public service announcement (PSA[1]). Notice the boldfaced words.

With only a few pieces of information, it's easy for a thief to **(a) commit** identity theft. Fortunately, there are ways to **(b) protect** yourself and reduce the **(c) risk** of becoming a victim. One helpful **(d) tip** is to **(e) shred** important documents before you throw them away.

2 Match the boldfaced words from the message with the definitions. Write the correct letter in the blank.

_____ 1. a helpful piece of advice

_____ 2. the possibility that something bad may happen

_____ 3. to do something (illegal)

_____ 4. to keep someone or yourself safe from harm

_____ 5. to cut something into small pieces

Shredding papers helps reduce the risk of identity theft.

---

[1] **PSA:** PSAs are short presentations that give people helpful information. You often hear them on radio, TV, or online.

Go to **MyEnglishLab** for more vocabulary practice.

NOTE-TAKING SKILL

Taking Notes with Lists

When taking notes, make lists of similar ideas, such as a list of examples or steps in a process. This helps to keep your notes organized and easy to read.

> **Fraud Types**
> phishing
> ID theft
> credit card

> **Stop Fraud**
> call credit card co.
> report to police
> notify bank

Notice that the lists have the same kind of information. The ideas in the first list are things (nouns), and the ideas in the second list are actions (verbs).

▶ **Listen to the excerpt. You will hear about actions to deal with bills. Make a list of the actions.**

Deal with bills:

_____

_____

_____

▶ **Listen to the excerpt. List the actions that criminals take when they are phishing.**

Criminals' actions:

_____

_____

_____

▶ **Listen to the excerpt. List the actions that people can take to stay safe from phishing.**

Stay safe from phishing:

_____

_____

_____

🔾 Go to **MyEnglishLab** for more note-taking practice.

COMPREHENSION

1 ▶ **Listen to two PSAs about how to protect yourself from identity theft. Create a chart like the one below to take notes. Try to make lists in your notes when you hear examples or steps in a process.**

TAKE NOTES Public Service Announcements	
Main Ideas	**Details**

2 Check (✓) the tips you heard. Use your notes to help you.

☐ 1. Get a locked mailbox.

☐ 2. Be careful about giving out personal information.

☐ 3. Check your bank and credit card statements every month.

☐ 4. Shred important papers before throwing them away.

☐ 5. Leave your identification at home if you don't need it.

> **USE YOUR NOTES**
>
> Compare your notes with a partner's. How can you improve your notes next time?

LISTENING SKILL

1 ▶ **Listen to an excerpt from PSA one. What question does the announcer ask? What is the answer? Why do you think the speaker asks a question?**

Recognizing Rhetorical Questions

Rhetorical questions can be used to direct the listener's attention. The speaker doesn't expect an answer from the listener. Instead, a rhetorical question makes the listener pay attention to an important idea.

▶ **Read and listen to the example. Notice the rhetorical question.**

Example

ANNOUNCER: Think you're safe from identity theft? Think again.

The rhetorical question directs the listener to the idea *Don't think you are safe from identity theft.*

NOTE: The speaker uses a shortened, informal form of the question "Do you think you're safe . . . ?"

2 ▶ **Listen to PSA two. The speaker asks two rhetorical questions. What does the speaker want us to pay attention to? Write the important ideas.**

1. "Hear that sound? That's the sound of a crime being committed."

   Important idea: _____

   _____

2. "Hear that sound? That's the sound of someone protecting himself from becoming a victim of identity theft."

   Important idea: _____

   _____

🡒 Go to **MyEnglishLab** for more skill practice.

CONNECT THE LISTENINGS 🔍

ORGANIZE

> **USE YOUR NOTES**
>
> **APPLY** Review your notes from Listening One and Two. Use the information in your notes to complete the chart.

Complete the chart with the details about identity theft.

	LISTENING ONE: Lily's Story	LISTENING TWO: PSA 1
1. How do thieves steal personal information?	• _____ _____ _____ • take information from receipts	• steal your mail • _____ _____ _____ • _____ _____
2. How can people prevent identity theft?	• rip up receipts • _____ _____ _____	• _____ _____ _____ • _____ _____ _____ • shred documents before throwing them away

SYNTHESIZE

Work with a partner. One person is a victim of identity theft. The other person is a security expert. Complete the conversation using information from Organize. Read the conversation out loud. Then switch roles and repeat the conversation.

VICTIM: I don't understand how this happened. How do thieves steal personal

information?

SECURITY EXPERT: Well, there are many ways. For example, _____

Give examples. _____

_____ .

So, what do you do now to keep your personal information safe?

VICTIM: Hmm, well I _____

Give examples. _____

_____ .

SECURITY EXPERT: That's good, but it's not enough. _____

Ask a rhetorical
question. _____ ?

Give examples. _____

_____ .

 Go to **MyEnglishLab** to check what you learned.

VOCABULARY

REVIEW

A word can have a meaning that is positive (good), negative (bad), or neutral (neither good nor bad). This is called the *connotation* of a word or expression. For example:

POSITIVE	NEGATIVE	NEUTRAL
safe	fraud	department store

1 **Work with a partner. Think about how these words were used in Lily's story and in the PSAs. Complete the chart with the words from the box.**

authorize	confirm	file a complaint	protect	shred
charge	deal with	paranoid	purchase	tip
commit	exposed	proof of identification	risk	victim

2 **Compare your chart with another pair's chart. Discuss the reasons for your choices.**

EXPAND

1 Read the text messages between two friends. Notice the boldfaced words.

2 Circle the correct synonym or definition for each boldfaced word.

1. **rip off**   steal   keep

2. **clean out**   steal everything   pay

3. **turn out**   cause   result

4. **watch out for** ignore   be careful of

5. **put away**   let out of jail   put in jail

CREATE

APPLY **Work in a group of three. Play the game To Tell the Truth. Follow the steps.**

1. Think of a time when something was stolen from you. Form a group with two other students and share your story.

2. One member of your group will tell his or her *true* story to the class. The other two members will each tell a story that is not true. Decide who will tell the truth and who will lie. Each group member writes down five words or phrases from the vocabulary box or the boldfaced words and vocabulary from Review and Expand to use in his or her story.

authorize	confirm	paranoid	put away	tip
charge	deal with	proof of identification	rip off	turn out
clean out	exposed	protect	risk	victim
commit	file a complaint	purchase	shred	watch out for

3. Present your stories to the class (Remember: One story is true; the other two are false. Each story contains five words from the vocabulary box.) After each story, take questions from the class. At the end, ask the class to guess which story is true.

4. Return to your seat to listen to another group's stories.

⟲ Go to the **Pearson Practice English App** or **My**English**Lab** for more vocabulary practice.

GRAMMAR FOR SPEAKING

1 Look at the picture and read the conversation. Notice the boldfaced modals of advice.

MOTHER: You **should** be careful about posting so much personal information on social media.

DAUGHTER: What do you mean?

MOTHER: You**'d better** delete details like your birthday and address. Thieves can use them to open credit cards in your name.

DAUGHTER: Mom, you **ought to** stop worrying so much.

Modals of Advice

1. Use **should** to ask for advice.	**Should** I report this to the police?
	What **should** I do if someone steals my passport?
2. Use **should, should not,** and **ought to** to give advice. NOTE: **Ought to** is generally not used with a negative in American English.	He **should** delete that phishing email.
	You **shouldn't** post your birth date on social media.
	They **ought to** choose strong internet passwords.
3. Use **had better ('d better)** and **had better not ('d better not)** to give strong advice.	We**'d better** shred those papers.
	You**'d better not** throw those papers in the trash.

2 **Choose the correct answer to complete each statement.**

1. Nasir wants to throw away some old bank statements. He _____ shred them.

   a. should   b. ought   c. better

2. Mira's mail was stolen. She _____ better buy a locked mailbox.

   a. should   b. ought   c. had

3. Someone called Azim and asked for a donation. He _____ give out his credit card number over the phone.

   a. should   b. shouldn't   c. better not

4. Lily got a bill for charges she didn't make. She _____ to file a complaint.

   a. ought   b. should   c. had better

5. Misako got an email asking for her credit card account number. She _____ not send the information.

   a. shouldn't   b. had better   c. ought

6. Chong Li gets money from a bank machine. He _____ make sure nobody is watching him.

   a. should   b. ought not   c. ought

7. Nicola likes to share a lot of personal information on social media. She _____ not do that.

   a. better   b. should   c. ought to

8. Abraham got a passport. He _____ lose it.

   a. ought   b. should   c. had better not

3 APPLY **Work in a group of three. Use the situations below to take turns asking for and giving advice.**

Example

STUDENT A: I haven't received any mail for three days. What **should** I do?

STUDENT B: You **should** check with the post office to see whether someone is stealing your mail.

STUDENT C: If someone is stealing your mail, you **ought to** contact the police.

1. I saw someone take a letter out of my neighbor's mailbox.

2. I get phone calls every day from a man I don't know. He's trying to sell me magazines.

3. My friend shares too much personal information online.

4. I think I lost my credit card.

5. I buy things from an online company. I just saw in the news that thieves stole customer information from the company.

6. An online store sent me an email asking for my credit card number.

Go to the **Pearson Practice English App** or **MyEnglishLab** for more grammar practice. Check what you learned in **MyEnglishLab**.

PRONUNCIATION

Recognizing and Pronouncing Compound Nouns

Compound nouns (compounds) are two nouns used together to name one thing, for example, *mailbox*. In *mailbox* the two nouns are written together as one word. These compounds are easy to recognize. Other compounds, like *identity theft* and *credit card*, are written as two words. Compounds have a special pattern of stress and pitch.

Read and listen to the compounds. Repeat them.

Examples

1. **post** office
2. **credit** card
3. **identity** theft
4. **garbage** can

5. **mail**box
6. **police** station
7. **bank** account
8. **room**mate

The first word has the heavier stress and higher pitch. The second word is not stressed as much and has lower pitch: ***post*** *office* / ***credit*** *card*

Sometimes another noun follows a compound, making a three-word compound: *identity theft victim*. The first word has the heaviest stress and highest pitch. The following words have less stress and lower pitch: ***identity*** *theft victim*.

1 ▶ **Read and listen to the nouns. Repeat them. Circle the words that are pronounced as compounds, with heavy stress and high pitch on the first word. Compare your answers with a partner's.**

1. diamond ring
2. charge accounts
3. online
4. email

5. internet fraud
6. police report
7. five thousand dollars
8. ID

9. website
10. personal information
11. 10-dollar bill
12. mailbox key

2 **APPLY** **Work with a partner. Answer the questions. Pronounce the compounds correctly.**

1. What's in your wallet?

2. What should you do if you lose your wallet or if someone steals it? Has this ever happened to you? What did you do?

SPEAKING SKILL

Keeping a Conversation Going

To keep a conversation going, both speakers need to show that they are listening and sometimes encourage the other person to keep talking.

▶ **Read and listen to the example. Notice the boldfaced words and the rising or falling intonation for each.**

Example

A: So, I got a call from this guy . . .

B: **Uh-huh**.

A: And he wanted me to give money to some organization called Amazon Rainforest something or other. You know what I'm talking about?

B: **Yes. Go on**.

A: Anyway, I got this weird feeling from him. Basically, I didn't trust him.

B: **So, what did you do**?

A: Well, I just hung up on him. You'd better be careful about these things, right?

B: **Right**.

TO SHOW YOU ARE LISTENING	TO ENCOURAGE THE SPEAKER TO KEEP TALKING
Yeah . . . (rising)	*Yes. Go on.* (falling)
Uh-huh . . . (rising)	*And?* (rising)
OK . . . (rising)	*So?* (rising)
Right. (falling)	*And then what?* (falling)
Wow! (falling)	*So what did he / she say / did you do / happened next?* (falling)

1 **Work with a partner. Complete the conversations. Choose language to show you are listening, or to encourage the speaker.**

Conversation One

A: So, I saw a man outside looking through my garbage.

B: _____

A: Well, at first I thought it was a neighbor, but then I realized I didn't recognize him.

B: _____

A: So, I asked my roommate to go outside with me. Better not to go alone, right?

B: _____

A: So, we went up to the guy, and I said, "Are you looking for something?"

B: _____

A: And he got really scared, dropped some papers he was holding, and ran. So, I quickly grabbed the papers . . .

B: _____

A: And they were my bank statements.

Conversation Two

A: Remember that apartment I tried to rent?

B: _____

A: Well, the owner tried to rip me off. He took information from my application form and opened a credit card in my name!

B: _____
How did you find out?

A: I started getting all these bills for charges on an account that I didn't open.

B: _____

A: And then I remembered John Day was the last person I'd given my personal information to.

B: _____

A: Well, I found out that he's done this before. Two years ago he was caught and put away for identity theft.

2 **Practice reading the conversations out loud with your partner. Switch roles and repeat.**

3 **APPLY Work with a new partner. Choose one of the topics below and tell your story. Listen to your partner's story. Use the words and phrases from the box on page 44 to show that you are listening and encourage your partner to keep talking.**

Talk about . . .

- an experience with identity theft (you or someone you know)

- a time when someone committed a crime against you or someone you know

- a crime that you heard about in the news

🔊 **Go to MyEnglishLab for more skill practice and to check what you learned.**

A role-play is a short performance in which you take on roles, or become characters, and act out a situation. Often the situations are similar to experiences that people might have in real life.

In this activity, you will create and perform a 3- to 5-minute role-play about identity theft. Work in a group of three. Follow the steps.

PREPARE

1 Choose a situation for the role-play. Choose from the following ideas:

- filing a police report
- receiving a fraudulent bill from a department store
- calling a credit card company about a theft
- giving advice to a friend about identity theft

2 Decide on the place, characters, and story. Choose from the following ideas:

Place:

- at a police station
- in a department store
- on the phone

Characters (think about age, personality, and feelings about the situation):

- identity theft victim
- police officer
- store employee
- identity thief

Story:

- Background: What happened before the role-play starts?
- Plot: What happens during the role-play?

3 Create the role-play. Write a script with the lines the characters will say.

PRACTICE

1 **APPLY** **Review your script and consider how to apply the vocabulary, grammar, pronunciation, and speaking skills from the unit. Use the checklist to help you.**

☐ **Vocabulary:** Read through the list of vocabulary on page 47. Add words from the list into your script.

☐ **Grammar:** Identify the modals of advice in the script. If there aren't any, add at least five.

☐ **Pronunciation:** Find the compounds in the script and mark the stress. If there aren't any, add at least two.

☐ **Speaking Skill:** Make sure your script has phrases to show that the characters are listening to each other and encouraging conversation. Draw arrows to mark the intonation for these sentences.

2 Practice the role-play several times until you can perform it without the script.

PRESENT

Perform your role-play for the class. Act like your character and speak naturally.

LISTENING TASK

Watch the role-plays. After each one, be prepared to answer this question: "What advice would you give the victim to solve his or her problem?"

ALTERNATIVE SPEAKING TOPIC

APPLY Discuss the questions in small groups. Use the vocabulary, grammar, pronunciation, and speaking skills you learned in the unit.

As technology has changed, the dangers of identity theft have also changed. What is the connection between technology and identity theft? What new kinds of identity theft might we have to deal with in the future?

CHECK WHAT YOU'VE LEARNED

Check (✔) the outcomes you've met and vocabulary you've learned. Put an X next to the skills and vocabulary you still need to practice.

Learning Outcomes
- ☐ Infer emotion from intonation
- ☐ Take notes with lists
- ☐ Recognize rhetorical questions
- ☐ Use modals of advice
- ☐ Recognize and pronounce compound nouns
- ☐ Keep a conversation going

Vocabulary
- ☐ authorize
- ☐ charge (n.)
- ☐ commit AWL
- ☐ confirm AWL
- ☐ expose AWL
- ☐ paranoid
- ☐ protect
- ☐ purchase (n.) AWL
- ☐ risk (n.)
- ☐ shred (v.)
- ☐ tip (n.)
- ☐ victim

Multi-word Units
- ☐ deal with
- ☐ file a complaint
- ☐ proof of identification

Go to **MyEnglishLab** to watch a video about identity theft, access the Unit Project, and take the Unit 2 Achievement Test.

LEARNING OUTCOMES

> Infer factual information from context

> Take notes with abbreviations

> Recognize and understand pronoun references

> Use present perfect and simple past

> Pronounce *-ed* endings

> Use eye contact in a presentation

🔵 Go to **MyEnglishLab** to check what you know.

Why Explore Space?

1 FOCUS ON THE TOPIC

1. What are some different kinds of space exploration? What is the purpose of this exploration?
2. What are the benefits of exploring space? What are the risks?

LISTENING ONE | The Space Junk Problem

VOCABULARY

1 ▶ **Read and listen to the article about a satellite from Ecuador. Notice the boldfaced words. Try to guess their meanings.**

Ecuador's Satellite Hit by Russian Spacecraft

An Ecuadorian communication **satellite** was hit by pieces of an old **spacecraft** about 1,500 kilometers (930 miles) above the southeastern coast of Africa. The satellite, called *Pegaso*, was sent into space in 2011. It was Ecuador's first satellite to **orbit** Earth.

Scientists knew the satellite would pass near the aging spacecraft, which was sent up in 1985 by the Soviet Union. The old rocket broke into **fragments** and is now surrounded by a cloud of **debris**. Scientists believe that *Pegaso* **collided** with the debris. The tiny satellite weighed only 1.2 kilograms (2.6 pounds), so even a small **particle** of debris could have caused **damage**.

Ecuador's space agency, EXA, said that the satellite continues to orbit but cannot send or receive signals. *Pegaso* was designed to send pictures and video back to Earth. Scientists are **tracking** the satellite to see if it stays on course or stops working completely.

Pegaso communication satellite

Despite the accident, Ecuador and Russia still **cooperate** on their space programs.

The National Aeronautics and Space Administration (NASA) said that no American satellites are in danger.

2 Match the words with the definitions. Write the words in the blanks.

damage	fragment ﺗﻜﮥ	orbit *circle*	satellite	track

1. ___satellite___ : machine that is sent into space and goes around Earth and is used for radio, video, and other electronic communication
2. ___fragment___ : a piece of something that has broken off something larger
3. ___damage___ : physical harm that is done to something
4. ___track___ : to follow the movements of something
5. ___orbit___ : to travel in a curved path around a much larger object such as the Earth or sun

collide ﻛﺮﺧﮥ	cooperate ﻫﻤﻜﺎری	debris درزه	particle	spacecraft ﻓﻀﺎﺋﯽ ﺟﻬﺎز

6. ___spacecraft___ : a vehicle that is able to travel in space
7. ___particle___ : a very small piece of something
8. ___debris___ : the pieces of something that are left after it has been destroyed
9. ___collide___ : to hit something that is moving in a different direction
10. ___cooperate___ : to work with someone else to do something that you both want

⏩ Go to the **Pearson Practice English App** or **MyEnglishLab** for more vocabulary practice.

PREVIEW

Trash has been a problem on Earth for many years. Now there is also trash in space. In this radio report, you will learn about space junk.

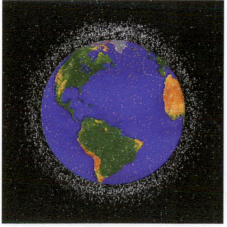

an orbital debris cloud

damage to the Mir Space Station from space debris

▶ **Listen to an excerpt from the report. Answer the question.**

Is space junk[1] dangerous? Why or why not? _____

_____

_____

[1] **junk:** unwanted old object

space debris

1 ▶ **Listen to the whole report. Create a chart like the one below to take notes.**

TAKE NOTES The Space Junk Problem	
Main Ideas	**Details**
NASA—old satellite falling to Earth	• 6 tons • into ocean

2 **Compare your notes with a partner's. How can you improve your notes?**

Go to **MyEnglishLab** to view example notes.

MAIN IDEAS

Choose the correct answer to complete each statement. Use your notes to help you.

1. Most space debris is created when satellites _____ .

   a. stop working

   (b.) collide or explode

   c. fall back to Earth

2. Falling debris _____ .   _in 207 chi   - Rushain_

   a. sometimes causes injury to people on Earth

   (b.) usually burns up before it reaches the ground

   c. frequently falls into cities and towns

3. Debris fragments in space are dangerous because they _____ .

   a. all move in the same direction

   b. orbit close to Earth

   (c.) travel very fast

4. Space debris presents the biggest danger to _____ .

   (a.) space crafts and satellites

   b. oceans and rivers

   c. people and animals

5. _____ must cooperate to solve the problem of space debris.

   a. Scientists and researchers

   (b.) The international community

   c. Governments and businesses

1 ▶ **Listen again and add to your notes. Choose the correct answer to complete each statement. Use your notes to help you.**

1. A six-ton piece of space debris the size of a bus fell to Earth in _____ .

   a. 2001   b. 2010   c. 2011

2. Two events created _____ of the debris in space.

   a. one-half (1/2)   b. one-quarter (1/4)   c. one-third (1/3)

3. NASA tracks _____ large debris fragments that orbit Earth.

   a. 2,100   b. 21,000   c. 210,000

4. There may be _____ of tiny debris particles.

   a. hundreds   b. millions   c. hundreds of millions

5. Each day, an average of _____ of space debris falls to Earth.

   a. one piece   b. five pieces   c. ten pieces

6. Space debris travels at _____ kilometers per second.

   a. 8   b. 8.8   c. 18

7. There are more than _____ working satellites in orbit around Earth.

   a. 1,000   b. 5,000   c. 10,000

8. _____ countries formed an organization to solve the problem of space debris.

   a. Two   b. Twelve   c. Twenty

2 **With a partner, take turns summarizing your notes. Then discuss how your notes and your answer in Preview helped you understand the listening.**

▶ Go to **MyEnglishLab** for more listening practice.

Inferring Factual Information from Context

A speaker may give facts indirectly. The listener can infer the facts based on the context.

▶ **Read and listen to the example. Notice how Michaela Johnson corrects the reporter. Based on inference, who do you think Michaela Johnson means when she says "we"?**

Example

REPORTER:	But this made us wonder: How much space junk is up there? And are we in danger?
MICHAELA JOHNSON:	Well, **we** call it orbital debris, not space junk.

Michaela Johnson means "scientists." She doesn't say directly that scientists use the term *orbital debris*. However, you can infer the information from the context because she is a scientist, and she says, "we call it . . ."

▶ **Listen to the excerpts. Choose the correct answer to complete each statement. Then write the key words from the excerpt that helped you decide.**

Excerpt One

NASA can't track most of the debris fragments because they _____ .

a. are not important

b. move too fast

c. are too small

Key words: _____

Excerpt Two

People _____ being hit by space debris.

a. should

b. should not worry about

c. should look out for

Key words: _____

Excerpt Three

_____ are dangerous to spacecraft.

a. Only large fragments

b. Only small fragments

c. Fragments of all sizes

Key words: _____

Work in a small group. Read the questions. Discuss your ideas.

USE YOUR NOTES

APPLY Find information in your notes to use in your discussion.

1. In the report, Michaela Johnson indicates that the space debris problem "will only get worse unless we can stop the creation of more space debris." Imagine that in an effort to find a solution to the space debris problem, you decide to make a public service announcement to educate people about the problem of space debris. What information would you include? What type of images?

2. The report described the need for countries to work together to solve the problem of space debris. What can be done about the problem? How can countries cooperate to find a solution?

➤ Go to **MyEnglishLab** to give your opinion about another question.

VOCABULARY

1 Read the fact sheet about space. Notice the boldfaced words.

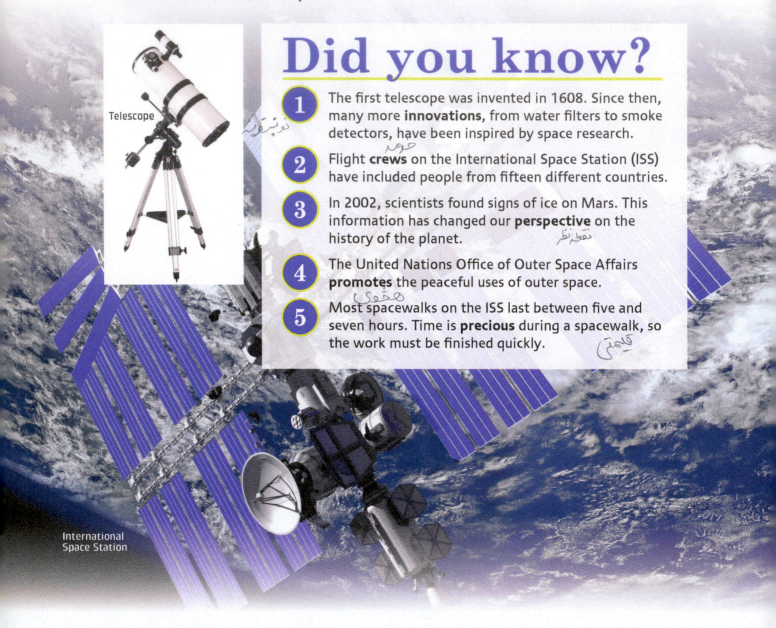

Telescope

Did you know?

1 The first telescope was invented in 1608. Since then, many more **innovations**, from water filters to smoke detectors, have been inspired by space research.

2 Flight **crews** on the International Space Station (ISS) have included people from fifteen different countries.

3 In 2002, scientists found signs of ice on Mars. This information has changed our **perspective** on the history of the planet.

4 The United Nations Office of Outer Space Affairs **promotes** the peaceful uses of outer space.

5 Most spacewalks on the ISS last between five and seven hours. Time is **precious** during a spacewalk, so the work must be finished quickly.

International Space Station

2 Write each boldfaced word from Exercise One next to its definition.

_____ a. groups of people who work together on a boat or aircraft

_____ b. new ideas or inventions

_____ c. way of thinking about something

_____ d. valuable and should not be wasted

_____ e. helps something to develop or increase

Go to the **Pearson Practice English App** or **MyEnglishLab** for more vocabulary practice.

Taking Notes with Abbreviations

An **abbreviation** is a short form of a word or phrase. Abbreviations are useful for note-taking because they can help you write information more quickly.

Abbreviate a word or phrase by using the first few letters:

space	sp
program	prog
government	gov
billion	bil
space exploration	sp explor

Abbreviate proper nouns with multiple words by using the first letter of each word:

United States	US
International Space Station	ISS

1 ▶ **Listen to the words and phrases and write abbreviations. Compare your abbreviations with a partner.**

a. _____   d. _____   g. _____

b. _____   e. _____   h. _____

c. _____   f. _____   i. _____

2 ▶ **Listen to the excerpt from the first vocabulary section. Fill in the blanks with information you hear. Use abbreviations.**

Main Ideas	Details
Ecuadorian _____	* _____ hit 1,500 _____ above Africa
hit by old _____	* was Ecuador's 1st _____ (Pegaso)
	* old rocket broke into _____

↖ Go to **MyEnglishLab** for more note-taking practice.

COMPREHENSION

1 ▶ Listen to an interview with Ray Santos, who is a scientist in the space exploration industry. Create a chart like the one below to take notes. Try to use abbreviations as you take notes.

TAKE NOTES The View from Space	
Main Ideas	**Details**

2 Label the three main points from the listening. Choose from the ideas in the box. (There is one extra choice.) Then, under each main point, cross out the supporting detail that is not mentioned. Use your notes to help you.

| Curiosity | ~~Innovation~~ | International Cooperation | Scientific Knowledge |

1. _____ Innovation _____

- We have had to solve new problems in space.
- ~~Space travel has become easier and cheaper.~~
- New products have been developed for use on Earth.

2. _____

- Countries help each other send satellites into space.
- Countries work together to run the International Space Station.
- Countries develop positive relationships.

3. _____ Curiosity _____

- There is still a lot to find out about space.
- Space exploration has given us a new perspective.
- ⊗ We can look for life on other planets.

USE YOUR NOTES
Compare your notes with a partner's. How can you improve your notes next time?

1 ▶ **Listen to an excerpt from the interview with Ray Santos. What does the word *it* refer to?**

INTERVIEWER: One criticism of the space program is the cost. The U.S. government is spending over 18 billion dollars on space exploration. Is **it** worth the price?

Recognizing and Understanding Pronoun Reference

Speakers use pronouns *(I/me, he/him, she/her, we/us, they/them, you, it, this/these, that/those)* to refer to people, things, and ideas. It is important to understand which people, things, or ideas a speaker is referring to.

A pronoun may refer to something mentioned before or to an idea that is not directly stated.

▶ **Read and listen to the example. Notice the boldfaced pronouns.**

Example

RAY SANTOS: Space exploration has a lot of benefits. One is innovation. The research for the space program has led to all kinds of innovations.

INTERVIEWER: Can you tell us about some of **those**?

RAY SANTOS: Think about **it**: To get into space **we** had to solve all kinds of problems.

- *Those* refers to innovations.
- *It* refers to space exploration.
- *We* refers to scientists or people in general.

2 ▶ **Listen to the excerpts. Then write the meaning of the boldfaced words.**

	Pronoun	Refers to
Excerpt One	a. **It** has brought together international flight crews . . .	it = _____
	b. **This cooperation** promotes positive relationships . . .	this cooperation = cooperation between _____
Excerpt Two	c. . . . **we**'ve had a great curiosity . . .	we = _____
	d. **This curiosity** has led us to explore . . .	this curiosity = curiosity about _____
	e. And **it** doesn't just give us answers—**it** gives perspective . . .	it = _____
	f. . . . we see how precious **it** is.	it = _____

▶ Go to **MyEnglishLab** for more skill practice.

CONNECT THE LISTENINGS 🔍

ORGANIZE

Complete the chart with information about how space exploration affects individual people, countries, and space. Circle the positive effects of space exploration. Draw a box around the negative effects.

USE YOUR NOTES

APPLY Review your notes from Listening One and Two. Use the information in your notes to complete the chart.

WHAT ARE THE EFFECTS OF SPACE EXPLORATION?		
	LISTENING ONE: *The Space Junk Problem*	**LISTENING TWO:** *The View from Space*
Effects on individual people	• Space debris falls _____ _____ . • Space debris may damage satellites, causing problems with _____ _____ .	• It promotes innovation. • It gives us _____ .
Effects on countries	• Countries must work _____ _____ .	• Countries work _____ _____ . • The U.S. spends $1.8 billion per year.
Effects in space	• Space debris damages spacecrafts. • Collisions create _____ _____ .	

SYNTHESIZE

Work with a partner. Discuss the questions about space exploration. Use the details and examples from Organize.

1. What are the positive effects of space exploration?

2. What are the negative effects?

Switch partners and repeat the discussion.

🅝 Go to **MyEnglishLab** to check what you learned.

3 FOCUS ON SPEAKING

VOCABULARY

REVIEW

Read each question and notice the boldfaced word. Then choose the correct answer.

1. What happens when two things **collide**?

   a. They crash.

   b. They go faster.

   c. They turn around.

2. How can countries **cooperate** on the space junk problem?

   a. They can argue about what to do.

   b. They can work together to clean it up.

   c. They can cancel their space programs.

3. A rock hit the space station. What did the **damage** look like?

   a. a small planet

   b. a hole

   c. a piece of metal

4. What should we do with the **debris**?

   a. clean it up

   b. sell it

   c. create more of it

5. Where would you find a flight **crew**?

   a. on a boat

   b. on an airplane

   c. on a train

6. What is a **fragment**?

   a. a piece of a larger object

   b. two pieces of an object joined together

   c. an unbroken object

7. What **innovation** has improved communication?

   a. the water filter

   b. the telescope

   c. the internet

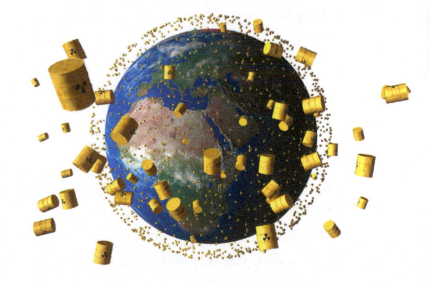

8. What **orbits** the Earth?

   a. the sun

   b. the moon

   c. planets

9. What does a **particle** look like?

   a. a tiny piece of dirt

   b. a large rock

   c. a long piece of metal

10. What is a person's **perspective**?

    a. the person's point of view

    b. the person's goals

    c. the person's language

11. What's an example of something that is **precious**?

    a. a rock from California

    b. a picture of a rock from Mars

    c. a rock from Mars

12. How can you **promote** something?

    a. put it in a safe place

    b. take good care of it

    c. tell people about it

13. Where can you see a **satellite**?

    a. under the ground

    b. in the night sky

    c. at a store

14. Where might a **spacecraft** go?

    a. to New York

    b. to China

    c. to Mars

15. How do scientists **track** moving objects in the sky?

    a. They discuss them.

    b. They destroy them.

    c. They watch them.

1 **Read the online article about space tourism. Notice the boldfaced words.**

SPACE TOURISM

Have you ever wanted to travel into space? Virgin Galactic, an American space exploration company, wants to take **commercial** passengers into space—for a price.

In April 2018, Virgin Galactic completed a successful test of a spacecraft to take six tourists into space. The spacecraft takes off from the ground like a plane and then goes almost straight up. After leaving Earth's **atmosphere**, the engines turn off. Outside of Earth's **gravity**, travelers experience weightlessness for several minutes. They also get an amazing view of Earth. Then the spaceplane descends 62 miles back to Earth. The cost is $250,000 per person.

Another space exploration company, SpaceX, is planning an even bigger trip. They have two tourists who have paid millions of dollars to make a trip around the moon. The chance to see the **surface** of the moon would give travelers a view that only a few **astronauts** have seen.

Both Virgin Galactic and SpaceX have a similar **mission**—to give regular people an opportunity to experience space.

to do

2 **Complete the definitions. Write the correct letter in the blank.**

1. A seat on a commercial spaceflight is _____ .

2. Earth's atmosphere is _____ .

3. Gravity is _____ .

4. A mission is _____ .

5. The surface is _____ .

6. An astronaut is _____ .

a. a person who travels and works in space

b. a trip by a spacecraft to complete a specific task

c. sold by a business to make money

d. the force that causes something to fall to the ground

e. the mixture of gases that surrounds Earth

f. the top area of something

CREATE

APPLY Work in a small group. Make a prediction about the future of space exploration. Agree or disagree with others' predictions. Use the expressions and verbs from the box and at least three of the boldfaced words from Review and Expand.

EXPRESSIONS

In 10 years . . .	there will / won't be _____	announce
In 50 years . . .	many nations will / won't	cause
In 100 years . . .	_____	create
In the future . . .	people will / won't	send
		solve
		travel

Example

A: In fifty years, people will travel to Mars on commercial missions, as tourists.

B: Maybe, but I don't think there will be enough innovation or money to do that in fifty years.

A: In the future, space flight will become more dangerous. There will be more debris orbiting Earth.

B: Right. That means the debris might collide with a spacecraft.

🔗 Go to the **Pearson Practice English App** or **MyEnglishLab** for more vocabulary practice.

GRAMMAR FOR SPEAKING

1 **What do you know about space? Take the Space Quiz. Check (✓) the statements that are true. Notice the boldfaced verbs.**

SPACE QUIZ

- ☐ 1. Twelve astronauts **have walked** on the moon.
- ☐ 2. Astronomer Carl Sagan's 1980 TV series *Cosmos* **created** popular interest in space.
- ☐ 3. NASA **has sent** school children to the International Space Station.
- ☐ 4. In 1970, the *Apollo 13* spacecraft **collided** with a satellite.
- ☐ 5. Astronauts **haven't landed** on Venus yet.

Discuss these questions with the class.

1. How is the time period different for statement 1 and statement 2?

2. How is the time period different for statement 3 and statement 4?

3. What rules can you make about simple present and present perfect?

Present Perfect and Simple Past

1. To form the present perfect use:	
have / has + past participle	Astronauts **have landed** on the moon.
have / has + not + past participle (negative)	Tourists **have not landed** on the moon.
have / has + subject + past participle (question)	**Have tourists landed** on the moon?
2. Use the present perfect to talk about events that **started in the past and continue to the present**. NOTE: often used with *since* and *for*	Astronauts **have traveled** in space since 1961. (The first astronaut is space was in 1961. Astronauts continued to travel in space from 1961 until the present.)
3. Use the present perfect to talk about events that happened at an **indefinite time in the past**. The event happened, but the exact time is not mentioned.	Astronauts **have been** to the moon. (Astronauts have been at a specific time in the past, but the exact time isn't mentioned.)
4. Use the present perfect and adverbs like *twice* or *many times* to talk about repeated actions at an indefinite time in the past.	The astronaut **has gone** to the International Space Station many times. How many times **has** he **gone** there?
5. Use the present perfect with *not . . . yet* to talk about something that has not happened before now but will likely happen in the future.	Astronauts **haven't traveled** to Mars **yet**.
6. Use the simple past to talk about things that happened at **specific times in the past**. The time when an event happened is an important focus of simple past.	Astronauts first **landed** on the moon in 1969. When **did** they **land** on the moon?

2 Complete the sentences. Write the simple past or the present perfect form of the verbs.

1. Russian astronaut Valentina Tereshkova (be) ___was___ the first woman to go into space. Since then, more than fifty-five women astronauts (fly) ___flew___ in space.

2. (hear) ___have___ you ___ever heard___ of Sally Ride? In 1983, she (become) ___becam___ the first American woman to travel in space.

3. After taking a break from space travel, astronaut Sunita Williams (return) ___returned___ to the International Space Station in 2018. From the beginning of her career until today, she (live) ___has lived___ on the Space Station for more than 322 days.

4. In 2012 and 2013, China (send) ___sent___ two female astronauts into space: Liu Yang and Wang Yaping. Many space programs (not / send) ___hasn't sended___ any female astronauts yet.

5. Last summer I (visit) ___visited___ the International Women's Air and Space Museum in Ohio. I know my sister (be) ___has been___ there many times, but I don't know when.

3 **APPLY** Read the History of the Space Age on page 192. Take turns making statements about the facts, using the simple past and present perfect.

Example

A: Let's see . . . sixty women **have gone** into space.

B: Right, and the first woman in space **was** Valentina Tereshkova. She **went** into space in 1963.

▶ Go to the **Pearson Practice English App** or **MyEnglishLab** for more grammar practice. Check what you learned in **MyEnglishLab**.

PRONUNCIATION

Pronouncing -ed Endings

The ending -ed is pronounced three ways:

- As /əd/ when the base verb ends in a /t/ or /d/ sound. This adds a syllable.[1]
- As /t/ when the base verb ends in a voiceless[2] sound
- As /d/ when the base verb ends in a vowel or voiced[3] sound

▶ **Read and listen to the examples and repeat.**

Examples

/əd/: *started, decided*

/t/: *stopped, worked, passed, watched*

/d/: *played, caused, changed, returned, traveled*

1 ▶ **Listen to the -ed sound in the underlined words. Check (✓) the sound you hear.**

	/əd/	/t/	/d/
1. The satellite <u>exploded</u>.	✓	☐	✓
2. The debris <u>damaged</u> the spacecraft.	☐	✓	☐
3. Scientists have <u>tracked</u> its orbit for many years.	☐	☐	✓
4. Have they <u>solved</u> the problem yet?	☐	☐	✓
5. Debris <u>surrounded</u> the planet.	✓	☐	☐
6. How many astronauts have <u>walked</u> on the moon?	☐	✓	☐
7. NASA <u>decided</u> to end the program.	☐	☐	✓
8. What <u>caused</u> the damage?	☐	☐	✓
9. They <u>finished</u> the spacewalk in less than an hour.	☐	✓	☐

---

[1] **syllable** = speech sound

[2] **voiceless** = consonant sound with no vibration

[3] **voiced** = consonant sound with vibration

2 ▶ **Listen and repeat the words from Exercise One.**

3 **Work with a partner. Take turns asking and answering questions. Use words from the box to complete the conversations. Remember to use -ed endings with correct pronunciation.**

cause	collide	create	injure	tour	visit	want	work

1. **A:** What happened to the Ecuadorian satellite?

   B: It _____ with an old spacecraft.

2. **A:** Would you like to go into space?

   B: Yes, I've always _____ to be an astronaut. / No, I've never

   _____ to be an astronaut.

3. **A:** Have you ever _____ the National Air and Space Museum in

   Washington, D.C.?

   B: Yes, I have. I _____ it in _____ (year). / No, I haven't

   _____ it.

4. **A:** What was Sally Ride's profession?

   B: She _____ as an astronaut for NASA.

5. **A:** Who _____ the space debris problem?

   B: Every country with a space program has _____ it.

6. **A:** Has space debris ever hurt anyone?

   B: No, it hasn't _____ anyone yet.

SPEAKING SKILL

When talking to people during oral presentations, it is important to look at them directly in the eyes. This is called **eye contact**.

Look at the following pictures. Who is demonstrating good eye contact—the person in photo A or photo B?

A

B

Using Eye Contact in a Presentation

Why Make Eye Contact?

When giving an oral presentation, eye contact is important because it . . .

- creates a connection between the speaker and the listeners.
- shows that the speaker is confident.
- helps the speaker to speak more naturally (instead of reading).

Making Eye Contact with a Group

- Look into the eyes of one person to say a complete thought (usually a sentence). Then look at a different person.
- Pause and look at the information in your notes. Then look up and speak to your audience.
- Use key words, phrases, and abbreviations in your notes. Don't write complete sentences. Sentences will cause you to read instead of looking at your audience.

1 Work with a partner. Take notes to answer the following question: "Would you like to travel in space? Why or why not?" Include two reasons for your opinion and details to support them.

2 Practice making eye contact while presenting to a partner. Explain your opinion while making eye contact. Remember: Talk to the person, not the paper.

3 **APPLY** Practice making eye contact while presenting to a small group. Take turns explaining your opinion.

a. Before a speaker begins to talk, the listeners all hold a pencil or pen in the air.

b. Speaker: As you present, make eye contact with each person.

c. Listeners: After the speaker looks at you for 4–5 seconds, put down your pencil or pen.

d. At the end of each presentation, notice whether the speaker made eye contact with everyone in the group.

⟲ Go to MyEnglishLab for more skill practice and to check what you learned.

In an oral presentation, a speaker prepares ideas and presents them to the class.

In this activity, you will give a 2- to 3-minute oral presentation to a small group of classmates on the benefits and problems caused by space exploration.

PREPARE

1 Divide into four groups.

Each group will read and discuss the information for one of the following topics about the U.S. space program (Student Activities, pages 193–194):

- Finance and Economy
- Environment
- Innovation and Development
- Human Relations

2 In your group:

1. Read only the information for your topic. (For example, if your topic is Finance and Economy, only read the information in that section.)

2. Work together to prepare your oral presentation. Take notes that include information about these questions:

   - Benefits: How has space exploration helped people and the world?
   - Problems: What problems has space exploration caused?

PRACTICE

1 APPLY **Consider how to apply the vocabulary, grammar, pronunciation, and speaking skills from the unit. Use the checklist to help you.**

☐ **Vocabulary:** Read through the vocabulary list on page 71. Then read through your notes. Put a star (*) above the vocabulary from the list. Choose two or three words or phrases and add them to your notes.

☐ **Grammar:** Scan your notes and underline verbs that are present perfect and simple present. Are you using them correctly? Add one or two more present perfect or simple present verbs.

☐ **Pronunciation:** Find verbs in your notes with *-ed* endings and mark the pronunciation of the endings. Record yourself saying the verbs. Did you pronounce the *-ed* endings correctly?

☐ **Speaking Skill:** In your notes, draw an eye 👁 in places when you can pause to look down at your notes and back at the audience.

2 Work with a partner from your group. Practice giving your oral presentation to your partner.

3 Give feedback to your partner.

- Did you understand the speaker's ideas?

- Did the speaker talk about the benefits and problems of space exploration?

- Did the speaker use vocabulary from the unit?

- Did the speaker use the simple past and present perfect with correct pronunciation?

- Did the speaker use eye contact?

PRESENT

1 Divide into four new groups. Each group should have an "expert" from one of the four topic areas (one person from Finance and Economy, Environment, Innovation and Development, and Human Relations).

2 Take turns giving a 2- to 3-minute oral presentation about your topic to the group.

3 After the presentation, consider all the information as a group and decide: "Should we continue to explore space? Why or why not? Should we work to send humans farther into space at this point? Or would it be better to continue to use unmanned space exploration technology?" Choose a student from your group to report the group's answer to the class.

A Mars rover, an example of unmanned space exploration technology

ALTERNATIVE SPEAKING TOPIC

APPLY **Discuss the topics in small groups. Use the vocabulary, grammar, pronunciation, and speaking skills you learned in the unit.**

People have wondered if there is other intelligent life in the universe. Although we have not found any extraterrestrials[1] yet, scientists have found other planets that could support life. We have tried to send messages into space and listened for signals from other planets, but so far there has been no communication.

a. Do you think it is a good idea to look for extraterrestrials? Should we try to communicate with them? Why or why not?

b. There are many images of extraterrestrials in movies, TV shows, and books. If we found real extraterrestrials, do you think they would be similar to those fictional beings?

_____
[1] **extraterrestrial:** living being from another planet

CHECK WHAT YOU'VE LEARNED

Check (✔) the outcomes you've met and vocabulary you've learned. Put an X next to the skills and vocabulary you still need to practice.

Learning Outcomes
- ☐ **Infer factual information from context**
- ☐ **Take notes with abbreviations**
- ☐ **Recognize and understand pronoun references**
- ☐ **Use present perfect and simple past**
- ☐ **Pronounce -ed endings**
- ☐ **Use eye contact during an oral presentation**

Vocabulary
- ☐ **collide**
- ☐ **cooperate** AWL
- ☐ **crew** (*n.*)
- ☐ **damage** (*n.*)
- ☐ **debris**
- ☐ **fragment** (*n.*)
- ☐ **innovation** AWL
- ☐ **orbit** (*v.*)
- ☐ **particle**
- ☐ **perspective** AWL
- ☐ **precious**
- ☐ **promote** AWL
- ☐ **satellite**
- ☐ **spacecraft**
- ☐ **track** (*v.*)

🔵 Go to **MyEnglishLab** to watch a video about space, access the Unit Project, and take the Unit 3 Achievement Test.

LEARNING OUTCOMES

- > Infer a speaker's purpose
- > Take notes with columns
- > Recognize and understand speaker emphasis

- > Use superlative adjectives
- > Highlight important information with word stress
- > Use appropriate volume and pacing in a presentation

Go to **MyEnglishLab** to check what you know.

Words That Persuade

1 FOCUS ON THE TOPIC

1. Look at the photo. What do you think the man is talking about? What do you think he is doing to persuade his audience?

2. There is a saying that "A good salesperson can sell you what you need. A great salesperson can sell you what you don't want and can't afford." What is the meaning of this saying?

3. Think of a time when a salesperson persuaded you (or someone you know) to buy something. What did the salesperson say? Why was it persuasive?

LISTENING ONE | Corporate Euphemisms

VOCABULARY

1 ▶ Read and listen to the article about how we use language. Notice the boldfaced words. Try to guess their meanings.

Watch Your Language: For People Who Love Languages

Fool[1] Me Once

Most people like to think that they are truthful, but studies show that, in reality, adults often tell "little white lies"—small, harmless lies—in social situations. For example, if a friend cooks dinner and asks, "How do you like it?" most people will say, "It's delicious," even if they think it tastes terrible. In this **context**, a lie is acceptable because it is used to avoid hurting someone's feelings.

Harmless Euphemisms

People also use euphemisms to avoid hurting people's feelings. **Euphemisms** are polite words or expressions that people use to talk about—and around— upsetting or embarrassing topics. For example, many people feel uncomfortable talking **directly** about death, so they use euphemisms. They might say "pass away" instead of "die." "Pass away" is less upsetting because it suggests that death is only a **transition** to another place.

In the business world, advertisers use euphemisms to sell products that solve embarrassing problems. For example, one company advertises mouthwash for "morning breath," which has a much better **connotation** than the more common term "bad breath." By using the positive image of a new morning instead of the negative word "bad," the euphemism promotes a more positive feeling about the product.

Deceptive Euphemisms

While most white lies and euphemisms have no real victims, some language can be used to hide the truth and can be quite **deceptive**.

Take the advertising expression "new and improved." We see this everywhere. It makes us think that we are paying for a better product, but the only difference is a change in the packaging.

Corporate Euphemisms

Deceptive language is also found in the **corporate** world. A recent news report quoted the head of a large business as saying, "The company experienced a significant **reduction** last year." What he really meant was, "We lost money and **fired** a lot of people." The statement influences our opinion of the company by hiding the true financial situation.

There is an **excessive** amount of deceptive language in the world today. Why? Because it works! But, as the expression goes, "Fool me once, shame on you. Fool me twice, shame on me." As language lovers, we can be smarter by learning to listen closely to the words we hear.

---

[1] **fool:** to trick someone into believing something that is not true

2 Choose the correct definition for each word.

1. **context**
   - a. the situation or information that helps you understand something
   - b. the situation or information that makes you confused about something

2. **euphemism**
   - a. a lie used to hurt someone
   - b. a polite word or expression used to make something seem more positive

3. **directly**
   - a. say something without being clear
   - b. say exactly what you mean

4. **transition**
   - a. when a person stays in the same situation
   - b. when a person changes from one situation to another

5. **connotation**
   - a. a positive or negative feeling suggested by a word
   - b. the basic meaning of a word

6. **deceptive**
   - a. intended to make someone believe something that is not true
   - b. intended to tell the truth about something

7. **excessive**
   - a. much more than necessary
   - b. not enough

8. **corporate**
   - a. relating to a big company or a group of companies
   - b. relating to individual people

9. **reduction**
   - a. a decrease in size or amount
   - b. an increase in size or amount

10. **fire**
    - a. to force someone to leave a job
    - b. to give someone a new job

Go to the **Pearson Practice English App** or **MyEnglishLab** for more vocabulary practice.

A businessman gives an online lecture about euphemisms used in the corporate world.

▶ **Listen to an excerpt from the lecture. What do you think is the purpose of this lecture? Choose your prediction.**

a. to argue in favor of using corporate euphemisms

b. to compare corporate and non-corporate euphemisms

c. to explain why people use corporate euphemisms

LISTEN

1 ▶ **Listen to the whole story. Create a chart like the one below to take notes.**

TAKE NOTES Corporate Euphemisms	
Main Ideas	**Details**
Corps. use euphemisms	• Ex: "workplace reduction"

2 **Compare your notes with a partner's. How can you improve your notes?**

↖ **Go to MyEnglishLab to view example notes.**

MAIN IDEAS

Choose the correct answer to complete each statement. Use your notes to help you.

1. Euphemisms are _____ used in the corporate world.

    a. often

    b. seldom

    c. never

2. Businesses try to _____ words with negative connotations.

    a. create

    b. avoid

    c. use

3. The same euphemisms are often used _____ .

    a. at work and with friends

    b. in different contexts

    c. in more than one conversation

4. Over time, euphemisms can become more _____ .

    a. meaningful

    b. useful

    c. negative

5. Doublespeak is language that _____ .

    a. hides the truth

    b. is honest and clear

    c. confuses the speaker

DETAILS

1 ▶ **Listen again and add to your notes. Use your notes to help you fill in the missing information.**

  1. *Workforce reduction* is a corporate euphemism for _____ .

  2. *Sanitation worker* is a euphemism for _____ .

  3. _____ means the removal of dirt to protect public health.

  4. *Between jobs* and *going through a career transition* are euphemisms for _____ .

  5. *Funemployed* is an example of a euphemism you use with _____ , not employers.

  6. *Downsizing* is a corporate euphemism for _____ .

  7. _____ is an example of a euphemism that got a negative connotation over time.

  8. Using twenty-nine different euphemisms to mean "fire people" is an example of _____ .

2 **With a partner, take turns summarizing your notes. Then discuss how your notes and your answer in Preview helped you understand the listening.**

↖ Go to **MyEnglishLab** for more listening practice.

Inferring a Speaker's Purpose

A speaker may have a specific purpose for making a statement. For example, the speaker may want to define a new term, contrast two ideas, or persuade the listener to agree with an idea. The listener can infer the speaker's purpose by paying attention to the context.

It is important to be able to identify the purpose of a statement so that you can understand the speaker's overall intended meaning.

▶ **Read and listen to an excerpt from the lecture. What is the speaker's purpose when he makes the boldfaced statement?**

Example

> A friend of mine got a letter from his employer that said the company was having a "workforce reduction" because of "changes in the market environment." What they really mean is that **a bunch of people are going to be fired because the company is in financial trouble**.

The purpose of the statement is to define the terms *workforce reduction* and *changes in the market environment*. The speaker says the new terms slowly and carefully, and then he explains what they mean.

▶ **Listen to the excerpts. What is the speaker's purpose? Read each question. Choose the correct answer.**

Excerpt One

What is the speaker's purpose when he says, ". . . he's out of a job but now has the time to do fun things during the work week"?

a. to define the term *funemployed*

b. to contrast *unemployed* and *funemployed*

c. to persuade the listener that *funemployed* is a useful euphemism

Excerpt Two

What is the speaker's purpose when he says, "However, over the years, it's become just as bad—just like saying 'we're firing people.' The connotation is the same now!"?

a. to define the term *downsizing*

b. to contrast *downsizing* and *firing people*

c. to persuade the listener that *downsizing* has a negative connotation

Excerpt Three

What is the speaker's purpose when he says, "Twenty-nine—in one page! That's too much—people get angry at this kind of doublespeak. They want to be told the truth, not hear euphemisms that hide the truth"?

a. to define the term *doublespeak*

b. to contrast *doublespeak* and *euphemism*

c. to persuade the listener that using doublespeak is a bad idea

Work in a small group. Read the questions. Discuss your ideas.

1. Review your notes. What are some of the advantages and disadvantages of using euphemisms or deceptive language in a corporate context?

2. The speaker advises his audience to use euphemisms wisely. What examples does he provide? What examples can you provide?

🔎 Go to **MyEnglishLab** to give your opinion about another question.

VOCABULARY

1 Complete the internet survey. Notice the boldfaced words.

What's your Style?

Before you start looking for a new home, take this quiz!

1 I like rooms that have . . .
- ○ high ceilings and a lot of space
- ○ a **cozy**, warm feeling

2 I prefer furniture that has . . .
- ○ a **vintage** look from the 60s or 70s
- ○ a modern, up-to-date style

3 I like colors that are . . .
- ○ **vibrant** and bright
- ○ soft and pale

4 I'm looking for a house that . . .
- ○ needs some repairs and updates
- ○ doesn't need any **maintenance**

5 In the kitchen, I want . . .
- ○ a **compact** refrigerator that doesn't take up too much room
- ○ a large refrigerator that holds a lot of food

2 Write each boldfaced word from the survey next to its definition.

_____ a. designed to be small and not waste space

_____ b. full of activity or energy in a way that is exciting and attractive

_____ c. old, but high-quality

_____ d. the repairs that are necessary to keep something in good condition

_____ e. small and comfortable

⬆ Go to the **Pearson Practice English App** or **MyEnglishLab** for more vocabulary practice.

NOTE-TAKING SKILL

Taking Notes with Columns

Use columns to show comparisons clearly. For example, to show a euphemism and its real meaning, draw a vertical line in your notes and write the euphemism in one column and its meaning in the other column.

EUPHEMISM	MEANING
changes in the market environment	financial trouble
downsizing	firing people

▶ **Listen to an excerpt from Listening One. Fill in the chart to show the comparison between euphemisms and their meanings.**

EUPHEMISM	MEANING
Its cozy	2 bed This leaving its cozy

▶ Go to **MyEnglishLab** for more note-taking practice.

COMPREHENSION

1 ▶ **Listen to an episode from the TV series *Home Sweet Home*. In this scene, a real estate agent gives a tour of a house. Create a chart like the one below to take notes. Try to use columns to take notes on euphemisms and their meanings.**

TAKE NOTES House Hunting	
Main Ideas	**Details**

2 Use your notes to help you fill in the missing information.

What the client thinks . . .	What the agent says . . .
1. The living room is small.	The living room is _____ .
2. The neighborhood is noisy.	The neighborhood is _____ .
3. The kitchen is small.	The kitchen is _____ .
4. The cabinets are old-fashioned.	The cabinets have a _____ look.
5. The backyard has no garden.	The backyard is _____ .

USE YOUR NOTES

Compare your notes with a partner's. How can you improve your notes next time?

LISTENING SKILL

1 ▶ Listen to an excerpt from *Home Sweet Home*. Is the real estate agent making strong positive statements, or is she making polite negative comments? What word emphasizes her point?

Recognizing and Understanding Speaker Emphasis

Intensifiers are adverbs used to emphasize another word. Speakers use intensifiers to make a point sound stronger. They can also use intensifiers to make a negative idea less strong or make it sound more polite.

▶ Read and listen to the example. Notice the intensifier used for emphasis.

Example

REAL ESTATE AGENT:	Well, it's a compact kitchen. It's **very** well organized.
CLIENT:	Those cabinets are **sort of** old-fashioned.

2 ▶ Listen to the excerpts. Complete the statement with the intensifier you hear. Does the intensifier make the statement sound stronger or more polite? Choose the correct answer.

Excerpt One

It has some _____ great features.

The intensifier makes the statement   a. stronger   b. more polite

Excerpt Two

It seems _____ small.

The intensifier makes the statement   a. stronger   b. more polite

Excerpt Three

I'd _____ put the sofa over here along this wall . . .

The intensifier makes the statement   a. stronger   b. more polite

But it's _____ small, too.

The intensifier makes the statement   a. stronger   b. more polite

🔵 Go to **MyEnglishLab** for more skill practice.

CONNECT THE LISTENINGS 🔍

> **USE YOUR NOTES**
>
> **APPLY** Review your notes from Listening One and Two. Use the information in your notes to complete the chart.

ORGANIZE

Complete the chart with details about euphemisms.

	LISTENING ONE: Corporate Euphemisms	LISTENING TWO: House Hunting
Euphemisms Are Used by:	_____ when they are going to fire employees _____ people looking for a job	_____ trying to sell houses
Euphemisms Used to Make Something Sound Better:	fire people = _____ = _downsize_ garbage collector = _____ unemployed = _____ = _____ = _____	small = _cozy_ = _____ busy / noisy = _____ old-fashioned = _____ no grass = _____ I don't like it. = _____

SYNTHESIZE

Work in a group of four. Each person in the group speaks from a different point of view: a corporate leader, an employee, a real estate agent, or a home buyer. Take turns completing each statement and giving an example from Organize.

Statements

a. I think that euphemisms (hurt people / make people feel better). For example, . . .

b. In my view, euphemisms (are necessary / are used too much) in business. For example, . . .

c. From my perspective, euphemisms (are deceptive / make negative ideas sound more positive). For example, . . .

🔵 Go to **MyEnglishLab** to check what you learned.

VOCABULARY

REVIEW

Cross out the meaning that does not match the boldfaced word.

1. The TV commercial shows the new Micro, which is a **compact** car that easily fits into a tight parking space.

   a. small and well organized

   b. ~~fast~~

2. The word *spam* has a negative **connotation**, while *advertisement* is more neutral.

   a. dictionary definition of a word

   b. feeling about a word

3. The billboard reads "Don't!" above a burning cigarette. The cigarette provides the **context** for understanding the message.

   a. the situation or information that helps you understand

   b. a book that explains a situation or information

4. The **corporate** world relies on advertising to sell products.

   a. business

   b. entertainment

5. The ad describes the apartment as "**cozy**," which means his large piano won't fit.

   a. small and comfortable

   b. sunny and cheerful

6. The salesman was being **deceptive** when he said the car is in "excellent condition."

   a. truthful

   b. dishonest

The new Micro compact car

7. The commercial doesn't **directly** say what Milagrow is for, but the images show men with no hair.

    a. in a clear way

    b. secretively

8. Advertisements use **euphemisms** to sell things that are embarrassing to talk about.

    a. polite words

    b. pictures

9. There's an **excessive** number of pop-up ads on that website. It's annoying.

    a. not enough

    b. many more than necessary

10. When Kate's boss said he was "letting her go," she didn't understand that she was being **fired**.

    a. given a better job

    b. forced to leave a job

11. **Low-maintenance** clients are the best—they don't complain or need a lot of attention.

    a. requiring a lot of help

    b. needing little to stay satisfied

12. Because of budget **reductions**, the company had to close several offices.

    a. decreases

    b. increases

13. Advertisers quickly made the **transition** from TV, newspapers, and magazines to the internet.

    a. a change from one situation to another

    b. a payment for services

14. The real estate agent said the orange walls in the kitchen were "**vibrant**," but Sara and Max thought the color was horrible.

    a. soft, relaxing, cool

    b. bright, lively, happy

15. Be careful when shopping for "**vintage**" furniture—sometimes the furniture is new and just made to look old.

    a. made of wood and inexpensive

    b. made a long time ago and high-quality

1 Read the advertisements.

goodcentstraveler.com
Check out these HOT DEALS!

RT flight Chicago to San Francisco: $189 (originally $269)

Weekend compact car rentals: starting at $42

6-night Alaskan cruises: from $379

Fantastic bargain!

MARTINELLI FURNITURE
is going out of business!

Everything MUST go!

Bedroom sets

Living room sets

Dining room sets

Hurry!
Time is running out!

BACK TO SCHOOL specials this week at
PENCILS

TechSon tablet, 32 GB
$239.89
Mega flash drive, 8 GB
$6.99
Recycled printer paper, 500 sheets – **$5.69**

Smart buy!
Buy now and save!

2 Write the words in the box from the advertisements in the correct categories.

HOT DEALS!	Everything MUST go!	Time is running out!
Smart buy!	Fantastic bargain!	Buy now and save!

Buy quickly: _____

Low price: _____

Both: _____

3 Do you think these expressions are examples of deceptive language or are they truthful statements? Discuss your answers with the class.

CREATE

1 **APPLY** **Work with a partner. Choose a context from the bulleted list. Create a short conversation using the words or phrases from the lists on the next page. Each word is worth a different number of points. Try to get as many points as you can.**

Contexts

- an employer talking to an employee about changes at the company
- two corporate executives discussing how to tell their employees about a workforce reduction
- a real estate agent trying to sell a house to a client
- a salesperson trying to sell something to a customer
- your idea . . .

1 point	2 points	3 points
compact	buy now and save	context
corporate	everything must go	euphemism
deceptive	fantastic bargain	low-maintenance
directly	fired	positive / negative connotation
excessive	hot deal	transition
vintage	smart buy	vibrant
	time is running out	workforce reduction

Example

STUDENT A: This chair is a <u>fantastic bargain</u>! [2 points]

STUDENT B: It would go nicely with my <u>vintage</u> couch. [1 point]

STUDENT A: The sale ends today, so <u>time is running out</u>! [2 points]

2 **Perform your conversation for the class. Have the class guess the context and identify the three words or phrases you used. Calculate who got the most points.**

🔵 Go to the **Pearson Practice English App** or **MyEnglishLab** for more vocabulary practice.

GRAMMAR FOR SPEAKING

1 **Look at the picture and answer the questions. Notice the boldfaced superlative adjectives.**

1. Which person has **the longest wait** in line?

   a. the woman at the ticket window

   b. the man in the green hat

   c. the woman with the purse

2. Which ticket is **the most expensive**?

   a. adults

   b. seniors

   c. children

3. Which movie has **the latest** show time?

   a. *Winter's Chill*

   b. *Summer Fun*

   c. *Spring Song*

WINTER'S CHILL	7:00	10:00
SUMMER FUN	6:45	8:15
SPRING SONG	7:30	9:00
ADULTS $10	SENIORS $8	CHILDREN $6

1. Use superlative adjectives to compare one person, place, or thing with two or more people, places, or things.	We have **the lowest** prices on golf clubs in the area. Martinelli's has **the cheapest** furniture in town.
Use superlatives to describe something that is **more** than other things.	This is **the most amazing** resort on the coast.
Use superlatives to describe something that is much **less** than other things.	He got **the smallest** room in the hotel. I picked **the least expensive** car.
2. For one syllable adjectives, use: **the** + adjective + **-est**	old—**the oldest** neighborhood.
For two syllable adjectives ending in **-y**, **remove -y** and **add -iest**.	pretty—**the prettiest** yard
For adjectives with two or more syllables, use **the most / the least** + adjective.	beautiful—**the most beautiful**
There are some irregular superlatives.	a good deal—**the best** deal a bad location—**the worst** location

2 **Complete the sentences. Write superlatives using the boldfaced adjectives. Some of the sentences may have more than one answer. Then work with a partner and compare answers.**

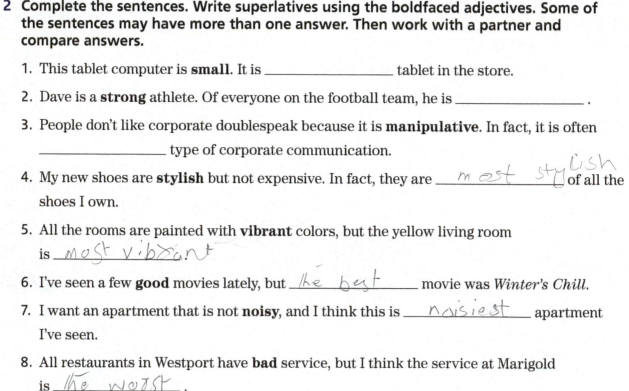

1. This tablet computer is **small**. It is _____ tablet in the store.

2. Dave is a **strong** athlete. Of everyone on the football team, he is _____ .

3. People don't like corporate doublespeak because it is **manipulative**. In fact, it is often _____ type of corporate communication.

4. My new shoes are **stylish** but not expensive. In fact, they are __*most stylish*__ of all the shoes I own.

5. All the rooms are painted with **vibrant** colors, but the yellow living room is __*most vibrant*__

6. I've seen a few **good** movies lately, but __*the best*__ movie was *Winter's Chill*.

7. I want an apartment that is not **noisy**, and I think this is __*noisiest*__ apartment I've seen.

8. All restaurants in Westport have **bad** service, but I think the service at Marigold is __*the worst*__ .

3 APPLY With your partner, take turns talking about the features you like most and least in each living room. Use superlative adjectives. Use words from the list or think of your own.

Example

STUDENT A: I like Room 2 because it's *the biggest* room. But Room 1 is *the coziest*.

Talk about the . . .		Use the adjectives . . .	
decorations	sofa and chairs	attractive	interesting
furniture	view	colorful	large
pillows	walls	comfortable	modern
room		cozy	vibrant
		good	

Room 1

Room 2

Room 3

Room 4

↳ Go to the **Pearson Practice English App** or **MyEnglishLab** for more grammar practice. Check what you learned in **MyEnglishLab**.

Highlighting Important Information with Word Stress

In radio, TV, and internet ads, actors emphasize, or **highlight**, certain words to get the listener to focus on important information. The same pattern also occurs in everyday communication. When we speak, we stress key words to make our meaning clear.

To highlight, or emphasize, a word:

- Say the word with a higher pitch (tone).
- Say the word louder.
- Make the word longer.

▶ **Read and listen to the example. Notice how the boldfaced words sound.**

Example

> This is the living room. It has some really **great** features. Look at the **nice** wood floors and the **big** windows.

1 ▶ **Listen to a commercial for Mistyland, a vacation resort. Underline the words that the speaker highlights.**

WIFE:	I just love Mistyland. Our condo is so cozy and clean.
HUSBAND:	And low maintenance. There's nothing to do!
WIFE:	In fact, the only thing you can do at Mistyland is relax.
HUSBAND:	And it has the most amazing golf course! I've never seen such vibrant green grass.
WIFE:	Or such beautiful blue skies. This place is absolutely dreamy!
HUSBAND:	Come to Mistyland—for your dream vacation.

2 **Compare your answers with those of a partner and discuss any differences. Then practice the commercial two times so you can both read each part. Make sure to highlight the words you underlined. Repeat the activity with another partner.**

3 **Fill in the blanks with your own ideas for a commercial. Underline the words you will highlight.**

I just love my new _____ ! (for example, car / phone / house)

It's so _____ and _____ !

And it has the most amazing _____ .

It's absolutely _____ !

Walk around the classroom. Say your commercial to three students. Remember to highlight the words you underlined.

Using Appropriate Volume and Pacing in a Presentation

When giving a presentation, it is important to speak with full volume (loudly) and at a comfortable pace (not too quickly or too slowly).

▶ **Listen to an ad for Rico Jeans. You will hear it two times.**

1. Is the volume high enough? Can you hear the speaker easily?

2. Is the pace too fast, too slow, or just right?

Appropriate volume and pacing help to make a speaker interesting and understandable. If the volume is too soft, the audience won't be able to hear. If the pace is too fast, the audience might not be able to understand, and if it is too slow the audience might get bored.

To speak with appropriate volume . . .

- Take deep breaths before you speak.
- Look up at your audience (not your notes).
- Observe your audience to see if you should speak louder.

To speak with appropriate pacing . . .

- Practice your presentation so you can speak fluently, without hesitation.
- Pause between ideas and at the end of sentences.
- Observe your audience to see if you should slow down and speak more clearly.

1 **Work with a partner. One person is the speaker. One person is the listener. Sit facing your partner with about a car length of space between you.**

Speaker: Choose three to five of the one-sentence advertisements below. Say the sentences loudly, with careful pacing.

Listener: After each sentence, repeat the most important selling points from the one-sentence ad. For example, "The jeans have the best fit for the best price." If you can't understand your partner, ask him or her to repeat.

1. Rico jeans offer the best fit for the best price.

2. Rico jeans are the best fitting jeans you can buy for under $20.

3. If you don't love your Rico jeans, simply return them for a full refund.

4. For all-day comfort and style, choose Rico.

5. For style and quality that lasts, slip into a pair of Ricos.

6. Join thousands of satisfied customers and get a pair of Rico jeans today.

Switch roles and practice again.

2 APPLY With your partner, look at the pictures of products. Choose one and write a short radio advertisement (about six sentences) that uses two voices. Remember to use persuasive language and superlatives in your advertisement. Perform your ad for the class, paying attention to volume and pacing.

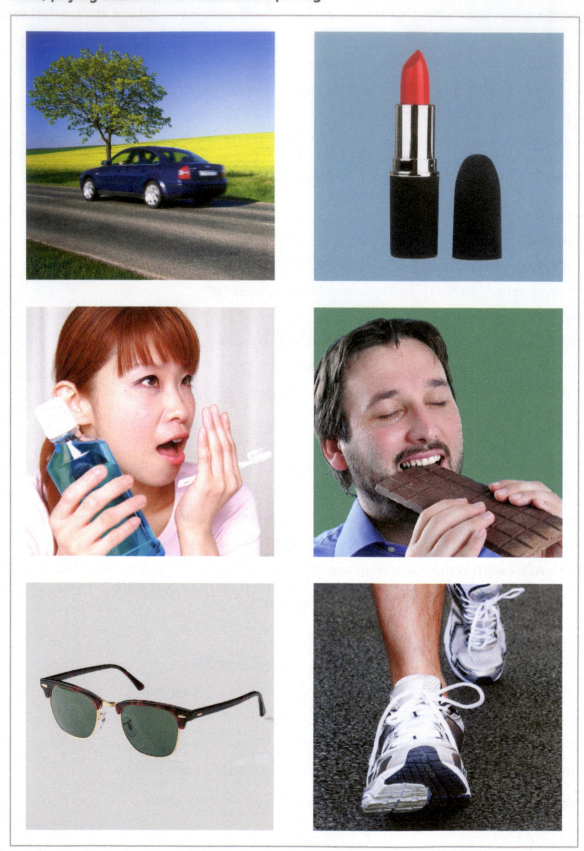

↪ Go to **MyEnglishLab** for more skill practice and to check what you learned.

Advertisements are created to persuade people to buy a product or service.

In this activity, you will create and perform a short TV, radio, or internet ad that uses persuasive language, including euphemisms, descriptive language, and superlative adjectives. As you perform, you will use highlighting, volume, and pacing to grab the attention of your listeners and focus on the main selling points.

PREPARE

Work in a group of two or three to plan the ad.

1 Choose a product from the list below or think of your own.

Products that solve an embarrassing problem	Products with a problem
wrinkle cream	used car
acne cream	compact car
diet pills	used cell phone
hair growth medicine	a very expensive product
hair dye	
mouthwash	
deodorant	
dandruff shampoo	

2 Decide on a situation for the ad (for example, two people talking in a grocery store).

3 Write a script.

- Write the script together. Use euphemisms and descriptive language to sell the product.
- Use superlatives to explain why this product is better (the best) than similar products
- Keep the ad short (about 60 seconds).
- Make sure each group member has a speaking part and a copy of the script.

PRACTICE

1 Work with your group to practice your ad. Be dramatic (show emotion) and use props (real objects) if you can.

2 [APPLY] Consider how to apply the vocabulary, grammar, pronunciation, and speaking skills from the unit. Use the checklist to help you.

☐ **Vocabulary:** Read through the list of vocabulary on page 95. Which words can you include in your ad to make it clearer and more interesting? Choose at least three words or phrases to use and add them to your notes.

☐ **Grammar:** Check your script for superlative adjectives. How many did you use? Try to include at least five. Add more if needed.

☐ **Pronunciation:** Read through your script and underline the words that should be emphasized. Practice the ad and make sure to highlight the important words (higher, louder, longer).

☐ **Speaking Skill:** As you practice, pay attention to your volume and pacing. Record yourself. Are you speaking too softly or too fast? Change your speech if necessary.

3 Evaluate your performance with your partners. What persuasive strategies are you using? What can you do to improve the ad?

PRESENT

Present the ad to the class. Give a brief introduction about the product. Then perform the ad. As you perform, use highlighting, volume, and pacing to emphasize key words and make sure your audience can hear and understand you.

LISTENING TASK

As you listen to the presentations, take notes on the questions.

1. What product is this ad selling?

2. What persuasive language and strategies do the performers use?

As a class, vote to choose the most persuasive ad.

ALTERNATIVE SPEAKING TOPIC

In addition to euphemism and doublespeak, here are more types of language used in certain contexts:

jargon: words and expressions used in a particular profession or by a particular group of people, which are difficult for other people to understand

> In police jargon, a police car is called a *unit*, and an ambulance is called a *bus*.

slang: very informal language that is used by a particular group, such as young people or criminals

> When a teenager says "I'm going to score some kicks," he means "I'm going to get some shoes."

exaggeration: a statement that makes something seem bigger or better than it really is

> She said there were "a million" people waiting in line for tickets, but we only had to wait a few minutes to get to the ticket window.

APPLY **Discuss the question as a class. Use the vocabulary, grammar, pronunciation, and speaking skills from the unit.**

What is the purpose of each of these different types of language? In what contexts are they used? Can you think of some more examples?

CHECK WHAT YOU'VE LEARNED

Check (✔) the outcomes you've met and vocabulary you've learned. Put an X next to the skills and vocabulary you still need to practice.

Learning Outcomes

- ☐ **Infer a speaker's purpose**
- ☐ **Take notes with columns**
- ☐ **Recognize and understand speaker emphasis**
- ☐ **Use superlative adjectives**
- ☐ **Highlight important information with word stress**
- ☐ **Use appropriate volume and pacing in a presentation**

Vocabulary

- ☐ **compact (*adj.*)**
- ☐ **connotation**
- ☐ **context** AWL
- ☐ **corporate** AWL
- ☐ **cozy**
- ☐ **deceptive**
- ☐ **directly**
- ☐ **euphemism**

- ☐ **excessive**
- ☐ **fire (*v.*)**
- ☐ **low-maintenance**
- ☐ **reduction**
- ☐ **transition (*n.*)** AWL
- ☐ **vibrant**
- ☐ **vintage**

↪ Go to **MyEnglishLab** to watch a video about gender and communication, access the Unit Project, and take the Unit 4 Achievement Test.

LEARNING OUTCOMES

> Infer feelings from context
> Take notes on details
> Recognize and understand reduced speech

> Use gerunds
> Use thought groups
> Use an introduction in a presentation

Go to **MyEnglishLab** to check what you know.

Follow Your Passion

1 FOCUS ON THE TOPIC

1. A *passion* is an activity that you love to do. More and more people, like the woman in the photo, are following their passions when they choose careers. What are the advantages of choosing a career that you love? What could be some disadvantages?

2. In order to follow your passion, you first need to know what your passion is. How can people find their passions?

2 FOCUS ON LISTENING

LISTENING ONE | Changing Career Paths

VOCABULARY

1 ▶ Read and listen to some myths and facts about college and careers from a university career center website. Notice the boldfaced words. Try to guess their meanings.

College and Career Myths[1] and Facts

1 MYTH: I want to change my **major** from math to biology, but I think it's too late.

FACT: Don't worry. About 70 percent of college students change their major. If your major isn't right for you, it's fine to **enroll** in another department next year.

2 MYTH: I should only take classes that prepare me for my future career.

FACT: Not true! Employers often look for people with a range of experiences. Don't get **tunnel vision**. Take a class outside of your major. Who knows? You might find a new talent!

3 MYTH: A career and a job are the same thing.

FACT: Not really. A career is a job that you have been trained for and which you do for a long time. A job can be long term, but it can also be something that you do for a short time that may or may not require special training.

4 MYTH: Choosing a major in college means deciding my career for the rest of my life.

FACT: Not so! Many college graduates get jobs that are not directly related to their major, and most will have one or more career **shifts** during their working lives.

5 MYTH: If I don't like college, I can **drop out**, start my own business, and become a billionaire.

FACT: This worked for Facebook founder Mark Zuckerberg, but most American billionaires are college graduates. So, if you want to be a billionaire, the best **strategy** is to graduate from college first.

6 MYTH: I shouldn't tell my professor that I'm having trouble in class.

FACT: Actually, most professors are very **supportive** of students who are having difficulties in class. Make an appointment with your instructor and ask for help.

7 MYTH: College is much harder than high school.

FACT: Not necessarily. College is "different," but not always "harder." College students have more freedom, so time **management** is important. Plan your time to make sure you get your work done.

For parents . . .
8 MYTH: My child isn't getting good grades. If I offer him money or some other **bribe**, that might encourage him to work harder.

FACT: Bad idea! Giving rewards is not the best way to encourage good grades. Talk to your child about the problem, but a student is **ultimately** responsible for his or her own success.

[1] **myth:** an idea that is not true

2 Match the words with the definitions. Write the correct letter in the blank.

_____ 1. major

_____ 2. enroll

_____ 3. tunnel vision

_____ 4. shift

_____ 5. drop out

_____ 6. strategy

_____ 7. supportive

_____ 8. management

_____ 9. bribe

_____ 10. ultimately

a. to offer a person something special in order to make the person do something

b. the main subject that a student studies at college or university

c. the act of controlling and organizing someone's work or time

d. to officially join a school, university, or course

e. a change

f. a planned series of actions for achieving something

g. giving help or encouragement

h. thinking about one part of a plan or problem instead of considering all the parts

i. finally, after everything else has been done or considered

j. to leave school before you finish a course

Go to the **Pearson Practice English App** or **MyEnglishLab** for more vocabulary practice.

PREVIEW

In these interviews, two professionals talk about the role their parents played in each one's choice of career.

Julie Hession is a cookbook author and founder of a company that makes breakfast cereal. She has developed her career by blogging about food, participating in cooking contests, and starting food companies.

Simon Sinek is an author and public speaker who teaches leaders and organizations how to inspire[1] people. He is the author of *Start with Why: How Great Leaders Inspire Everyone to Take Action.*

▶ **Listen to excerpts from the interviews. Make predictions.**

1. Do you think Julie's father was supportive of her career change? Why or why not?

_____

2. Do you think Simon's parents were supportive of his career change? Why or why not?

_____

_____

[1] **inspire:** to encourage someone to do or produce something good

1 ▶ Listen to the interviews. Create a chart like the one below to take notes.

TAKE NOTES Changing Career Paths	
Main Ideas	**Details**
2 professionals—parent influence on careers	• Dad—follow your passions

2 Compare your notes with a partner's. How can you improve your notes?

🌐 Go to **MyEnglishLab** to view example notes.

MAIN IDEAS

Choose the correct name to complete each statement. Use your notes to help you.

1. **Julie / Simon** studied hotel and restaurant management.

2. **Julie / Simon** went to law school.

3. **Julie / Simon** was unhappy in her / his first job.

4. **Julie's / Simon's** father advised changing jobs.

5. **Julie's / Simon's** parents advised finishing school.

6. **Julie / Simon** followed her / his parents' advice.

DETAILS

1 ▶ Listen again and add to your notes. Read the statements. Use your notes to help you decide which statements are true or false. Write *T* (true) or *F* (false).

_____ 1. Julie is the founder of a company named "Easy Breakfast."

_____ 2. In college, Julie learned about careers, like advertising and finance.

_____ 3. Julie's first job was at Wyndham Hotels.

_____ 4. Julie's father drove to Annapolis to talk with his daughter.

_____ 5. Simon wanted to be a tax lawyer.

_____ 6. Simon's parents tried to bribe him to make him stay in school.

_____ 7. Simon chose a career in finance.

_____ 8. Simon's parents never talked about his choice of career after he made his decision.

2 With a partner, take turns summarizing your notes. Then discuss how your notes and your answers in Preview helped you understand the listening.

🌐 Go to **MyEnglishLab** for more listening practice.

Inferring Feelings from Context

A speaker may express a feeling indirectly. The listener can infer a speaker's unspoken thoughts based on word choice, intonation, and the context.

▶ **Read and listen to the example. What is Julie thinking when she says, "I know that's a huge phrase right now . . . but I heard that from my dad a long time ago"?**

Example

> JULIE: My dad is the first person that ever told me to "follow your passion" and, you know, make money off of it. And I've always, I know that's a huge phrase right now, you hear that all the time, but I heard that from my dad a long time ago.

Here Julie is saying that her dad believed in "following your passion" before the idea became popular. Julie is thinking that her father is wise and that she respects his advice.

▶ **Listen to the excerpts. Read each question. Then choose the correct answer to complete each statement.**

Excerpt One

What is Julie thinking when she says, "This is going to be my life"?

She is _____ her career choice.

a. excited about

b. thankful for

c. not happy about

Write down the information (word choice, intonation, or context) that helped you find the answer.

_____

Excerpt Two

What does Simon imply when he says, "And I never fought so much with my parents than during this time"?

He _____ with his parents about his career decision.

a. was expecting to fight

b. was surprised that he fought

c. wanted to fight

Write down the information (word choice, intonation, or context) that helped you find the answer.

_____

What is Simon's father feeling when he says, "So?"

His father is _____ about his career.

a. open to hearing about Simon's decision

b. worried because he thinks Simon is making the wrong decision

c. angry because Simon is not listening to advice

Write down the information (word choice, intonation, or context) that helped you find the answer.

_____

DISCUSS 🔍

Work in a small group. Read the questions. Discuss your ideas.

1. Julie and Simon's parents were supportive of their children but in different ways. How was their support different? In your opinion, which parents provided more effective support? Explain your opinion.

2. What decisions did Julie and Simon make about their careers? Do you think they made the right decisions? Explain why or why not using examples from the interviews.

▶ Go to **MyEnglishLab** to give your opinion about another question.

> **USE YOUR NOTES**
>
> **APPLY** Find information in your notes to use in your discussion.

1 Read the introduction to a talk by Jeremy Brezden, in which he tells his story about finding a career that he loves. Notice the boldfaced words.

Jeremy Brezden
6.7M views

Follow Your Passion | Jeremy Brezden

What is your "passion"? Do you play sports in your spare time? Do you **volunteer** to help people at a school or organization? Do you love to play music?

Some people **take a chance** and follow their passion into a new career. In his talk, Jeremy Brezden describes going through a **process** of evaluating his work **environment**, finding his passion, and **figuring out** a new direction in life.

2 Match the words with the definitions. Write the correct letter in the blank. Then circle the correct word or phrase to complete the definition.

_e_ 1. environment   a. to do something **for money / without expecting money**

___ 2. volunteer   b. **a series of actions / one action** done to get a result

___ 3. process   c. to do something **risky / safe**

___ 4. take a chance   d. to **think about / ask for help with** a problem until you find a solution

___ 5. figure out   e. the **situations / decisions** that affect the way we live and work

Go to the **Pearson Practice English App** or **MyEnglishLab** for more vocabulary practice.

Taking Notes on Details

Details help support main ideas. Two main kinds of details are *examples* and *explanations*.

Details: Examples	Details: Explanations
An <u>example</u> is *someone or something* that you mention to show what you mean.	An <u>explanation</u> is *a statement* that you make to show what you mean.
I love sports! During the fall I play basketball and soccer, and in the summer, I like to go cycling and sailing.	*I love sports! Sports are a great way to stay healthy. I always feel good after exercising. Also, sports are great for my social life. I've met so many people through the sports I do.*
Examples: basketball, soccer, cycling, sailing	Explanations: help stay healthy / good for social life

▶ **Listen to the excerpts from Listening One. Write the details. Do not try to write every word.**

Write the *examples* in the Details column.

Main Ideas	Details (examples)

Excerpt One
undergrad. curric.
	hotel rest. <u>management</u>
	    " _____
	    " _____

Excerpt Two parents tried everything	_____ _____ _____

Write the *explanations* in the Details column.

Main Ideas	Details (explanations)
Excerpt Three had tunnel vision	_____
Excerpt Four parents supportive	_____

⚓ **Go to MyEnglishLab for more note-taking practice.**

1 ▶ **Listen to a talk by Jeremy Brezden as he gives advice about how to find your passion in life. Create a chart like the one below to take notes. Try to include examples and explanations in your details as you take notes.**

TAKE NOTES   Finding Your Passion

Main Ideas	Details

2 **Use your notes to help you complete the chart below.**

Main Ideas	Details (examples and explanations)
Check (✓) the three strategies that Jeremy Brezden suggests.	Draw a line to match the correct details with the strategies you checked.
☐ figure out what your talents are	realized that he liked working with people
☐ talk to your parents	his mother advised him to become a nurse
☐ get work experience in high school	volunteered for the Red Cross
☐ identify activities you like to do	helped friends with science homework
☐ decide what is important to you	worked as an assistant in a computer lab

3 **Look at the pictures. Which shows the job that Jeremy Brezden had after college? Which shows the job he has now? Write A or B.**

_____ job right after college   _____ job he has now

USE YOUR NOTES

Compare your notes with a partner's. How can you improve your notes next time?

A

B
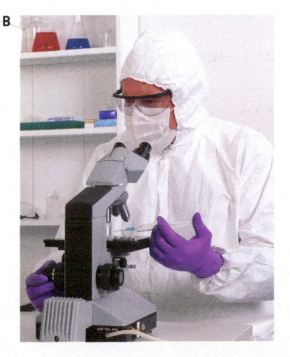

1 ▶ **Read and listen to an excerpt from Listening Two. How does the speaker pronounce the boldfaced words?**

JEREMY BREZDEN: ... but after a while, I realized that I didn't **want to** get up in the morning and go to work. I **had to** figure out what my real passion was.

Recognizing and Understanding Reduced Speech

English words are often reduced in speech. Speakers leave out some sounds and blend words together. Reduced speech is not careless speech. It helps a speaker to speak fluently.

▶ **Read and listen to these common reductions.**

Examples

Unreduced	Reduced
going to	gonna
got to	gotta
want to	wanna
should have	shoulda / should've
could have	coulda / could've
have to	hafta
What are you . . . ?	Wadaya . . . ? / Wada you . . . ?
Do you . . . ?	D'ya . . . ? / D'you . . . ?

2 ▶ **Listen to the conversation. Notice the reduced phrases. Then complete the conversation. Write the reduced form of each phrase. Remember, we don't usually write the reduced form of phrases. This is very informal and not suitable for most situations.**

A: ___What are you___ doing after college?
         1.

B: I'm ___goner___ look for a job. But there's a problem. I'm a business major, but

   I ___am___ *want wanna* be a teacher. I ___should have___ gotten a teaching certificate.
         3.   **4.** *shodda*

D'ya ___Do you___ think I could get a teaching job?
         5.

A: I think you should try. There's no rule that says you ___have to___ get a job that
                                                          6.
                                                          ha

   matches your major.

B: You're right, I've ___got o___ think about this some more.
                       7.

3 Now read the conversation out loud with a partner. Make sure to pronounce the reduced forms of the phrases.

▶ Go to **MyEnglishLab** for more skill practice.

ORGANIZE

Use the ideas from Listening One and Two to complete the chart.

USE YOUR NOTES

APPLY Review your notes from Listening One and Two. Use the information in your notes to complete the chart.

	LISTENING ONE: Changing Career Paths		LISTENING TWO: Finding Your Passion
	Julie Hession	Simon Sinek	Jeremy Brezden
How did the speaker realize he or she needed a career change?	• was unhappy with job and lonely in Annapolis	• _____ _____ _____	• _____ _____ _____
What help did the speaker get from his or her parents, if any?	• _____ _____ _____	• ultimately got support from father	
What strategies did the speaker use to change his or her career direction?	• _____ _____ _____	• _____ _____ _____ • told his parents	• _____ _____ _____ • went back to school

SYNTHESIZE

Work in a group of three. Discuss the questions. Support your answers with information from Organize. Then compare your answers with those of another group.

1. The people in Listening One and Listening Two came to their career change decisions in different ways. Compare the experiences of the three people. How were they similar / different?

2. Which person seems to have the closest relationship with his or her parent(s)? What leads you to think that this relationship is the closest? How did this relationship help this person to follow his or her passion?

3. Which person had the most effective strategies to change the direction of his or her career? Why do you believe these strategies were the most effective?

🅚 Go to **MyEnglishLab** to check what you learned.

3 FOCUS ON SPEAKING

VOCABULARY

REVIEW

Complete the paragraphs. Use the boldfaced words. You might have to change the form of some of the words.

1. **figure out / bribe / take a chance**

   My parents really wanted me to be an accountant. They tried to ____bribe____ me by saying, "If you study accounting, we'll pay for college." But my passion is fashion design. I had to ____figure out____ a way to pay for college myself. It was hard, but today I work in New York in the fashion industry. Sometimes you have to ____take a chance____ and do what you love.

2. **process / supportive / tunnel vision**

   I've always wanted to be a doctor, ever since I was a kid. Some people say I have _____ , but it's the only career I want. I know it's a long ____process____ to become a doctor, with many years of school. Thankfully, my family is very ____supportive____, so I know I can achieve my goal.

3. **management / strategy / environment**

   I started working in a restaurant after high school. I learned a lot about the restaurant business from that job, like how to work in a fast-paced ____environment____ and how to give great customer service. Slowly, I moved up into a ____management____ position. I had a simple ____strategy____ for getting here: I worked hard and learned as much as possible on the job.

4. **major / shift / volunteer**

   When I went to college, I wanted to study business. Then I ____shifted____ [volunteer] for an afterschool program and helped children with their homework. After that experience, my career goal ____shifted____ away from business. I decided to change my ____volunteer____ [major] to education, and today I'm a teacher.

5. **enroll / drop out / ultimately**

   I started studying to be a pharmacist, but I didn't like it. I ____dropped out____ of school and worked in a clothing store for a few years. Then I ____enrolled____ in a new school and studied computer programming. I ____ultimately____ graduated last year, and now I have a great job in software development.

EXPAND

1 Read the tips. Notice the boldfaced words.

Tips for New Employees

Congratulations! You are starting a new job. Here are some tips to help you **(1) play your cards right** and succeed in your new position.

1 Listen and learn
As a new employee, you should watch and listen. Don't try to give your opinion on every issue. Be ready to **(2) play second fiddle** to more experienced co-workers. With time, you can take more of a leadership role.

2 Ask questions
Make sure you understand your work assignments. If not, talk to your boss or co-workers and **(3) get the lowdown**. Get the information you need to complete your assignments effectively.

3 Be helpful
Look for things that need to be done, even if they aren't part of your job description: Copy and staple a report for a meeting? Clean up the break room? Show your co-workers that you are willing to **(4) get your hands dirty**.

4 Be flexible
Be ready to **(5) play it by ear**. Surprises happen, and you should know how to respond to unexpected situations.

5 Ask for help
You are new in your job, so you still have a lot to learn. Don't hide your problems or mistakes. Ask for help immediately and don't wait for problems to **(6) get out of hand**.

2 Match the boldfaced words or phrases from Exercise One with the definitions. Write the correct number.

_____ a. to accept that you have a lower position

_____ b. to act without preparation

_____ c. to become involved in all aspects of something, including work that is unpleasant or less interesting

_____ d. to become uncontrolled

_____ e. to do everything necessary to succeed

_____ f. to get the facts about something

CREATE

APPLY Work with a partner. Take turns giving and getting career advice. Use the boldfaced vocabulary from Review and Expand in your answers.

1. **Ask your partner the questions:**
   - What is your career goal? (If you are unsure, think about one or two careers that you might enjoy.)
   - What are the difficulties that might prevent you from reaching that goal?

2. **Give your partner advice about his or her career. Use expressions from the list.**

   Possible advice
   - **drop out** of a class and **enroll** in a new class
   - **shift** your career in a new direction
   - **take a chance**
   - **volunteer** somewhere
   - **figure out** a **strategy**
   - **major** in _____
   - don't have **tunnel vision**
   - talk to a **supportive** family member / friend
   - go through a **process** to find your passion
   - **get the lowdown** on new jobs in your city
   - **play your cards right** and follow up on opportunities

   ⬆ Go to the **Pearson Practice English App** or **MyEnglishLab** for more vocabulary practice.

GRAMMAR FOR SPEAKING

1 **Read the job advertisement. Underline the gerunds (verb + *-ing*).**

TOUR GUIDES NEEDED

130 reviews

Do you dream about visiting new countries and cultures?
Do you enjoy meeting new people?
Do you like living out of a suitcase?

Touring the world and getting paid for it. What could be better?
Call 502-476-3409.

26 days ago   save job   more...

Gerunds

1. A gerund is a verb that is **used like a noun.** It answers the question "What?"	***What*** *is your favorite sport?*
• Use base form of **verb + -ing**	***Swimming*** *is my favorite sport.*
• Sometimes there are spelling changes	***Working*** *for a tour company sounds fun.*

Base Form	Gerund
make	*making*
drop out	*dropping out*
lie	**lying**

NOTE: Don't confuse gerunds with progressive verbs

Gerund: ***Dancing*** *is her passion.*

Progressive: *She **is dancing.***

---

2. A gerund can be the **subject** of a sentence.

Teaching is a rewarding profession.

---

3. A gerund can be the **object** of some verbs.

Examples:

avoid	begin	consider	dislike
enjoy	finish	like	put off
love	prefer	start	try
go	hate	stop	keep (continue)

*I **dislike sitting** at a desk all day.*

*She **put off making** a decision about her career.*

*He **enjoys teaching** children.*

---

4. A gerund can be the **object of a preposition.**

Examples:

afraid of	interested in
worried about	good at
bad at	bored with
excited about	plan on
believe in	choose between
dream about	

*I am **excited about finishing** school.*

*She **dreams about becoming** a pilot.*

*He is **bad at planning** ahead.*

---

2 Work with a partner. Fill in the blanks with gerunds. Use each verb in the box once. Share your answers with the class.

~~cook~~   create   make   drop out   waste   follow   attend   change   experiment

_____Cooking_____ is my favorite hobby. Whenever I'm in the kitchen I love _____

with new spices and _____ dishes that look and taste beautiful. I'm so passionate

about food that I've considered _____ of college and _____ culinary

school to become a chef. _____ my career plan is a big deal, but I want to avoid

_____ time and money to get a degree in a profession I don't enjoy. Sometimes I

worry about _____ the wrong decision when it comes to my career, but I believe

in _____ my passions, so I'm pretty sure I'll do it!

3 **With your partner, take turns talking about jobs you might enjoy doing.**

Student 1: Suggest a job you might enjoy doing. Give reasons for your answers.

Example

STUDENT 1: I think I would enjoy working as a chef. Cooking is my favorite thing to do in my free time. So if I got a job as a chef, I would be able to do something I love all the time!

Student 2: Ask Student 1 the questions below. Add three of your own questions, using gerunds. Decide if your partner's job is a good fit. Explain your opinion.

Example

STUDENT 2: Is having a predictable schedule important to you?

STUDENT 1: Not really. I don't mind working odd hours.

STUDENT 2: Then it sounds like being a chef is a good fit for you!

Questions:

1. What subjects do you like *studying*?

2. What do you enjoy *doing* in your free time?

3. Do you dream about *owning* your own business?

4. Is *having* a predictable schedule important to you?

5. Do you dislike *working* in particular environments (e.g., an office, a classroom, outside)?

6. Do you prefer *being* a leader or a follower?

7. What ages of people do you like *working* with (e.g., adults, children)?

8. Are you afraid of *speaking* in front of large groups?

9. How do you feel about *working* with technology?

10. _____ ?

11. _____ ?

12. _____ ?

🔊 Go to the **Pearson Practice English App** or **MyEnglishLab** for more vocabulary practice.

Using Thought Groups

A **thought group** is a phrase that expresses a thought or idea. Sentences are made up of thought groups that are joined together. Thought groups help the listener understand the meaning of a sentence by breaking the sentence into shorter parts. Pronounce a thought group by pausing briefly between the groups of words.

▶ **Read and listen to the example. Notice how the slashes (/) separate the thought groups.**

Example

> I'm excited about / going to graduate school! / I'm tired of / working in an office. / Teaching / is my dream job!

Common Thought Groups	
Prepositional phrases	**Verb + preposition**
at the career center	He's excited about . . .
near the gate	I'm tired of . . .
with a counselor	She dreams about . . .
Short phrases	**Gerund phrases**
I saw an ad / for a job.	going to graduate school
	working in an office
	teaching kids

1 ▶ **Listen to the sentences. Mark the thought groups with a /.**

1. I'm good at / learning new languages.

2. I like / working at / the restaurant.

3. Helping / people / is important to me.

4. I'm not afraid of / speaking / in public.

5. I have experience / working in restaurants.

6. I am thinking about / becoming a pilot.

7. I don't mind / doing paperwork.

8. Making money / is my main goal.

9. I've considered / changing my major.

10. I enjoy / learning about careers from surfing the web.

2 **Work with a partner. Practice saying the sentences from Exercise One with the thought groups. Take turns and check each other's pronunciation.**

3 Complete the sentences to describe your skills and preferences. Say a sentence to your partner. Your partner will agree or disagree. Be sure to pronounce the thought groups.

Example

A: I'm good at / learning languages.

B: Me too. / I'm good at / learning languages.   OR   I'm not. / I'm bad at / learning languages.

a. I'm (good / bad) at _____ .

b. I (like / dislike) _____ .

c. _____ (is / isn't) important to me.

d. I'm (afraid of / not afraid of) _____ .

e. I (have / don't have) experience _____ .

f. I (dream of / can't imagine) _____ .

g. I (don't mind / can't stand) _____ .

h. _____ (is / is not) my main goal.

i. I've (considered / never considered) _____ .

j. I (enjoy / hate) _____ .

SPEAKING SKILL

Using an Introduction in a Presentation

A strong introduction in an oral presentation will grab the audience's attention and encourage listeners to focus on the main message. Here are some ways to start your oral presentations strongly.

1. Include one or more attention grabbers. An attention grabber "grabs" listeners' attention and makes them want to listen to you.

Attention Grabber	Example
a. Ask a question	"Have you ever heard the phrase *follow your passion*?"
b. Share a quote	"Steve Jobs, the CEO of Apple Computers, once said that "the only way to do great work is to love what you do."
c. Tell an anecdote (short story)	"I still remember the day when my father told me that he wished he could quit his job . . . "
d. Give a dramatic fact or statistic	"According to a recent Gallup World Poll, 85 percent of workers in 200 countries hate their jobs."

2. State the purpose or focus of your presentation in a clear statement.

Examples

"Today, I'm going to talk about . . . what led me to a career in medicine."

"For the next 2 or 3 minutes I'd like to talk about . . . "

"In this presentation, I'll share . . . "

"There are many skills and interests that led me . . . "

1 ▶ **Listen to the following attention grabbers for an oral presentation. Write the letter of the technique that is used.**

A = Question	B = Quote	C = Anecdote	D = Fact / Statistic

1. _____   3. _____   5. _____

2. _____   4. _____   6. _____

2 **Read the following oral presentation introductions and underline the statement of purpose or focus. Discuss your answers with the class.**

1. When I was seven years old, I remember bringing home a stray kitten. I found it on the side of the road, so I took it home and asked my mom if we could keep it. She said yes, as long as I took care of it. That was my first pet. Since then, I've had many animals in my life. I'm pretty sure I want a career that involves animals, but I'm not sure what. Loving animals is one thing, but there are many other skills and interests that could lead me in one direction or another.

2. Throughout my life, my parents have always encouraged me to follow my passions. But how can I figure out what my passions are? When I first thought of this question, I couldn't think of anything that excited me, so I started making a list. That's when I realized that there a lot of things that I think are fun or interesting. In this presentation, I'll share some of them. Not the whole list, but the most important things that I would call my passions.

3 APPLY **Work with a partner. Choose an oral presentation topic from the list below. Write an attention grabber and a statement of purpose or focus.**

Attention grabber: _____

_____

_____

Statement of purpose/focus: _____

_____

Oral Presentation Topics
- expectations of parents in my career choice
- careers that would not be a good match for me
- my main passion in life

Meet with students who chose the same topic as you. Share your work. Choose one example to share with the class. During the group and class discussions, think of the following questions:

1. Which is the most interesting attention grabber? What makes it interesting?

2. Which is the best statement of purpose / focus? Why is it the best?

↑ **Go to MyEnglishLab for more skill practice and to check what you learned.**

FINAL SPEAKING TASK: Oral Presentation APPLY

In this activity, you will give a 2- to 3-minute oral presentation to your classmates about your personal strengths, interests, and work preferences. The audience will listen and give suggestions for careers that might be a good match for you.

PREPARE

1 Write answers to these questions suggested in Listening Two.

    a. What are you good at doing?

    b. What do you like to do?

    c. What is important to you in a career?

        • work environment   • location and travel   • pay and benefits
        • type of work   • type of organization   • work schedule

2 Look at your answers. Is there enough useful information for the audience to be able to suggest careers? Add more details to your notes.

3 Use your answers from Exercise One to create an outline for your presentation, using either a pros and cons or point-by-point organization. Include the three main topics from your notes.

Introduction (with attention grabber and clear statement of purpose)

Topic 1: what you are good at

Topic 2: what you like to do

Topic 3: what is important to you

Conclusion

List the details you will include. Use only key words and phrases in your notes.

PRACTICE

1 APPLY Consider how to apply the vocabulary, grammar, pronunciation, and speaking skills from the unit. Use the checklist to help you.

☐ **Vocabulary:** Read through the list of vocabulary on page 117. Choose three to six words or phrases to use and add them to your notes.

☐ **Grammar:** Scan your notes for gerunds and add some if you don't have any. Are you using them correctly?

☐ **Pronunciation:** Record yourself practicing with thought groups. Then listen to the recording. Are your ideas clear?

☐ **Speaking Skill:** Look at your introduction. Did you use an effective attention grabber? How clear is your statement of purpose?

2 Practice the presentation several times. Remember to read your notes silently and then look up and speak to your audience.

PRESENT

Make your presentation to the class.

LISTENING TASK

Listen to your classmates. During each presentation, make a list of three possible careers that you think might be a good match for the presenter. Be prepared to share your ideas after the presentation.

ALTERNATIVE SPEAKING TOPIC

APPLY Read the quotes about careers. Do you agree with them? Why or why not? Share your thoughts with the class. Use the vocabulary, grammar, pronunciation, and speaking skills you learned in the unit.

1. No man can succeed in a line of endeavor which he does not like.

—Napoleon Hill, writer

Paraphrase: People cannot succeed in jobs they don't like.

2. I think everyone should experience defeat at least once during their career. You learn alot from it.

—Lou Holtz, coach, writer, speaker

Paraphrase: Everyone should fail at least once in a career. You can learn a lot from failure.

3. Each man has his own vocation; his talent is his call. There is one direction in which all space is open for him.

—Ralph Waldo Emerson, writer

Paraphrase: Everyone has a talent. There is one direction that is open for you to follow in life and that is the direction your talent takes you.

CHECK WHAT YOU'VE LEARNED

Check (✔) the outcomes you've met and vocabulary you've learned. Put an X next to the skills and vocabulary you still need to practice.

Learning Outcomes
- ☐ Infer feelings from context
- ☐ Take notes on details
- ☐ Recognize and understand reduced speech
- ☐ Use gerunds
- ☐ Use thought groups
- ☐ Use an introduction in a presentation

Vocabulary
- ☐ bribe (*n., v.*)
- ☐ enroll
- ☐ environment AWL
- ☐ major (*n.*) AWL
- ☐ management
- ☐ process (*n.*) AWL
- ☐ shift (*n.*) AWL
- ☐ strategy AWL
- ☐ supportive
- ☐ tunnel vision
- ☐ ultimately AWL
- ☐ volunteer (*v.*) AWL

Multi-word Units
- ☐ drop out
- ☐ figure out
- ☐ take a chance

Go to **MyEnglishLab** to watch a video about careers, access the Unit Project, and take the Unit 5 Achievement Test.

LEARNING OUTCOMES

> Infer opinion from word choice
> Take notes with an outline
> Recognize and understand opinions

> Use *will* and *if* clauses
> Pronounce the vowel *o*
> Make suggestions

 Go to **MyEnglishLab** to check what you know.

Culture and Commerce

1 FOCUS ON THE TOPIC

1. Look at the photo and read the title of the unit. *Commerce* means business. What is the relationship between culture and commerce in tourism? How can culture and commerce work together to increase tourism?

2. In what ways can tourism be helpful in a community? In what ways can it be harmful?

LISTENING ONE | Tourist Attraction or Human Zoo?

VOCABULARY

1 ▶ A travel blog is an internet site where people write about their trips. Read and listen to the travel blog about a trip to Thailand. Notice the boldfaced words. Try to guess their meanings.

Travel Blog: Northern Thailand

We've had a great time exploring Northern Thailand so far. It's really interesting, and there's so much to see!

One thing I've learned is that elephants are the national symbol of Thailand. They're very important in Thai history and cultural **(a) traditions**. Elephants are also a big **(b) tourist attraction**, so there are many different elephant parks for tourists to visit. We decided to visit one, but we soon found out that there's a lot of **(c) controversy** about them. Some parks treat the elephants very badly. They're not treated with respect and have to perform **(d) degrading** tricks for tourists, like playing basketball and dancing. The owners don't really care about the elephants; they just want to **(e) make a living** by showing the animals to tourists.

However, the elephant park we went to is very different. In this place, they're trying to **(f) preserve** the wild elephant population. It's a large, beautiful park where the elephants can walk around freely. They are so playful! I took this photo of two young elephants walking together with their trunks **(g) wrapped** around each other, just like two kids walking hand-in-hand. Going to the park was an amazing experience, much better than seeing elephants in a **(h) zoo**. I also bought some nice **(i) souvenirs**: a stuffed elephant toy for my niece and a carved wooden elephant for my parents.

Tomorrow we're going to see another unusual sight: the village of Nai Soi where the long-necked women of the Padaung tribe live. The women wear brass coils to **(j) stretch** their necks. More on that tomorrow!

2 Match the boldfaced words from Exercise One with the definitions. Write the correct letter in the blank.

_C__ 1. a strong disagreement among people

_h__ 2. a place where animals are kept so that people can look at them

_c__ 3. to keep something from being changed or harmed

_g i k_ 4. customs (special activities) that have existed for a long time

_____ 5. things you buy to help you remember a place

_____ 6. to make something longer by pulling it

_g__ 7. folded around something

_____ 8. showing no respect

_____ 9. something interesting for a tourist to see or do

_e__ 10. to earn money from

Go to the **Pearson Practice English App** or **MyEnglishLab** for more vocabulary practice.

PREVIEW

A journalist is reporting on the long-necked women of Padaung and the tourists who travel to Nai Soi to see them.

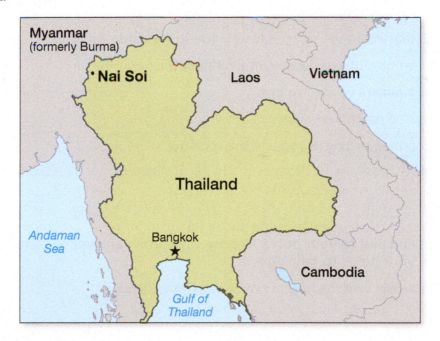

Listen to an excerpt from the report. Choose your prediction.

This news report will present the tourist attraction in _____ .

a. a positive way

b. a negative way

c. a way that is both positive and negative

1 ▶ **Listen to the radio report. Create a chart like the one below to take notes.**

TAKE NOTES Tourist Attraction or Human Zoo?	
Main Ideas	**Details**
Long-necked women bring tourists to Thai/Myanmar border	• around 10,000 tourist/yr

2 **Compare your notes with a partner's. How can you improve your notes?**

↳ Go to **MyEnglishLab** to view example notes.

MAIN IDEAS

Read the statements. Use your notes to help you decide if they are true or false. Write *T* (true) or *F* (false). Correct the false statements by crossing out the incorrect information and writing the correction.

The tradition of the long-necked women . . .

F **1.** . . . started in Thailand.

T **2.** . . . brings tourists to the village to buy souvenirs and take pictures.

T **3.** . . . allows women to earn money for their families.

F **4.** . . . makes women's necks stronger.

T **5.** . . . has caused controversy among tourists.

____ **6.** . . . will continue as long as tourists keep coming.

DETAILS

1 ▶ **Listen again and add to your notes. Choose the correct answer to complete each statement. Use your notes to help you.**

1. About ____ tourists visit the long-necked women every year.

   a. 1,000

   b. 10,000

   c. 100,000

2. When they lived in Myanmar, the Padaung ____ .

   a. sold souvenirs to tourists

   b. fought in a war

   c. farmed the land

3. A full set of brass coils _____ .

   a. weighs up to 22 pounds (10 kilograms)

   b. costs up to $22

   c. takes up to 22 years to put on

4. A long-necked woman cannot remove the coils because _____ .

   a. her neck is very weak

   b. they are made of brass

   c. her family won't let her

5. Back in Myanmar, the tradition of stretching women's necks _____ .

   a. has almost disappeared

   b. is still strong

   c. is becoming more popular

6. A long-necked woman can make $70 to $80 _____ from tourists.

   a. a week

   b. a month

   c. a year

7. Sandra feels that she is helping the Padaung women because she is _____ .

   a. spending money in the village

   b. not visiting the village

   c. bringing medicine to the village

8. Fredrick uses the image of _____ to describe the Padaung women.

   a. animals in a zoo

   b. prisoners in jail

   c. actors in a show

2 **With a partner, take turns summarizing your notes. Then discuss how your notes and your answer in Preview helped you understand the listening.**

🔾 **Go to MyEnglishLab for more listening practice.**

MAKE INFERENCES 🔍

Inferring Opinion from Word Choice

A speaker may use certain words to express his or her opinion indirectly. The listener can infer the speaker's opinion by paying attention to the connotation of the words the speaker chooses.

Example

> Brass coils are part of a tradition that brings joy to the Padaung women and to the tourists who come to see them.

We can infer from the positive connotation of the words *tradition* and *joy* that the speaker has a positive opinion about cultural traditions in general and does not have negative feelings about the brass coils.

> Brass coils do bring joy, but we must also consider the physical impact they have on the Padaung women.

We can infer from the negative connotation of the words *physical impact* and the use of the word *but* that the speaker has a negative opinion about the brass coils.

> The brass coils are made in the village.

The phrase *made in the village* is not positive or negative. It is neutral. The speaker is not expressing an opinion.

▶ **Read and listen to the example. Does Sandra feel positive, negative, or neutral about spending money in Nai Soi?**

Example

> SANDRA: . . . and so if I go, it's like I'm helping them to preserve it. Spending my money is also helping them. You know, they make a living from tourism, so they need us.

Sandra's feelings about spending money in Nai Soi are positive. She uses words such as *preserve* and *helping*, which have a positive meaning, so we can infer that she has positive feelings.

▶ **Listen to excerpts from the report and focus on the speaker's word choice. How does the speaker feel? Read each statement. Choose the correct answer.**

Excerpt One

The reporter's feelings about the Padaung's new lives in Nai Soi are ＿＿＿ .

a. positive

b. negative

c. neutral

What words did you hear that helped you find the answer? ＿＿＿＿＿＿＿＿＿＿＿＿＿＿＿＿＿＿＿＿＿＿＿

Excerpt Two

Fredrick's feelings about the tradition of neck stretching are ＿＿＿ .

a. positive

b. negative

c. neutral

What words did you hear that helped you find the answer? ＿＿＿＿＿＿＿＿＿＿＿＿＿＿＿＿＿＿＿＿＿＿＿

Work in a small group. Read the questions. Discuss your ideas.

1. According to the listening, what ways are the Padaung women helped by tourism in their village? What is your opinion of their situation?

2. How does tourism help preserve their cultural traditions? What is your opinion of this situation?

> **USE YOUR NOTES**
>
> **APPLY** Find information in your notes to use in your discussion.

🔘 Go to **MyEnglishLab** to give your opinion about another question.

LISTENING TWO | Town Hall Meeting in Cape Cod

VOCABULARY

1 Read the information about Cape Cod. Notice the boldfaced words. What can you conclude about this tourist destination?

Cape Cod, Massachusetts

Cape Cod is one of New England's most popular tourist attractions. Tourism has **developed** quickly, and now the area is visited by more than 5 million tourists each year. During the summer **season**, from June to September, tourists come to relax at the beach, shop in the small towns, and eat fresh seafood. During the rest of the year, the population drops to about 200,000, and Cape Cod becomes a small **community** again. Many summer businesses, such as restaurants and souvenir shops, close for the winter because they cannot **afford** to pay their workers' **salaries** once the tourists leave.

2 Match the words with the definitions. Write the correct letter in the blank.

__e__ 1. develop	a.	to have enough money to pay for something
_____ 2. season	b.	one of the four main periods (times) in the year
_____ 3. community	c.	a group of people who live in the same town
_____ 4. afford	d.	money that workers receive regularly as payment for their work
_____ 5. salary	e.	to grow into something bigger

➤ Go to the **Pearson Practice English App** or **MyEnglishLab** for more vocabulary practice.

NOTE-TAKING SKILL

Taking Notes with an Outline

Use outlines to show the relationship between main ideas and details (explanations and examples). Place the main ideas in the left column and use Roman numerals (I, II, III, . . .) to order the ideas as they're presented. Place details in the right column. and use capital letters (A, B, C, . . .) for each detail (explanation) related to the corresponding main idea. If there are examples supporting a particular explanation, list them using Arabic numbers (1, 2, 3, . . .) below the detail.

Main Ideas	Details (explanations and examples)
I. main idea	A. explanation
	B. explanation
II. main idea	1. example
	2. example

1 ▶ Listen to the excerpt from Listening One. Fill in the outline to show the difference between the main idea and the details.

Main Ideas	Details (examples and explanations)
I. _____	A. _____
	B. _____
	1. _____
	C. _____
	D. _____
	2. _____

2 Review your notes from Listening One. Rewrite your notes using an outline to show the relationship between main ideas and details.

➤ Go to **MyEnglishLab** for more note-taking practice.

COMPREHENSION

1 ▶ **Listen to a town hall meeting. The mayor (the town leader) is leading the meeting. The townspeople are listening and expressing their opinions. Create a chart like the one below to take notes. Try to take notes with an outline that shows the main ideas (their opinions) and details (reasons for their opinions and examples). Try to use indentation, numbers, bullet points, and / or dashes to indicate when a new idea begins.**

TAKE NOTES Town Hall Meeting in Cape Cod	
Main Ideas	**Details**

2 **Choose the correct answer to complete each statement. Use your notes to help you.**

1. The traffic on Cape Cod _____ .

   a. gets worse during the summer

   b. is bad all year

   c. is better now that there are buses

2. _____ is difficult to find on Cape Cod.

   a. Housing for regular people

   b. Housing near shops and restaurants

   c. Vacation housing

3. The restaurant owner knows a waitress who lives _____ .

   a. in her car

   b. far from her work

   c. in a hotel

4. The woman who runs the souvenir shop says _____ .

   a. she plans to open another store next year in a neighboring village

   b. she does most of her business during the summer

   c. her business is doing badly this year

5. The male business owner says he lost money because _____ .

   a. the same things are sold by too many stores

   b. tourists go to the beach instead of going shopping

   c. the rainy weather kept tourists away

> **USE YOUR NOTES**
>
> Compare your notes with a partner's. How can you improve your notes next time?

1 ▶ **Listen to an excerpt from the town hall meeting. What words does the speaker use to show that he is going to state an opinion?**

Recognizing and Understanding Opinions

It is useful to know when a person is going to state an opinion. Speakers use many different expressions to introduce opinions. For example:

In my opinion . . .   *I think that . . .*   *I believe . . .*

▶ **Read and listen to the example. Notice the signal words.**

Example

I agree that traffic gets bad, but, **in my mind,** the biggest problem is housing.

The speaker uses the phrase "in my mind" to signal that he is going to state an opinion. His opinion is that housing is the biggest problem caused by tourists.

2 ▶ **Listen to the excerpts. Complete each statement. Write the expression that signals an opinion in the blank. Then write the speaker's opinion on the line.**

Excerpt One

WOMAN 2:   OK, I know it's difficult to have all these tourists around during the

summer, but _I, for one_ am . . _very happy to have_

SPEAKER'S OPINION: _we need the tourism_

Excerpt Two

MAN 2:   But I'm a business owner, too, and one problem _I may see_ is

that . . .

SPEAKER'S OPINION: _we depend on the weather too much_

Excerpt Three

MAN 2:   _I would like to see_ us develop where we . . . _don't depend_

SPEAKER'S OPINION: _____

▶ **Go to MyEnglishLab for more skill practice.**

CONNECT THE LISTENINGS 🔍

ORGANIZE

1 Complete the chart with the details about the effects of tourism.

USE YOUR NOTES

APPLY Review your notes from Listening One and Two. Use the information in your notes to complete the chart.

	POSITIVE EFFECTS OF TOURISM	NEGATIVE EFFECTS OF TOURISM
LISTENING ONE: *Padaung Tribe*	1. _____ 2. Tourism is easier than farming. 3. _____	1. Women continue to wrap their necks. 2. _harting boddies degrading_
LISTENING TWO: *Cape Cod Residents*	1. _other make money_	1. Traffic gets bad. 2. _____ 3. _____

2 Draw a circle around the effect that is similar in both communities.

SYNTHESIZE

Work with a partner. Debate the topic: "Does tourism help or hurt people in tourist communities?" One person takes the pro position (Tourism has positive effects on people in tourist communities). The other person takes the con position (Tourism has negative effects on people in tourist communities). Each person has one to two minutes to present his or her position. Use the information from Organize to support your position.

Switch partners and repeat the debate two more times with new partners.

▶ Go to **MyEnglishLab** to check what you learned.

VOCABULARY

REVIEW

Three words in each group have related meanings. Find the word that doesn't belong in each group. Consult a dictionary if necessary.

1. **zoo**	museum	animal park	wildlife center
2. **afford**	have money for	pay for	borrow from
3. **controversy**	argument	debate	agreement
4. **degrading**	polite	embarrassing	painful
5. **make a living**	earn a **salary**	enjoy life	get paid
6. **preserve**	**develop**	save	care for
7. **season**	days of the week	time of year	period of time
8. **souvenir**	reminder	keepsake	equipment
9. **tourist attraction**	place to see	guidebook	point of interest
10. **tradition**	habit	change	belief
11. **community**	small town	village	city

EXPAND

1 Read the letter to the editor about the effects of tourism in Cape Cod. Notice the boldfaced words. Try to guess their meanings.

TO THE EDITOR

Effects of Tourism

Millions of tourists visit Cape Cod each year. Most tourists come here to relax at the beach and enjoy our delicious seafood. Others like to **get off the beaten path** and explore parts of the Cape that most tourists don't see. Whatever they do here, we appreciate the tourists because most **locals** have jobs that depend on tourism, such as shop owners and restaurant workers.

However, tourism can also **have a** negative **impact** on the area. The cost of housing is one example. The cost of housing keeps increasing, so many families can't afford to buy a home. **In the long run,** this problem will force families to leave the Cape and live elsewhere.

(continued on next page)

Problems like this affect our **way of life** here on the Cape. Life is becoming more difficult for the year-round residents. We need to **find a compromise** that will preserve the tourist income for the area and allow the locals to continue living here.

Michelle Connelly
Sandwich, Mass.

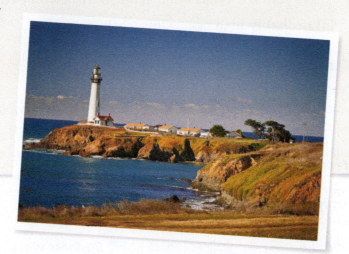

2 Match the words with the definitions. Write the correct letter.

_____ 1. get off the beaten path

_____ 2. locals

_____ 3. have an impact

_____ 4. in the long run

_____ 5. way of life

_____ 6. find a compromise

a. to have an effect on someone or something

b. customs and habits of daily living

c. far in the future

d. to go somewhere that most tourists don't visit

e. to look for ideas that opposing groups can agree on

f. people who live in a place all year

CREATE

APPLY **Work in a small group. Each person thinks of a tourist destination he or she has visited. Take turns making a short presentation about the destination. Answer the questions. Use the vocabulary from Review and Expand.**

Questions

1. What tourist destination did you visit?

2. What are the major tourist attractions?

3. What impact does tourism have on the locals?

4. What impact does tourism have on the environment?

Go to the **Pearson Practice English App** or **MyEnglishLab** for more vocabulary practice.

GRAMMAR FOR SPEAKING

1 Work with a partner. Read the conversation between two shop owners on Cape Cod. Then switch roles and repeat. Notice the boldfaced predictions.

A: Did you see the weather report today? They say it**'ll keep raining** all week.

B: Really? That's bad. If it keeps raining, the tourists **won't come**. They**'ll stay** home.

A: I know. I**'ll probably lose** money this week.

Will and *If* Clauses

1. Use *will* and *will not (won't)* to make predictions. *Will* is usually contracted in speech.	It **will rain** again next week. Tourists **won't come** to the shops and restaurants. They**'ll stay** home.
2. Use *probably* with *will* to show less certainty. **will + probably** **probably + won't**	 Business **will probably be** slow all week. I **probably won't make** enough money.
3. Use *if-clauses* to talk about possible results in the future. Use simple present in the main clause and *will* in the main clause. The result in the future can continue in the next sentence with *will*.	[*if*-clause] [main clause] If the rain **continues**, we**'ll have** a lot of problems. [main clause] [*if*-clause] We**'ll have** a lot of problems if the rain **continues**. We**'ll lose** a lot of business.

If + 1V. —

2 Work with a partner. Complete the paragraphs. Use the words in parentheses. Use contractions of *will* where possible. Then take turns saying the sentences.

1. If it _____rains_____ a lot this summer, fewer tourists _____will visit_____ .
   (rain)   (visit)

   Businesses _probably won't make_ enough money. Some shops _will probably close_ .
   (probably / not / make)   (probably / close)

2. If housing ___will gets___ more expensive, many families ___won't be able___
   (get)   (not / be able to)

   afford a house on Cape Cod. Some families ___will probab___ and others
   (probably / move away)

   _____ renting.
   (continue)

3. I heard that another seafood restaurant ___will___ in town.
   (probably / open)

   If it ___opens___ , there ___will be___ more jobs for the locals. But
   (open)   (be)

   the other restaurants in town ___will probably lose___ customers.
   (probably / lose)

4. Traffic ___will get___ worse if more tourists ___bring___ their cars
   (get)   (bring)

   to Cape Cod. There ___probably won't be___ enough parking spaces at the beach.
   (probably / not / be)

3 **APPLY** Work with a partner. Read about the people who live or go on vacation on Cape Cod. Take turns asking about the future and making predictions. What will happen to these people if tourism increases on Cape Cod? What will happen if tourism decreases?

Example

STUDENT A: What **will happen** to Joe if tourism increases?

STUDENT B: If tourism **increases**, Joe's restaurant **will probably get** busier.

STUDENT A: I agree. He**'ll serve** more seafood every day. He**'ll probably need** to hire more cooks and waitresses. . . .

CAPE COD RESIDENTS

Joe . . .

- owns Joe's Seafood Shack.
- serves 100 pounds of seafood each day.
- employs five cooks and four waitresses.

Sandy . . .

- is a high school student.
- works in a local souvenir shop during the summer.
- saves money to go to college.

Bill and Maureen . . .

- own the Cape Art Gallery.
- sell paintings and jewelry from local artists.
- employ two salesclerks.

The Harvey family . . .

- vacations on Cape Cod every summer.
- rents a house from a local.
- enjoys the area because the beaches aren't crowded.

Go to the **Pearson Practice English App** or **MyEnglishLab** for more grammar practice. Check what you learned in **MyEnglishLab**.

PRONUNCIATION

Pronouncing the Vowel *o*

The letter *o* is pronounced many different ways in English. In the words *hotel, shop, come, woman,* and *move,* the letter *o* is pronounced five different ways. Sometimes the letters around *o* can help you guess how to pronounce the vowel, but not always.

▶ **Read and listen to the example. Notice how the letter *o* is pronounced. Is it pronounced the same in any of the words?**

Example

> The **long**-necked **women** of Padaung talk with tourists, **pose** for pictures, and sell souvenirs. They have **become** an important source of **commerce** and **money** in small villages **along** the Thai / Myanmar border.

	Spelling	Pronunciation Tips
a)	*o* + a consonant + silent *e* *home, bone, pose, hope, close*	/ow/, like the vowel in *go*. Keep rounding your lips.
b)	*o* + one or more consonants *shop, lot, job, commerce, problem*	/a/, like the vowel in *father*; this vowel has no "o" sound. Do not round your lips.
c)	*o* + *ng, ss, st, ll, ff* *long, boss, lost, collar, office*	/ɔ/, like the vowel in *law*. This vowel is like /a/, but the lips are a little rounded. NOTE: Some Americans pronounce these words with /a/, like the vowel in *father*. You can use this vowel, too.
	Exceptions	
d)	*come, mother, brother, love, other*	/ə/, like the vowel in *cut*. Your mouth is almost closed.
e)	*move, lose*	/uw/, like the vowel in *do*
f)	*woman*	/u/, like the vowel in *could*
g)	*women*	/ɪ/, like the vowel in *sit*

1 ▶ **Listen to the words and repeat them.**

1. positive	7. won't	13. controversy
2. progress	8. money	14. sold
3. economic	9. vote	15. option
4. modern	10. popular	16. hospital
5. proposal	11. company	17. ocean
6. month	12. local	18. done

2 Work with a partner. How is the letter **o** pronounced in the words in Exercise One? Complete the chart. The number of lines in each column tells you how many words are in that column. Ask your teacher to repeat the words if you're not sure. Compare your answers with the class.

O SOUNDS LIKE . . .		
The Vowel in Father	**The Vowel in Go**	**The Vowel in Cut**
_____positive_____	_____	_____
_____	_____	_____
_____	_____	_____
_____	_____	
_____	_____	
_____		
_____		

3 Make phrases by writing words from the box in the blanks. Check your answers with a partner's. Practice saying the phrases to your partner. Pronounce the vowels carefully.

~~economic~~   local   modern   popular   positive

1. _____economic_____ progress (business, jobs)

2. a _____ controversy (not in earlier times)

3. a _____ proposal (one that will have good results)

4. a _____ option (one people like)

5. a _____ company (in this area)

Making Suggestions

When you make a suggestion, you give ideas about what you think someone should do. Suggestions can be *stronger* when you strongly believe the other person should follow your advice or *weaker* when you don't feel as strongly.

Stronger	We should (definitely) . . .	visit an elephant park.
	We (definitely) shouldn't . . .	
	Let's (not) . . .	
	I think / don't think we should . . .	
Weaker	One option is to . . .	visit an elephant park.
	We might (not) want to . . .	
	We could . . .	
	Why don't we . . .	
	What do you think of . . .	visiting an elephant park?
	How about . . .	

1 ▶ **Work with a partner. Read and listen to the conversation between two tourists in Thailand. Notice the boldfaced suggestions. Take notes to answer the following questions: "Which are stronger? Which are weaker?"**

A: What do you want to do tomorrow? **One option is to visit an elephant park.**

B: That's a great idea! Then **we could go to Padaung to see the long-necked women.**

A: **Let's not go there.** I think it's degrading for the women.

B: OK, but **we definitely shouldn't miss the elephant park.**

2 **Read each pair of suggestions with your partner. Choose the one that is stronger. Discuss the difference between the two suggestions.**

1. a. Let's take a guided tour.

   b. How about taking a guided tour?

2. a. We might want to buy souvenirs.

   b. We should definitely buy souvenirs.

3. a. I think we should eat at the hotel.

   b. One option is to eat at the hotel.

4. a. We could go to the elephant park today.

   b. Let's not go to the elephant park today.

5. a. What do you think of visiting the long-necked women?

   b. I don't think we should visit the long-necked women.

3 **Imagine that you are going to spend four days in Bangkok, Thailand. What would you like to do? Read the list of activity choices and take turns making suggestions with your partner. Use a different phrase to make strong suggestions about the most interesting activities and weaker suggestions about the less interesting activities.**

ACTIVITY CHOICES

Animals

- Go to Dusit Zoo to see wild animals.
- Visit the Snake Farm and see venom[1] removed from snakes to make medicine.
- Volunteer at an elephant park and help take care of the elephants.

Shopping

- Buy books about Thailand from Asia Books.
- Find fashionable women's clothing at Siam Square shops.
- Go to Lao Song Handicrafts to buy traditional Thai crafts and souvenirs.

Sightseeing

- Go to the National Museum and learn about Thai art.
- Visit the Grand Palace to see where Thai kings lived.
- Go to the Wat Sai floating market, where farmers sell food on boats.

Off the Beaten Path

- Spend a day at a spa, enjoying a massage, skin care, and a sauna.
- Take a Thai cooking class at the Blue Elephant Cooking School.
- Go on a bike tour of Bangkok.

---

[1] **venom:** poisonous liquid that snakes produce

🞂 **Go to MyEnglishLab for more skill practice and to check what you learned.**

An interactive poster presentation is an academic activity that combines presentation with discussion. Each presenter creates a poster about a topic. During the presentation, the presenter stands next to his or her poster. People walk around and look at the posters, and the presenter explains the information and answers questions about it.

In this activity, create and present a poster about a tour. The tour will have a theme and include several activities. Discuss your tour and its possible effects on the local community. Then look at other posters and discuss the tours with the presenters.

PREPARE

1 **Work with a partner to plan and create your poster.**

    a. **Choose a location for your tour. It can be a place that you know or a place that you research on the internet. You can choose a well-known area or somewhere off the beaten path.**

    b. **Choose a theme for the tour.**

Tour Theme	
Family Fun Tour	Do activities that are enjoyable for families with children
Culinary Tour	Visit the best restaurants and learn about the local cuisine
Adventure Tour	Explore the outdoors and try new outdoor activities
History Tour	Learn about history by visiting historic sites and museums
Cultural Tour	Understand a new culture by visiting a community and learning about their history, traditions, and way of life
Set-Jetting Tour	Visit locations that are settings for a book, TV show, or film
Other: _____	

    c. **Brainstorm activities that follow the theme for the tour. Where will the tourists go? What will they do? What can they buy? Make notes about the following activities:**

- tourist attractions (sites, museums)
- shopping and souvenirs
- restaurants
- places off the beaten path
- outdoor activities
- other: _____

2 Work together with your partner to create a poster advertising the tour. The posters should include:

- the location
- the theme
- at least five highlights of the tour

Make your poster interesting and eye-catching. Include pictures and colorful writing to grab people's attention and generate interest in your tour.

PRACTICE

1 Work with another pair to form a group of four. Practice explaining your poster. Give suggestions to help improve your classmates' explanations.

2 During the poster session, the audience will ask, "What will happen to the local community if this tour becomes popular?" Prepare for this question by making a list of the positive and negative impacts. Give suggestions to your partner about the possible impacts.

	Positive Impact	Negative Impact
Businesses		
Jobs		
Transportation		
Environment		
Local culture		
Other: _____		

3 **APPLY** Consider how to apply the vocabulary, grammar, pronunciation, and speaking skills from the unit. Use the checklist to help you.

☐ **Vocabulary:** Read through the list of vocabulary on page 141. Which words can you include in your poster or explanation to make it clearer and more interesting? Choose at least three words or phrases to use and add them to your notes.

☐ **Grammar:** Use *will* to make predictions about the future impact of the tour on the local community. Are you using it correctly?

☐ **Pronunciation:** Notice the words that are spelled with the letter *o*. Make sure you are pronouncing them correctly.

☐ **Speaking Skill:** Make suggestions about how your partner can improve his or her poster or presentation. Also make suggestions about how to reduce the impact of the tour on the local community. Use different phrases to make stronger and weaker suggestions.

PRESENT

1 Divide the class into two groups, with one student from each pair in Group A and the other in Group B (so each student in a group has a different poster).

- Students in Group A put their poster on the wall. Be ready to explain the tour to the students viewing the poster.

- Students in Group B walk around the room, look at the posters, and listen to the presenters. Ask follow-up questions:

  o Ask, "How will this tour impact the local community if it becomes popular?"

  o Listen to the possible impacts of the tour. Make suggestions for how to reduce the negative impacts and increase the positive impacts.

  o Ask other questions about the tour.

2 When students have visited all the posters, switch roles so that Group B presents and Group A looks at the posters and asks questions.

APPLY **Discuss the topics in small groups. Use the vocabulary, grammar, pronunciation, and speaking skills you learned in the unit.**

For some places, tourism is the most important way to make money. For example, Thailand used to make most of its money from growing rice, but now more money comes from tourism.

a. What are the pros and cons of relying on tourism as a source of money?

b. What are some things places that rely on tourism to make money can do to lessen the negative effects?

CHECK WHAT YOU'VE LEARNED

Check (✔) the outcomes you've met and vocabulary you've learned. Put an X next to the skills and vocabulary you still need to practice.

Learning Outcomes	Vocabulary		Multi-word Units
☐ Infer opinion from word choice	☐ afford	☐ season (*n.*)	☐ make a living
☐ Take notes with an outline	☐ community AWL	☐ souvenir	
☐ Recognize and understand opinions	☐ controversy AWL	☐ stretch (*v.*)	
☐ Use *will* and *if* clauses	☐ degrading (*adj.*)	☐ tourist attraction	
☐ Pronounce the vowel *o*	☐ develop	☐ tradition AWL	
☐ Make suggestions	☐ preserve (*v.*)	☐ wrapped (*adj.*)	
	☐ salary	☐ zoo	

 Go to **MyEnglishLab** to watch a video about ecotourism, access the Unit Project, and take the Unit 6 Achievement Test.

LEARNING OUTCOMES

> Infer a speaker's core beliefs

> Review and reflect on your notes

> Recognize phrases that describe thoughts or feelings

> Use *and, but, so,* and *because*

> Use expressive intonation to show confidence and interest

> Use signal words to persuade

 Go to **MyEnglishLab** to check what you know.

Restorative Justice

1 FOCUS ON THE TOPIC

1. Restorative justice helps people change their bad behavior by having the guilty person and the victim meet and talk. This photo shows a restorative justice meeting among a school counselor, a bully, and the victim of the bully. What do you think happens in a restorative justice meeting?

2. In the United States, 70 percent of people released from prison commit another crime within five years. Why do you think this happens? What are some things that can be done to prevent this?

LISTENING ONE | What Is Restorative Justice?

VOCABULARY

1 ▶ **Read and listen to an article about restorative justice. Notice the boldfaced words. Try to guess their meanings.**

What Is Restorative Justice?

Most criminal justice systems focus on punishment. When a crime is committed, the government decides who is guilty and **ensures** that the criminal is punished. The **offender** pays a fine, is **incarcerated**, or, in some places, faces physical punishment or death.

In contrast, restorative justice focuses on the effect of crime on people and relationships. Restorative justice is based on the idea that crime harms relationships between people **affected** by the crime—the victim, the offender, and members of the community—and that the justice system should heal the relationships. Restorative justice may be used in addition to traditional punishments like jail time, or it can be used as an alternative to traditional punishment.

Typically, this happens through a restorative justice meeting between the victim and offender. The meeting is led by a trained **facilitator** who plans the meeting and leads the discussion. The victim is able to tell the offender how the crime affected him or her. The offender has the opportunity to show **remorse** and apologize, take responsibility for the harm caused, and make **restitution**. The **outcome** of the meeting depends on the needs of the victim. For example, the offender may agree to pay the victim for stolen or damaged items.

There are many benefits. Victims often feel better after they participate in restorative justice. They can let go of the **tension**, fear, and anger they feel and are able to **move on** with their lives. Also, research has shown that offenders are less likely to commit another crime when they see the effects of the crime on the victim. This is one of the most powerful results of restorative justice—to give an offender the chance to be rehabilitated.[1]

---

[1] **rehabilitate:** to help someone live a healthy, useful, or active life again after they have been seriously ill or in prison

2 Match the words with the definitions. Write the words in the blanks.

affect	facilitator	move on	outcome	remorse
ensure	incarcerate	offender	restitution	tension

1. ___tension___ : a nervous or worried feeling that makes it impossible to relax
2. ___remors___ : to feel sorry for something negative that happened
3. ___facilitator___ : someone who helps a group of people discuss things with each other
4. ___affec___ : to do something that produces an effect or change in something
5. ___offender___ : someone who is guilty of a crime
6. ___ensure___ : to make sure something will happen in the right way
7. _____ : the act of giving something back to the victim of a crime
8. _____ : to put or keep someone in prison
9. ___outcome___ : the final result of a meeting or discussion
10. ___move on___ : to let negativity go and then change and improve your life

⬅ Go to the **Pearson Practice English App** or **MyEnglishLab** for more vocabulary practice.

PREVIEW

▶ **In this interview, a restorative justice facilitator describes the restorative justice process. Listen to an excerpt from the interview.**

1. What step in the restorative justice process is the facilitator describing?

   a. during the crime

   b. when the offender is arrested

   c. when the victim and offender meet

   d. after the restorative justice meeting is over

LISTEN

1 ▶ **Listen to the interview. Create a chart like the one below to take notes.**

TAKE NOTES What Is Restorative Justice?	
Main Ideas	**Details**
– What is restorative justice?	• offenders + victims communicate
	• harm repaired

2 **Compare your notes with a partner's. How can you improve your notes?**

⬅ Go to **MyEnglishLab** to view example notes.

MAIN IDEAS

All the statements contain some FALSE information. Use your notes to help you determine which information is false. Rewrite the statements so they are true. Some statements can be corrected in more than one way.

1. Communication between the victim and offender helps decide how long the offender should go to jail.

   _____

2. Victims participate in restorative justice because they want the offender to be punished.

   _____

3. The facilitator makes sure that the offender apologizes for the crime.

   _____

4. Before meeting a victim, offenders must first finish their prison sentences.

   _____

5. Victims and offenders do not express their emotions during the meeting.

   _____

6. Restorative justice is often life-changing for the victim but doesn't usually help the offender.

   _____

DETAILS

1 ▶ **Listen again and add to your notes. Answer the questions. Use your notes to help you.**

   1. What happens during a restorative justice meeting?

      a. What does the victim do?

         _____

      b. What does the offender do?

         _____

      c. What does the facilitator do?

         _____

   2. What are the reasons for participating in restorative justice?

      a. Why do victims participate?

         _____

      b. Why do offenders participate?

         _____

   3. What are some outcomes of restorative justice for the victims and the offenders?

      _____

2 **With a partner, take turns summarizing your notes. Then discuss how your notes and answer in Preview helped you understand the listening.**

▶ Go to **MyEnglishLab** for more listening practice.

Inferring a Speaker's Core Beliefs

A core belief is a principle or idea that affects your view of the world and the decisions you make. Restorative justice is based on several core beliefs about victims, offenders, and how to repair the harm caused by a crime. When the facilitator talks about the restorative justice process, he does not explicitly state his core beliefs. However, his beliefs are implied by the words he chooses.

▶ **Read and listen to the example. When he says, "It's an opportunity to fill that need," what core belief is he indirectly talking about?**

Example

FACILITATOR: But for others, it's not enough. They're frustrated. They want answers to their questions. They want the chance to tell the offender how they feel. So, some victims want to meet with the offender personally. It's an opportunity to fill that need.

The facilitator describes several things that the victim may want to tell the offender and then says the offender can "fill that need." This indirectly expresses the core belief that **offenders need to listen to the victims**.

▶ **Listen to the excerpts. Read each question. Then choose the correct answer to complete each statement.**

Excerpt One

What does the facilitator imply when he says, "We don't just throw people in a room together and say: 'Talk!'"?

A successful restorative justice meeting must _____ .

a. have a time for both people to talk

b. take place in a quiet room

c. be carefully planned

Excerpt Two

What does the facilitator imply when he says that offenders may think of their victims as "someone's name on a piece of paper" or someone the offender "saw in court"?

To understand the victim, an offender must realize that victim is _____ .

a. angry and afraid

b. a real person

c. easy to talk to

(continued on next page)

What does the facilitator imply when he says emotion is "part of the process"?

That expressing anger or sadness is a _____ part of the restorative justice process.

a. common

b. dangerous

c. unhelpful

DISCUSS 🔍

Work in a small group. Read the questions. Discuss your ideas.

USE YOUR NOTES

APPLY Find information in your notes to use in your discussion.

1. Summarize the core beliefs in restorative justice that relate to the victim, the offender, and the justice process. What do you think of this approach to justice? Do you agree or disagree with the core beliefs?

2. In what type of situations and crimes should restorative justice be used? When would it be most helpful? When should it not be used?

🔵 Go to **MyEnglishLab** to give your opinion about another question.

LISTENING TWO | Derek and Marcus

VOCABULARY

1 Read the story about Derek and Marcus. Notice the boldfaced words

Derek is a widower who has lived alone since his wife died. One day, his house was robbed and his television, his laptop computer, and all his wife's jewelry were stolen. "I was **shocked**. I'd always felt safe in this neighborhood." The crime was deeply upsetting to him. "I tried to forget about it, but I couldn't. My daughter asked how I was doing, and it all came **pouring out**—all the anger and sadness."

Marcus is a nineteen-year-old man who lives in the next town. The police arrested him for the robbery. Marcus pleaded guilty and was sentenced to one year in jail. The crime has affected his family as well. "When my mom found out, I thought she would **lose it**. I hope she can **forgive** me one day."

After Marcus was sentenced, Derek and Marcus agreed to participate in restorative justice. Sonia, the facilitator, hopes it will help both of them. "It's more than someone **just breaking the law**. Crimes like this hurt the victim, the offender, and the community."

2 Write each boldfaced word from Exercise One next to its definition.

_____ 1. become very angry or upset

_____ 2. doing something illegal

_____ 3. stop being angry at someone, although they did something wrong

___Shoukeed___ 4. surprised and upset by something unpleasant

_____ 5. telling someone all your feelings because you are unhappy

🎧 Go to the **Pearson Practice English App** or **MyEnglishLab** for more vocabulary practice.

Reviewing and Reflecting on Your Notes

It is important to review and reflect on your notes in order to remember the important information from what you heard. It is preferable to do this within 24 hours of taking the notes. Actively interacting with your notes will help put the information into your long-term memory.

One way to review your notes is to write questions about the information. Circle a detail in your notes. Write a question that is answered by the details you circled. Then review the questions and notes to help you remember the information.

1 **Read the example notes for Listening One. Look at the circled information. Write questions about the information. Compare your questions with a partner's.**

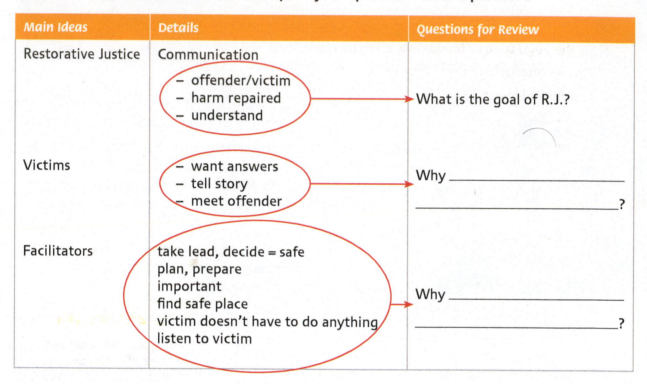

Main Ideas	Details	Questions for Review

Restorative Justice	Communication
	  – offender/victim
	  – harm repaired
	  – understand
		What is the goal of R.J.?

Victims	– want answers – tell story – meet offender	Why _____ _____?
Facilitators	take lead, decide = safe plan, prepare important find safe place victim doesn't have to do anything listen to victim	Why _____ _____?

2 **Review your notes from Listening One. Try to add at least one new question to your notes to help you remember the important information from the interview.**

↳ Go to **MyEnglishLab** for more note-taking practice.

COMPREHENSION

1 ▶ **Marcus was convicted of robbery for stealing from Derek's house. After the trial, Derek and Marcus met in a restorative justice meeting. Listen to Derek and Marcus reflect on their experience. Create a chart like the one below to take notes. After taking notes, use questions to review and reflect on your notes.**

TAKE NOTES Derek and Marcus' Story	
Main Ideas	**Details**

2 **Choose the correct answer to complete each statement. Use your notes to help you.**

1. At the beginning of the meeting, Derek felt _____ .
   a. nervous and angry
   b. relieved and hopeful
   c. sad and afraid

2. Derek was upset that the ring was stolen because _____ .
   a. he planned to give it to his daughter
   b. he kept it to remember his dead wife
   c. it was very expensive

3. Derek thought that Marcus _____ his crime.
   a. didn't understand the effect of
   b. felt remorse for
   c. tried to explain the reasons for

4. After the meeting, Derek _____ Marcus.
   a. started to forgive
   b. still felt angry at
   c. wanted to stay in touch with

5. At the beginning of the meeting, Marcus felt _____ .
   a. angry and annoyed
   b. calm and confident
   c. nervous and unsure

6. When Marcus robbed a house, he didn't think about _____ .
   a. feeling guilty afterward
   b. hurting the people who lived there
   c. getting arrested and sent to jail

7. By the end of the meeting, Marcus wanted to _____ .
   a. become a better person
   b. rob more houses
   c. pay Derek back for the ring

USE YOUR NOTES

Compare your notes with a partner's. How can you improve your notes next time?

1 ▶ **Read and listen to an excerpt from Derek and Marcus' story. How does Derek feel?**

DEREK: I **was afraid** I'd lose it.

Recognizing Phrases That Describe Thoughts or Feelings

When speakers tell a story, they may use a variety of words and phrases to describe what they are thinking or feeling about the events. Recognizing these phrases helps listeners understand how a speaker feels about the events in the story.

▶ **Read and listen to the example. Notice the phrases that describe thoughts or feelings.**

Example

MARCUS: When I saw him first, he looked real serious, and, like, mad. **Part of me wanted to run out of the room . . .**

Marcus uses the phrase "part of me wanted to run out of the room" to express that he was nervous and scared to meet Derek, but he wasn't going to run away from the situation. Part of him wanted to leave, but there was still a part of Marcus that wanted to stay and find out what would happen.

2 ▶ **Listen to the excerpts. Write the missing words that express the speaker's thoughts or feelings. Then identify how the speaker felt.**

1. DEREK: At first, I ___did not___ what to say.

   What is Derek thinking or feeling?

   _____

2. MARCUS: I ___never though___ the people who lived in the house.

   What is Marcus thinking or feeling?

   ___didn't really care___

3. MARCUS: I ___though like___ I wasn't hurting anyone.

   What is Marcus thinking or feeling?

   ___its ok___

4. DEREK: I ___reilea zee___ that I can move on.

   What is Derek thinking or feeling?

   _____

5. MARCUS: . . . but I ___feel like___ now I want to be better, be a better person.

   What is Marcus thinking or feeling?

   _____

▶ **Go to MyEnglishLab for more skill practice.**

ORGANIZE

1 Complete the chart with main ideas about restorative justice from Listening One and specific examples that illustrate those ideas from Listening Two.

USE YOUR NOTES

APPLY Review your notes from Listening One and Two. Use the information in your notes to complete the chart.

LISTENING ONE: What Is Restorative Justice?	LISTENING TWO: Derek and Marcus' Story
Victim – tell story	V _____ _____
Offender _____ _____	O – "didn't hurt anyone"
O – chance to repair harm	O _____ _____ V _____ _____
V & O _____ _____	V – not afraid – start to forgive O _____ _____

SYNTHESIZE

Discuss the questions in a small group. Be prepared to share your answers with the class.

1. What steps in the restorative justice process did Derek and Marcus talk about? What other steps are part of the restorative justice process?

2. How were Derek and Marcus helped by the restorative justice process? How does restorative justice help other victims and offenders?

3. What difficulties did Derek and Marcus have with restorative justice? What else could be difficult about the restorative justice process?

ⓚ Go to **MyEnglishLab** to check what you learned.

VOCABULARY

REVIEW

Complete the crossword puzzle with words and phrases from Listening One and Two. Write one letter in each square.

ACROSS

5. The best ___outcom___ is when both the criminal and the victim come to an agreement together about how to repair the damage from a crime.

6. In restorative justice, the victim and the ___opender___ meet together to talk about the crime.

10. It is important to ___ensure___ that the victim feels safe.

12. If the offender is _____, the meeting could take place in a conference room in the prison.

13. People who ___break___ _____ ___the___ _____ ___law___ may be arrested and sent to trial for their crimes.

14. The victim is sometimes able to ___forgive___ the offender for committing the crime.

15. Once the conference starts, victims often become emotional and let their feelings _____ ___pour___ _____ ___out___ _____ .

DOWN

1. If victims are afraid that they are going to _____ ___Lost___ _____ ___it___ _____ , the facilitator can help them stay calm.

2. Offenders may feel ___remors___ for their crime, but the traditional justice system does not give them a way to express it.

3. A crime can negatively ___affect___ the victim and his or her family in many ways.

4. There may be ___tension___ when the victim and the offender meet because both people are unsure what will happen.

7. The ___faciitatos___ prepares the victim and offender for the restorative justice meeting.

8. Offenders are often _____ to hear details about how their crimes hurt the victim.

9. The victim sometimes cannot _____ ___move___ _____ ___on___ _____ and heal from the crime because of feelings of fear or anger.

11. An offender can make ___restitution___ , such as paying the victim back for something stolen or damaged.

1 Read the police report. Notice the boldfaced words.

POLICE REPORT

Philip Sunbury is a twenty-one-year-old male. On November 29, 2018, police officers stopped him for driving 60 miles per hour in a 40-mile-per-hour area. When officers searched the car they found stolen jewelry and computers. Police **arrested** Mr. Sunbury and **detained** him in Los Angeles City Jail for two weeks. Mr. Sunbury was **tried** in court and **convicted** of burglary. The judge **sentenced** him to three years of incarceration at Los Angeles Correctional Facility.

Philip Sunbury, age 21

2 Choose the correct synonym or definition for each boldfaced verb.

1. **arrest**

   a. take someone away

   b. talk with someone

2. **detain**

   a. stop someone from entering

   b. stop someone from leaving

3. **try**

   a. judge an offender in court

   b. release an offender from court

4. **convict**

   a. announce that someone may have broken the law

   b. state based on evidence that someone has broken the law

5. **sentence**

   a. ask for restitution

   b. tell an offender his or her punishment

CREATE

1 Read the situation.

Mandy is an eighteen-year-old college student. One evening, she went to a party and drove home late. It was dark and raining, and she was driving fast. All of a sudden, she saw a stop sign at an intersection, but she couldn't stop in time. She hit a parked car on the other side of the intersection and damaged it badly. Another driver saw the accident and called 9-1-1. Mandy got scared and ran away. The police arrived and called the owner of the car. The owner had a tow truck take his car to a mechanic to see how much it would cost to get it fixed. The police searched the area near the accident and found Mandy hiding behind a tree. The police arrested Mandy and detained her at the police station while they called her parents. She will be tried in court to determine her punishment.

2 Discuss the questions with a partner and give reasons for your opinions.

1. Should Mandy be tried as an adult or a youth?

2. Should she be incarcerated?

3. What should her sentence be?

4. Would restorative justice be a good way to provide restitution for the owner of the damaged car?

5. Do you think Mandy would express remorse during a restorative justice conference?

6. What are some ways to ensure a good outcome for Mandy and the owner of the damaged car?

3 **APPLY** **Work with your partner to create a plan that could help Mandy and the owner of the damaged car to move on. Present your plan to the class.**

 Go to the **Pearson Practice English App** or **MyEnglishLab** for more vocabulary practice.

GRAMMAR FOR SPEAKING

1 Read and listen to the telephone conversation. Practice the conversation with a partner. Then switch roles and repeat. Notice the boldfaced connectors.

WOMAN: Hi, Tom. How's it going?

MAN: Not good. My son has to go to driving school **because** he was speeding.

WOMAN: That's actually not so bad! My daughter had to do the same thing. The police stopped her because she was driving 10 miles an hour over the speed limit **and** not using her turn signals. She had just gotten her driver's license, **so** the class was actually very helpful.

MAN: Josh signed up for the class, **but** he doesn't want to go. He thinks it's a waste of time.

And, But, So, and Because

1. Use **and** to connect two or more ideas. The ideas can be independent or dependent clauses.*	*Josh paid $100 **and** attended a driving class.* (independent clause + dependent clause) *Josh paid $100, **and** the judge sent him to a driving class.* (two independent clauses)
2. Use **but** to connect two opposing ideas. The ideas can be independent or dependent clauses.	*Josh signed up for the class **but** didn't go.* (independent clause + dependent clause) *The judge sent him to the class, **but** Josh didn't want to go.* (two independent clauses)
3. Use **so** to connect a cause and a result. The cause and result must be two independent clauses.	*Josh was driving too fast, **so** he had to take a driving class.* (two independent clauses)
4. Use **because** to give a reason. *Because* connects an independent clause with an adverb clause (*because* + subject + verb).	*He had to attend a driving class* (independent clause) ***because** he was driving too fast.* (adverb clause) ***Because** he was driving too fast* (adverb clause)*, he had to attend driving class.* (independent clause)

****independent clause:** a structure with a subject + verb that can stand alone as a sentence. In a sentence with two independent clauses, a comma is used between the two clauses, before the connecting word.

dependent clause: a structure that cannot stand alone as a sentence. It must be connected to an independent clause. In a sentence with a dependent clause and an independent clause, a comma is not used between the two clauses.

2 Work with a partner. Complete the sentences with *and*, *but*, *so*, or *because*. Add commas as necessary.

1. Josh doesn't want to go to driving class ____Because____ he thinks it will be boring.

2. His dad wants him to go ____so____ he's trying to convince Josh it's important to learn about the dangers of speeding.

3. The class is free ____and____ close to Josh's house.

4. If Josh attends, he might learn some new driving rules , ____and____ his father would be happy.

5. Sarah wants to take the class ____but____ the time doesn't work with her schedule.

6. She changed her schedule ____so____ now she can attend.

7. Sarah wants to take a driving class ____so be____ she wants to be a better driver.

8. She asked her boss if she could skip work and go to the class , ____but____ he said "no."

3 **APPLY** Work with a partner. Look at the picture and answer the questions. Use connectors in your answers.

1. What happened? Was anyone hurt?

2. What is the police officer doing?

3. Why is the girl upset?

4. What is the mother doing? Why is she talking on the phone?

5. What is the other woman doing? What do you think she is saying to the police officer?

6. What are the two women in the background doing?

Take turns describing the scene with your partner. Use connectors in your descriptions.

🔵 Go to the **Pearson Practice English App** or **MyEnglishLab** for more grammar practice. Check what you learned in **MyEnglishLab**.

Using Expressive Intonation to Show Confidence and Interest

When speakers use a monotone—a low pitch with little variation—they may sound uncertain or uninterested. When speakers speak with a variety of pitches, they can sound confident and interested.

1 ▶ **Listen to the speakers and label the photos. Which speaker sounds uncertain and uninterested (A)? Which speaker sounds confident and interested (B)?**

1. ____    2. ____

To Show Confidence and Interest with Intonation

Content words (nouns, main verbs, adjectives, adverbs) are usually stressed, with higher pitch.	There **must** be **other ways** to **deal** with **criminals**.
Function words (prepositions, articles, conjunctions, etc.) are usually unstressed, with lower pitch.	There *must* be *other ways* to *deal* with *criminals*.
To vary the pitch of your voice, focus on using higher pitch to stress key syllables of the most important content words.	There **must** be **OTHer ways** to **deal** with **CRIminals**.

Restorative justice is not only used in the criminal justice system. Many schools now use restorative justice to help resolve conflicts between students.

2 ▶ **Listen to the sentences and repeat them. Circle the most important content words pronounced with stress and a higher pitch. Compare the words you circled with a partner.**

1. When teenagers fight in schools, they are often sent home . . .

2. . . . but many schools are using restorative justice instead of punishment.

3. Restorative justice in schools is about communication.

4. The teenagers talk about their conflict.

5. They express their feelings and listen to each other.

6. The goal is to come to an agreement and repair the relationship.

7. It's a good way to teach teens how to solve problems . . .

8. . . . and it keeps them in school!

3 Listen to the sentences again. Work with a partner. Take turns saying the sentences. Use expressive intonation.

4 Work with your partner. Circle the important content words that you will say with stress and a higher pitch. Perform the conversation using expressive intonation. Take turns being each character.

PRINCIPAL: I'm thinking of starting a restorative justice program at our school.

TEACHER: That's a great idea! We had one at my last school.

PRINCIPAL: I think it will help our students. When there's a problem, we can help the students talk about it and find a resolution.

TEACHER: It's very helpful for bullying. The victim and the bully can both benefit.

PRINCIPAL: Right. The victim can tell his or her story, and the bully has a chance to make restitution.

TEACHER: Yes, I saw that outcome many times. I'd be happy to talk to other teachers about my experience.

SPEAKING SKILL

Using Signal Words to Persuade

Signal words help a listener follow a speaker's thoughts. In a persuasive speech, the speaker uses signal words to "signal," or show, when the speaker is introducing a position (A) or a supporting argument (B).

A. Signal Words for Introducing a Position

▶ Read and listen to the excerpts from two oral presentation introductions. Underline the speaker's position. Then circle the signal words used to introduce the opinion.

Excerpt One

Solitary confinement is a punishment in which a criminal is put in a room alone for long periods of time. Some people think that solitary confinement is too cruel and should be stopped. Others feel that it is an effective way to stop a criminal from hurting other people. In my opinion, solitary confinement should not be used as a punishment, especially with offenders under the age of eighteen.

Excerpt Two

I think restorative justice should be an option for some crimes. One argument is that it can help judges decide which punishment will help the victim. In New Zealand, for instance, the results of a restorative justice conference can be sent to a judge and influence the final decision.

Signal words to introduce positions include:

I believe (that) . . .

I feel (strongly) (that) . . .

I support (that) . . .

In my opinion . . .

I think . . .

B. Signal Words to Introduce Supporting Arguments

Points of Equal Importance	Points from Least to Most Important[1]
One argument (is / is that) . . .	My first argument (is / is that) . . .
Another point (is / is that) . . .	Another important argument (is / is that) . . .
My first/second/third argument (is / is that) . . .	An even more important point (is / is that) . . .
My final argument (is / is that) . . .	The most important argument (is / is that) . . .

[1] You can also choose to organize your presentation from most to least important.

1 **Complete the outlines below with signal words. Make sure to decide whether or not the supporting arguments are equally important when adding the appropriate signal words. Discuss your answers with a partner. Then discuss as a class.**

Position: _____ restorative justice should not be used when the victim is a child.

Argument 1: _____ children might be forced to participate in restorative justice even if they don't want to.

Argument 2: _____ children are too young to deal with the emotions that can arise from restorative justice.

Argument 3: _____ children might not know how to communicate with an offender.

Position: _____ people should not be allowed to own guns.

Argument 1: _____ people are more likely to be hurt by a gun if they have one in their home.

Argument 2: _____ if people are allowed to own guns, police officers face greater danger.

Argument 3: _____ if guns are easy to buy, criminals could get them more easily.

2 Work in a small group. Make a list of other signal words that you could use to introduce positions and supporting arguments.

Introducing Positions	Introducing Supporting Arguments

Work with your classmates to create two big lists on the board that everyone can use.

3 APPLY Pick a topic from the list below. In a small group, practice using signal words to introduce your opinion and supporting arguments.

- solitary confinement
- restorative justice with children
- ownership of guns
- corporal punishment

Go to **MyEnglishLab** for more skill practice and to check what you learned.

FINAL SPEAKING TASK: Persuasive Oral Presentation 🔍 APPLY

In a persuasive oral presentation, the speaker states a position and then gives arguments in order to persuade the audience to agree with the opinion.

In this activity, you will give a 3- to 5-minute persuasive oral presentation on a controversial topic related to justice and punishment.

PREPARE

1 Read the list of questions. Choose a topic for your presentation or think of your own topic.

- Should restorative justice be the main way to provide restitution for a crime?

- Should the main purpose of prison be punishment or rehabilitation?

- Should teenagers who commit crimes receive the same punishments as adults?

- Is the death penalty an effective punishment for serious crimes?

- If a person acts in self-defense and hurts someone, should he or she be prosecuted?

- How should people who drink and drive be punished?

- Should people who use illegal drugs be incarcerated?

- Your idea: _____

2 **Research your topic on the internet to help you decide a position about the question. Think of two or three persuasive arguments to support your position. Write your position and arguments below.**

Position: _____

    Argument 1: _____

    Argument 2: _____

    Argument 3: _____

3 **Meet with a partner and share your question, position, and arguments. Ask your partner for thoughts and suggestions about your ideas.**

- Is the position clear?

- Do the arguments support the position?

Switch roles and give your partner suggestions for their presentation.

4 **Write an outline for your presentation, following the guidelines below:**

Introduction (1/2–1 minute)

- Introduce the question and briefly explain the situation.

- Present two different sides of the situation.

- State your position.

Body (2–3 minutes)

- Give two or three arguments to support your position.

- State each argument. Use signal words to introduce each point.

- Explain each argument using explanations and examples.

Conclusion (1/2 minute)

- Restate your opinion.

- Make a concluding statement.

PRACTICE

1 **APPLY** **Consider how to apply the vocabulary, grammar, pronunciation, and speaking skills from the unit. Use the checklist to help you.**

- ☐ **Vocabulary:** Read through the list of vocabulary on page 167. Choose three to five words or phrases to include in your presentation.

- ☐ **Grammar:** Make sure your ideas are correctly connected with *and, but, so,* and *because.*

- ☐ **Pronunciation:** Use expressive intonation (high and low pitches) to show confidence and interest.

- ☐ **Speaking Skill:** Use signal words to introduce your position and supporting arguments.

2 Practice giving your presentation to a friend or in front of a mirror. Or videotape yourself with a cell phone or computer and review the video. Evaluate your performance.

- Is your position strong and clear?
- Do your arguments support your position?
- Is your presentation organized and easy to follow?
- Are you using expressive intonation to sound confident and interested?
- Do you make good eye contact with your audience?

PRESENT

Give your presentation to the class. When presenting, make eye contact with the audience and use your outline as a guide. Speak loudly with expressive intonation.

LISTENING TASK

Listen to your classmates' presentations. Be prepared to discuss these questions: "Do you agree with the presenter's opinion? Why or why not?"

ALTERNATIVE SPEAKING TOPIC

APPLY Work in a small group. Read the information in the chart. Then discuss the questions below. Use the vocabulary, grammar, pronunciation, and speaking skills you learned in the unit.

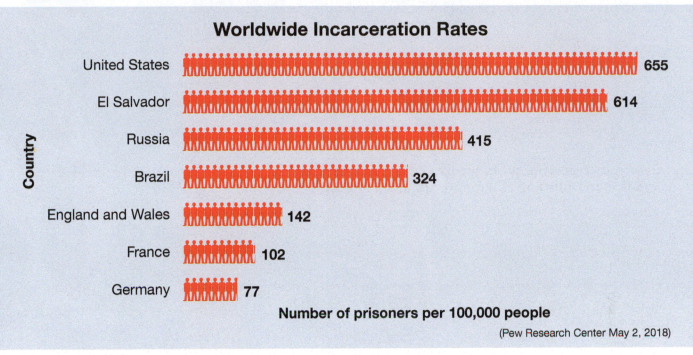

Worldwide Incarceration Rates

Country	Number of prisoners per 100,000 people
United States	655
El Salvador	614
Russia	415
Brazil	324
England and Wales	142
France	102
Germany	77

(Pew Research Center May 2, 2018)

What do you think are some of the reasons for the high incarceration (prison) rate in the United States? What are some things that could be done to reduce incarceration?

CHECK WHAT YOU'VE LEARNED

Check (✔) the outcomes you've met and vocabulary you've learned. Put an X next to the skills and vocabulary you still need to practice.

Learning Outcomes
- ☐ Infer a speaker's core beliefs
- ☐ Review and reflect on your notes
- ☐ Recognize phrases that describe thoughts or feelings
- ☐ Use *and, but, so,* and *because*
- ☐ Use expressive intonation to show confidence and interest
- ☐ Use signal words to persuade

Vocabulary
- ☐ affect (*v.*) AWL
- ☐ ensure AWL
- ☐ facilitator AWL
- ☐ forgive
- ☑ incarcerate
- ☐ offender
- ☐ outcome AWL
- ☐ restitution
- ☑ remorse
- ☑ shocked (*adj.*)
- ☐ tension AWL

Multi-word Units
- ☐ break the law
- ☐ lose it
- ☐ move on
- ☐ pour out

🔘 Go to **MyEnglishLab** to watch a video about the death penalty, access the Unit Project, and take the Unit 7 Achievement Test.

LEARNING OUTCOMES

> **Infer contrast from context**
> **Use symbols to take notes**
> **Identify repetition to emphasize a point**

> **Use modals of necessity**
> **Use final intonation**
> **Interrupt politely and hold the floor**

🔵 Go to **MyEnglishLab** to check what you know.

Reducing Your Carbon Footprint

1 FOCUS ON THE TOPIC

1. Climate change has many effects. One of these is global warming, which is an increase in temperatures all over the world. What might be some of the causes of global warming?

2. There are many things that we can do as individuals to help the environment. Look at the photo. How is this family helping reduce their impact on the environment? What are some other lifestyle choices you can make to help the environment?

LISTENING ONE | Living Small

VOCABULARY

1 ▶ **Read and listen to the article about how our lifestyle can affect global warming. Notice the boldfaced words. Try to guess their meanings.**

Your *personal carbon footprint* is the amount of carbon dioxide (CO_2)[1] that you put into the air when you drive a car, fly in an airplane, or use electricity made by burning coal[2] or gas.

CO_2 and other **greenhouse gases** have a serious impact on the environment. They make Earth warmer, causing climate change.

Even the food you eat affects your personal carbon footprint. A diet that includes a lot of meat creates a bigger footprint, while the footprint of a vegetarian diet is smaller. This is because a lot of **resources** are used to raise animals and **transport** meat from the farm to your table.

Ways to Reduce Your Personal Carbon Footprint

Install **solar panels** to make electricity for your house.

Grow vegetables in a raised **bed** in your garden.

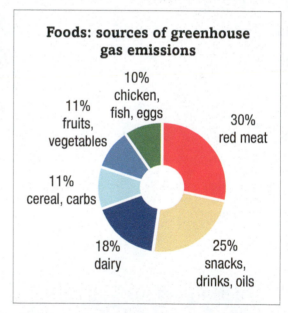

Foods: sources of greenhouse gas emissions

- 10% chicken, fish, eggs
- 11% fruits, vegetables
- 30% red meat
- 11% cereal, carbs
- 18% dairy
- 25% snacks, drinks, oils

What can we do to protect the environment for future **generations**? **Collectively**, we must reduce our energy **consumption**. Start with simple changes to reduce your own carbon footprint. For example, skip a serving of meat each week. It may seem like a **drop in the bucket**, but it's equal to driving 320 miles (515 kilometers) in a car.

Protect and plant trees. **Dense** forests around the world are being cut down to make room for farms. This causes a faster increase in greenhouse gasses. Trees have a positive impact on climate by taking CO_2 out of the air. Forests take in nearly 40 percent of human-made CO_2.

---

[1] **carbon dioxide:** often called CO_2 in speech and writing
[2] **coal:** a hard, black mineral that is dug out of the ground and burned to produce heat

2 Complete the definitions. Choose the correct answer.

1. greenhouse gas: a gas, especially carbon dioxide (CO_2) or methane (CH_4), that traps _____ above the Earth and causes global warming

   a. water

   b. heat

   c. pollution

2. resource: a supply of something _____ such as land, oil, or coal

   a. useful

   b. expensive

   c. big

3. transport: to _____ goods or people _____

   a. keep . . . in one place

   b. take . . . from one place to another in a vehicle

   c. look for . . . that can be helpful

4. generation: all people _____

   a. living together

   b. of about the same age

   c. in the same country

5. collectively: _____

   a. as a group

   b. alone

   c. with friends

6. consumption: the _____ of energy, oil, or electricity

   a. use

   b. cost

   c. selling

7. a drop in the bucket: an action that has _____ effect

   a. a big

   b. little or no

   c. an unexpected

8. solar panel: equipment that makes energy from the _____

   a. sun

   b. wind

   c. ocean

9. (raised) bed: an area in a garden that is used to _____

    a. keep chickens

    b. collect trash

    c. grow plants

10. dense: made of a lot of things that are very _____

    a. small

    b. far apart

    c. close together

○ Go to the **Pearson Practice English App** or **MyEnglishLab** for more vocabulary practice.

PREVIEW

Julia Peters is trying to leave a small carbon footprint. She describes her life in a podcast.

▶ **Listen to an excerpt from Julia's podcast. Which topics will she mention in the podcast? Check (✓) your predictions.**

_____ a. driving an hour to work

_____ b. growing food

_____ c. using solar energy

_____ d. cutting forests to build houses

_____ e. living with other people

_____ f. starting a large chicken factory

Julia Peters taking care of her chickens

LISTEN

1 ▶ **Listen to the whole podcast. Create a chart like the one below to take notes.**

2 **Compare your notes with a partner's. How can you improve your notes?**

○ Go to **MyEnglishLab** to view example notes.

TAKE NOTES Living Small	
Main Ideas	**Details**
JP: sm personal footprint imp	• live small b/c so many ppl on Earth

Choose the correct answer to complete each statement. Use your notes to help you.

1. Julia lives with a small carbon footprint to _____ .

    a. save money

    b. protect Earth for future generations

    c. live a healthy life

2. Julia grows her own food because _____ .

    a. food from the store has been transported from far away

    b. the stores near her house don't have fresh vegetables

    c. her garden has many raised beds

3. Julia has solar panels to _____ .

    a. produce all the energy for her house

    b. avoid using energy that comes from coal

    c. encourage her neighbors to use clean energy

4. Julia shares her house with other people because _____ .

    a. she likes living with friends

    b. the government gives her money for sharing

    c. it saves energy

5. Julia believes that the efforts of _____ can help to make a change.

    a. the government

    b. one person

    c. her family

Fresh eggs from chickens
kept in the backyard

1 ▶ **Listen again and add to your notes. All the statements below contain some FALSE information. Use your notes to help you determine which information is false. Cross out the parts that are untrue and write corrections.**

1. The speaker's name is Julia ~~Smith~~. *Peters*

2. Julia lives in San Francisco, California.

3. She lives in an old house.

4. Julia says that she grows carrots, basil, and squash in her yard.

5. For most Americans, the food they eat has traveled 500 miles.

6. In the summer, Julia's chickens lay about two eggs a day.

7. If we don't reduce our coal consumption, the average temperature of the earth will increase two or three degrees.

8. There are three people living in Julia's house.

9. It's difficult for one person to have an impact on climate change when there are almost 8 billion people on the planet.

2 **With a partner, take turns summarizing your notes. Then discuss how your notes and your answer in Preview helped you understand the listening.**

↘ **Go to MyEnglishLab for more listening practice.**

Growing your own food in your backyard

MAKE INFERENCES

Inferring Contrast from Context

A speaker may indirectly express a contrast between two situations. The listener can infer the contrasting ideas based on the context.

▶ **Read and listen to the example. Notice the boldfaced words. What is Julia implying?**

Example

> JULIA: Here in the backyard, you can see, **it's not much of a yard. There's not much grass**. We've taken out most of the grass to put in raised beds so that we can grow more of our own food.

In the example, she is *implying* that her yard is different from most other yards and that most Americans have grass instead of raised beds.

▶ **Julia explains what she does and implies what most Americans do. Complete the chart.**

	What Julia Does	**What Most Americans Do**
Excerpt One		
Excerpt Two		

DISCUSS

Work in a small group. Read the questions. Discuss your ideas.

1. Julia says her efforts are just "a drop in the bucket." Why does she say this? In your opinion, can her actions have an impact on global warming? Explain.

2. In what ways is Julia's lifestyle different from the way people live in your home country? In what ways is it similar? Would Julia's lifestyle be culturally acceptable in your country? Why or why not?

▶ Go to **MyEnglishLab** to give your opinion about another question.

USE YOUR NOTES

APPLY Find information in your notes to use in your discussion.

LISTENING TWO | A Call to Action

1 Read the fact sheet. Notice the boldfaced words.

FACT SHEET

1. Motor vehicle manufacturing is one of the top ten **industries** in the United States.

2. **Factories** in China produce 25 percent of the automobiles in the world.

3. Newer cars are more **energy-efficient**, so they need less gasoline than older cars.

4. New **technology**, such as radar to help cars drive in reverse, will make cars easier and safer to drive.

5. Newer cars use less gasoline, which reduces their carbon dioxide (CO_2) **emissions**.

2 Write each boldfaced word from Exercise One next to its definition.

_____ a. gases that go into the air

_____ b. using less of a resource (gas, oil, water)

_____ c. buildings where products are made by machines

_____ d. groups of businesses, each of which makes the same type of product

_____ e. machines that are based on modern knowledge of science and computers

🍀 Go to the **Pearson Practice English App** or **MyEnglishLab** for more vocabulary practice.

Taking Notes with Symbols

Symbols are marks or signs that represent ideas, relationships, or processes. They are useful for note-taking because they can help you write information quickly and clearly.

Some examples of symbols:

°	degrees (temperature)
=	equals, same
%	percent
2, 3, 4	two, three, four (numbers)
↑	increase, more
↓	decrease, reduce
→	causes, leads to
△	change
1/3, 1/2	one-third, one-half (fractions)

1 ▶ **Listen to the excerpts from Listening One. Each excerpt will be read twice. Fill in the blanks with symbols.**

1. If we don't ___reduce↓___ coal, avg temp. will ___↑___ by ___having onto two 1~2°___

2. ___Four___ people using ___=___ amount energy, split by ___4___

3. If ___more↑___ people do it, can make a ___change   △___

2 ▶ **Listen to the excerpts. Take notes using symbols.**

1. _____

  _____

2. _____

  _____

3. _____

  _____

⊙ Go to **MyEnglishLab** for more note-taking practice.

1 ▶ **Listen to a speech at an environmental rally. Create a chart like the one below to take notes. Try to use symbols to write information quickly.**

TAKE NOTES A Call to Action	
Main Ideas	**Details**

2 Use your notes to help you complete the tasks.

1. Label the percentages in the graph with the source of CO_2 emissions.

   a. making electricity

   b. transportation

   c. industry (businesses and factories)

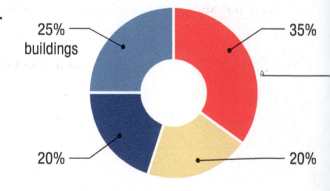

2. What is the main point the speaker is trying to make? Choose the correct answer.

   a. Factories and businesses produce a lot of pollution.

   b. Government and industry need to do more to reduce carbon emissions.

   c. Individuals should do more to reduce their personal carbon footprints.

USE YOUR NOTES
Compare your notes with a partner's. How can you improve your notes next time?

1 ▶ **Listen to the excerpt. What words or phrases does the speaker repeat?**

Identifying Repetition to Emphasize a Point

Speakers repeat words, phrases, and grammatical patterns to make their points stronger or to signal that they are important. The repetition also creates a rhythm (like a song or poem) that sounds good to the listener. Repetition is especially common in public speeches.

▶ **Read and listen to the example. Notice the boldfaced words and the underlined patterns.**

Example

It's not enough for individuals to **change**. <u>We need</u> governments to **change**. <u>We need</u> industry to **change**. <u>We need</u> big **changes** if we want to stop global warming from destroying our planet.

The speaker repeats the word *change* and the pattern *we need . . . to change*. The repetition makes the statement stronger and emphasizes the need for change.

2 ▶ **Listen to the excerpts. Fill in the missing words in the repeated grammatical patterns. Then answer the questions.**

Excerpt One

___*we need*___ government and industry ___*to work*___ together to lower these emissions. ___*to devel op*___ new, cleaner technology to heat our homes, power our factories, and ___*keep*___ the lights on.

1. What words and / or grammatical patterns are repeated? _____

2. What ideas is the speaker trying to emphasize? _____

Excerpt Two

___*we + need*___ government and industry ___*to work*___ together to build more energy-efficient cars and trucks. ___*to build*___ more public transportation.

1. What words and / or grammatical patterns are repeated? _____

2. What ideas is the speaker trying to emphasize? _____

● Go to **MyEnglishLab** for more skill practice.

ORGANIZE

Complete the chart with ideas that show the contrast between individuals, and government and industry.

USE YOUR NOTES

APPLY Review your notes from Listening One and Two. Use the information in your notes to complete the chart.

	LISTENING ONE: *Living Small*	LISTENING TWO: *A Call to Action*
Individuals	• Grow _____ _____ • Use _____ _____ • Live _____ _____	• Reduce _____ _____ • Tell _____ _____
Government and Industry		• Work _____ _____ • Develop _____ _____ • Build _____ _____ • Reduce _____ _____

SYNTHESIZE

Form two groups, Group A and Group B, to have a jigsaw discussion. Follow the steps.

1. Work with a partner in your group. Discuss the question assigned to your group. Use the details and examples from Organize.

   Group A: What can individuals do to reduce carbon dioxide emissions?

   Group B: What can government and industry do to reduce carbon dioxide emissions?

2. Find a partner in the other group. Work in a pair: one person from Group A and one person from Group B.

3. Take turns explaining the answer to your group's question to your partner. Use details and examples from Organize.

4. Change partners two more times so that you talk to three people total.

🔘 Go to **MyEnglishLab** to check what you learned.

3 FOCUS ON SPEAKING

REVIEW

Complete the statements. Use the words from the boxes.

emissions	resources	transported

1. _____ from burning coal increase greenhouse gases.

2. We increase our personal carbon footprint when we eat food that is _____ long distances to get to our grocery stores.

3. The sun and the wind are two natural _____ that produce clean energy.

consumption	dense	raised beds	solar panels

4. My city is very _____ . There are so many people living in a small area.

5. In our backyard, we grow food in _____ .

6. Our electricity bill decreased when we put _____ on our roof.

7. I try to reduce my _____ of gasoline by riding my bike instead of driving my car.

energy-efficient	factories	industry	technology

8. The automobile _____ has made changes to reduce CO_2 emissions, but it needs to do more.

9. Modern factories can become more efficient by using computers and other new _____ .

10. Cars make CO_2 emissions, and the _____ that make cars also produce emissions.

11. Newer, more _____ cars use less fuel than old cars.

(continued on next page)

a drop in the bucket	collectively	generations	greenhouse gases

12. We are beginning to see some of the effects of _____ , but we won't know the full impact of climate change on the environment for many years.

13. If we don't stop global warming, future _____ will have to deal with the effects of climate change.

14. When I think of the big problem of global warming, the little things I do to reduce my footprint often seem like _____ .

15. If individuals, government, and industry work _____ , it is possible that the effects of global warming can be reversed.

EXPAND

1 Complete the chart with the missing word forms. Use a dictionary to help you.

Noun	Verb	Adjective
transportation	**transport**	X
consumption		X *consumable*
emissions	*to emit*	X
	X	**energy-efficient**
generation[1]	*generat*	X *generative*
density	X *den*	**dense**
resource	X *to resource*	*resourceful*
industry	X *industrialize*	*industrious*
technology	X *technologize*	

[1] Generation has two meanings: (1) people of a similar age and (2) the creation of something.

test

2 **Read the sentence pairs. Each sentence has a different form of the same word (for example, *transportation, transport*). Complete each sentence. Write the correct word form. Be sure to use the correct singular or plural noun, and subject-verb agreement.**

1. I use buses, trains, and other kinds of public ___transportation___ to get to and from work.

   I use my car when I have to ___transport___ large or heavy things.

2. The sun is an important _____ for people who use solar energy.

   My brother is very _____ . He found a government program to pay for his solar panels.

3. Trees can help prevent global warming because they _____ CO_2.

   To protect our forests, we should reduce our _____ of paper.

4. The auto _____ needs to do more to stop global warming.

   The air is polluted because we live in an _____ area.

5. Traveling by public transportation is more _____ than traveling in a personal car.

   The _____ of automobiles has increased in recent years with new electric and hybrid (gas / electric) cars.

6. New _____ for solar and wind energy will reduce the cost of those energy sources.

   There have been many _____ changes in the automobile industry over the past 100 years.

7. Climate change is caused by carbon _____ from burning coal, oil, and natural gas.

   Wood stoves also _____ carbon dioxide.

8. Cities are _____ living areas. People live close together in small spaces.

   The _____ of cities encourages people to use public transportation. Parking can be difficult, so people often find it more convenient to take buses and trains.

9. Future _____ will have to deal with the effects of climate change.

   Luckily, scientists are discovering new ways to _____ power from the wind and the sea.

CREATE

APPLY **Work in a small group. Each student reads one of the statements aloud. The other students agree or disagree and explain why. Use the target words and vocabulary from Review and Expand in your answers.**

<u>Agreeing / Disagreeing Language</u>

I agree / disagree with this statement because . . .

I think / don't think _____ because . . .

I think this is / isn't a good idea because . . .

Use the vocabulary from the box in your answers. Check off the words as you use them.

collectively	emissions	greenhouse gases	solar panels
consume	energy-efficient	industry	technology
density	factory	raised beds	transportation
a drop in the bucket	generate	resourceful	

Statements

1. New technology will solve the problem of climate change.

2. Industries should pay extra for the energy they consume and the emissions they release.

3. To reduce greenhouse gases, more countries should generate their energy from nuclear power.

4. All countries should limit the number of cars on the road and increase public transportation.

5. Even if individuals work collectively to reduce their personal carbon footprints, their efforts are still just a drop in the bucket.

▶ Go to the **Pearson Practice English App** or **MyEnglishLab** for more vocabulary practice.

GRAMMAR FOR SPEAKING

1 Read the interview with an environmental activist. Notice the boldfaced modals of necessity. Then answer the questions.

HOST: What do individuals **have to** do to reduce their personal carbon footprint?

ACTIVIST: Well, we all **have to** drive less. We also need better public transportation so that we **don't have to** take our cars everywhere.

HOST: What else?

ACTIVIST: Everyone **must** work together. We **can't** solve this problem alone. And we **must not** wait too long to make these changes—or else our climate will change forever.

1. What is the difference between *have to* and *must*? _____
_____

2. What is the difference between *doesn't have to* and *must not*? _____
_____

Modals of Necessity

1. Use *have to* and *must* to tell when something is necessary.	
Have to is usually used in conversation and informal writing.	We *have to* find ways to reduce emissions.
Must is used most often in writing.	We *must* stop global warming.
2. Use the correct form of *have to* for all tenses.	We *have to* make changes today.
	We *had to* start making changes years ago.
	We'll *have to* make more changes in the future.
Use *must* only for present and future tenses.	We *must* make changes today.
	We *must* make more changes in the future.
3. Use *have to* for questions.	What do individuals *have to* do?
NOTE: *Must* is almost never used in questions.	Do they *have to* stop driving?
4. Use *don't / doesn't have to* when something is not necessary (when there is a choice).	We *don't have to* drive everywhere.
Use *must not* when something is prohibited (when there is no choice).	We *must not / can't* wait too long to make changes.
NOTE: In spoken English, *can't* is often used instead of *must not*.	

2 Read the rest of the interview. Circle the correct answers.

HOST: What do businesses have to do to reduce emissions?

ACTIVIST: First of all, business leaders **(1) must / don't have to** find new ways to reduce emissions from industry.

HOST: Will that cost a lot?

ACTIVIST: Reducing emissions **(2) can't / doesn't have to** be expensive. In fact, businesses often save money.

HOST: How can our government help?

ACTIVIST: Governments **(3) don't have to / must not** ignore the emissions problem. They **(4) can't / have to** create new laws to help reduce emissions.

HOST: Do we need new taxes to pay for this?

ACTIVIST: No, we **(5) don't have to / must** have new taxes. There are other ways to raise money.

HOST: Any other thoughts?

ACTIVIST: Sometimes people feel that this problem is impossible to solve, but we **(6) must not / don't have to** quit. And we **(7) must / can't have** everyone's help.

HOST: We're out of time, so we **(8) don't have to / have to** stop now. Thanks very much.

ACTIVIST: Thank you.

3 APPLY Work with a partner. Read the list of suggestions and add at least five more to the list. Discuss how to reduce our personal carbon footprints. Use *have to / must, don't have to,* and *must not / can't.*

Example

Student A: I think that we must build more public transportation.

Student B: Yeah, I agree. We have to stop driving everywhere. We can't rely on cars so much.

Suggestions

1. _buy more solar panels_ _____

2. _stop using electricity_ _____

3. _ignore the problem of global warming_ _____

4. _____

5. _____

6. _____

7. _____

8. _____

↰ Go to the **Pearson Practice English App** or **MyEnglishLab** for more grammar practice. Check what you learned in **MyEnglishLab**.

PRONUNCIATION

Using Final Intonation

When you finish speaking, your voice should fall to a low note. When you have more to say but need some time to think, your voice doesn't fall to a low note—it stays on the same note as the previous word or rises.

▶ Read and listen to the way *I know* is pronounced in this conversation. Is *I know* used to end a statement, or is there more after it?

Example

A: If you're worried about the environment, you shouldn't drive to work.

B: I know.   _yes_

A: You should take the bus.

continue **B:** I know . . . but I think it's faster when I drive.

Note: You can use *I know* to agree or disagree. When we use *I know* to disagree, we often follow it with *but*.

1 ▶ **Listen to the sentences. Is the speaker finished or not? If the speaker is finished, put a period (.) after the sentence. If the speaker is going to continue, put an ellipsis (. . .). Check your answers with a partner's.**

1. I'm going to start riding my bike to work

2. I'm not going to use the air conditioner so much

3. I'm going to volunteer to clean up the park

4. I always turn off the lights

5. I drive to school once a week

6. I'm going to buy a hybrid[1]

7. I'm going to vote for green candidates

8. I'm going to recycle bottles and cans

2 **Look at the unfinished sentences from Exercise One. Choose a sentence and finish it. Say your sentence to the class.**

3 **Work with a partner. Practice using intonation to let your partner know whether you've finished speaking or not. Read the sentences from Exercise One to your partner. Let your voice fall if your sentence is finished. Don't let your voice fall if your sentence isn't finished. Your partner will tell you whether he or she thinks your sentence is finished or not. Then switch roles.**

4 **Read statements about the environment to your partner. Your partner gives his or her opinion, agreeing with _I know_ or disagreeing with _I know, but_ . . .**

Student A's Statements

1. I don't think there's anything we can do about CO_2 levels. We all produce carbon dioxide when we breathe.

2. Wealthy countries create more pollution than poorer countries. They should have to pay to clean it up.

3. I'm worried about global warming, but I don't know if I can do anything to make a difference.

Student B's Statements

1. A lot of people in the automobile industry are going to lose their jobs if we raise taxes on gasoline.

2. A lot of storms hit coastal areas. The government shouldn't permit new building in coastal areas.

3. I need a new car, and I'd like to buy a hybrid. But they're more expensive than gas-powered cars.

---

[1] **hybrid:** A car that uses electric power at lower speeds and gasoline power at higher speeds. It produces less pollution.

SPEAKING SKILL

Interrupting Politely

During a discussion, you can politely interrupt the speaker and take a turn. A person might interrupt to share an idea or opinion, to ask a question, or to ask the speaker to repeat.

Interrupt Politely	Ask for Clarification or Explanation
Sounds and Gestures	*Could you repeat that?*
Clear your throat (say "ahem").	*Could you say that again?*
Raise your hand.	*Could you explain that?*
Raise your index finger.	*Can I ask you something?* [Then ask a question.]
Make eye contact with the speaker.	*Can I ask a question?*
Words	**Make a Comment**
I'm sorry . . .	*I'd like to add something . . .*
Excuse me . . .	*I'd like to make a point . . .* [Then make a comment.]
	Can I say something?
	But . . .

Holding the Floor

If you are speaking and someone interrupts, you can "hold the floor," or keep talking, if you aren't ready to be interrupted.

Sounds and Gestures	Words for Holding the Floor
Keep talking.	*Just a minute / second.*
Speak louder.	*Hold on a minute / second.*
Don't look at the person interrupting.	*Let me finish, please.*
Put your hand up to show that you want the other person to wait.	*I'm not done yet.*

NOTE: When interrupting and holding the floor, it is usually most effective to combine sounds and gestures with the words and phrases.

1 Look at the cartoon and answer the questions.

1. Where are the man and the woman?

   _____

2. What is the man doing?

   _____

3. How is the woman responding to him?

   _____

2 Work with a partner. Complete the classroom discussion. Write phrases for interrupting and holding the floor. Then practice the conversation in a group of three. Switch roles and repeat.

KYOO HYUN: . . . So, what are the effects of global warming? One is that cyclones are bigger and more frequent. . . .

BRIDGET: (asking for clarification) _____ , could you repeat that?
  1.

KYOO HYUN: Cyclones. They're getting bigger and more frequent.

BRIDGET: (asking for clarification) _____
  2.

KYOO HYUN: Yes?

BRIDGET: What's a cyclone?

KYOO HYUN: Oh, it's a really big storm that has very fast wind, like a hurricane or typhoon. As I was saying . . .

SAM: (making a comment) _____ There've been a lot of strong cyclones
  3.
recently, but I think they might not be caused by global warming.

KYOO HYUN: Some people say that, but most scientists don't agree.

SAM: (making a comment) _____ I've heard that . . .
  4.

KYOO HYUN: (holding the floor) _____ . I want to finish this idea. . . .
  5.

3 APPLY Take a role: an individual, a government official, a businessperson. Review the chart on page 180 for ideas and vocabulary. Work in a small group. Discuss the question for 4 minutes. Each person should interrupt at least once to ask for clarification or make a comment. Each person should also hold the floor at least once, if interrupted. Use the Speaking Skill strategies.

Question: What can individuals, government, and industry do to reduce carbon emissions?

Go to MyEnglishLab for more skill practice and to check what you learned.

FINAL SPEAKING TASK: Academic Discussion 🔍 APPLY

An academic seminar is a kind of discussion in which a leader manages a discussion on an academic topic. The leader presents information to the group and leads a discussion.

In this activity, you will lead a seminar discussion on a topic related to climate change. You will also participate in your classmates' seminar discussions.

PREPARE

1 Work in a group of four. Choose a seminar topic. Each group member should choose a different topic.

Topic A: Global CO_2 Emissions

Topic B: Vehicle Use Worldwide

Topic C: Natural Disasters and Global Temperature

Topic D: Sea Level Rise

2 Prepare to lead a seminar.

a. Work independently. Look at charts and tables in Part A of the Student Activities section on page 195. Read the information in Part B of the Student Activities section on page 196. Make sure you understand the ideas and vocabulary.

b. Answer the data analysis questions in Part B. Make brief notes.

c. Prepare a 1-minute introduction of your topic for the seminar. Explain the charts and the information you learned from the data analysis in Part B.

Introduction: Sample Outline (1 minute)

- Introduce the topic and give background information.

- Explain each chart. "Look at figure _____ on page _____ . This chart shows . . . "

- Explain how the information in the two charts is connected.

PRACTICE

1 Compare answers and practice leading a discussion seminar.

Meet in a small group with other students who are preparing the same topic.

a. As a group, review the information and compare your answers to the data analysis questions in Part B.

b. Take turns practicing your 1-minute introduction for the seminar discussion. Make suggestions to help your classmates improve their introductions.

c. As a group, read the discussion questions in Part B. Then write at least one more discussion question.

2 APPLY As you work in your group, consider how to apply the vocabulary, grammar, pronunciation, and speaking skills from the unit. Use the checklist to help you.

☐ **Vocabulary:** Read through the list of vocabulary on page 191. Choose at least two words or phrases to include in your explanation.

☐ **Grammar:** Use the modals of necessity *have to* and *must* to discuss the topic.

☐ **Pronunciation:** During the discussion, listen for intonation that shows when a person has finished a thought. Use intonation to show if your thought is finished or not.

☐ **Speaking Skill:** Interrupt politely to ask for clarification or explanation, or to make a comment. If you are interrupted and want to keep speaking, use strategies for holding the floor.

PRESENT

Hold the discussion seminars.

Meet in a group of four with one person from each topic group. Take turns leading a seminar. Participate in the discussions for the other seminars.

Seminar format:

- Introduction—1 minute

  - Discussion Leader: Introduce your topic and explain the charts in Appendix A. You may use notes, but do not read the explanation. Answer any clarification questions.

  - Seminar Members: Listen to the introduction and refer to the charts in Appendix A. Ask clarification questions if needed.

- Discussion—3 minutes

  - Discussion Leader: Ask one or two discussion questions. Lead the discussion. Make sure everyone in the group participates. Share your ideas and opinions about the discussion question(s).

Repeat until each student has led a seminar.

ALTERNATIVE SPEAKING TOPIC

APPLY **Discuss the questions in small groups. Use the vocabulary, grammar, pronunciation, and speaking skills you learned in the unit.**

How has climate change affected you or your community? What are people doing to reduce carbon emissions? What lifestyle changes could you make to reduce your own carbon footprint?

CHECK WHAT YOU'VE LEARNED

Check (✔) the outcomes you've met and vocabulary you've learned. Put an X next to the skills and vocabulary you still need to practice.

Learning Outcomes
- ☐ Infer contrast from context
- ☐ Take notes with symbols
- ☐ Identify repetition to emphasize a point
- ☐ Use modals of necessity
- ☐ Use final intonation
- ☐ Interrupt politely and hold the floor

Vocabulary
- ☐ (raised) bed
- ☐ collectively
- ☐ consumption AWL
- ☐ dense
- ☐ emission
- ☐ energy-efficient
- ☐ generation AWL

- ☐ greenhouse gas
- ☐ factory
- ☐ industry
- ☐ resource AWL
- ☐ solar panel
- ☐ technology AWL
- ☐ transport (v.) AWL

Multi-word Units
- ☐ a drop in the bucket

🔾 Go to **MyEnglishLab** to watch a video about a family living the simple life, access the Unit Project, and take the Unit 8 Achievement Test.

STUDENT ACTIVITIES

Read the History of the Space Age. Take turns making statements about the facts, using the simple past and present perfect.

Example

A: Let's see . . . sixty women **have gone** into space.

B: Right, and the first woman in space **was** Valentina Tereshkova. She **went** into space in 1963.

HISTORY OF THE SPACE AGE

The modern Space Age began in 1942 when the first rocket entered outer space. Since then, many new records for space travel have been set.

Category	Total Number During Space Age	Fun Fact
Women in space	more than fifty-five women	First woman in space: Valentina V. Tereshkova, 1963
Satellites in orbit	thousands of satellites	First satellite to orbit Earth: *Sputnik 1*, 1957
People in space	more than 500 astronauts	First person in space: Yuri Gagarin, 1961
People in space for more than one year	four people	Longest time in space: Valeri Polyakov, 437 days
People on the moon	twelve astronauts	First humans on the moon: crew of the *Apollo 11*, 1969
Spacewalks	more than 130 so far[1]	First spacewalk: 23 minutes, Alexi Leonov, 1965[2] Longest spacewalk: 8 hours 56 minutes, Susan J. Helms and James Voss, 2001
Number of manned spaceflights	About 300 so far	Most spaceflights: seven trips, Jerry Ross (between 1985 and 2002) and Franklin Chang-Diaz (between 1986 and 2002)

[1] Spacewalks usually involve two or more people.

[2] Leonov floated in space for about 10 minutes; however, he was outside the spacecraft for at least 20 minutes.

GROUP 1: Finance and Economy

- The United States spends over $19.5 billion a year on space exploration.

- The money spent on the United States space program is less than 1 percent of the total budget for the country.

- One dollar ($1) spent on the space program results in eight dollars ($8) of economic benefit, through the creation of new jobs and new products that are sold around the world.

- The space program creates new jobs. For example, the project to send the Curiosity Rover to Mars created at least 7,000 jobs in eight years.

- Some people say that the products that have been invented through the space program (such as water filters and smoke detectors) might have been invented more cheaply on Earth.

- Other: _____

_____

GROUP 2: The Environment

- Satellites in space allow us to observe environmental problems. For example, we can observe global warming (rising temperatures) by seeing the ice melting at the North Pole. We can also see pollution in the oceans and the destruction of the rainforests.

- Satellites allow us to track big storms, such as cyclones and hurricanes, as well as large fires.

- The space program has invented a process for cleaning chemicals out of water. This process is now used on Earth to take harmful chemicals out of dirty water from factories.

- When rockets travel into space, harmful chemicals are put into the air. Spacecraft also burn a lot of fuel.

- Spacecraft leave orbital debris in space. These fragments can damage satellites, the International Space Station, and other spacecraft. They can also fall to Earth.

- Other: _____

_____

GROUP 3: Innovation and Development

- Many high-quality, innovative products have been invented as a result of the space program. Some examples are sunglasses, paint that doesn't burn in a fire, safety systems for cars, medical equipment, and equipment to help us see at night.

- Satellite communications have changed people's lives with cell phone service, GPS navigation, and weather prediction. They have also changed business with better communication, faster banking services, video conferencing, and other new technologies.

- Some products invented through the space program might have been invented more cheaply on Earth.

- Asteroids contain precious metals that we can use on Earth. Companies are working now to find a way to go into space, get the metals from the asteroids, and bring them back to Earth.

- Space tourism is a growing industry. There are many people who would like to travel to space as a tourist. Space tourists have already paid $20 million to $35 million to travel to the International Space Station.

- Other: _____

_____

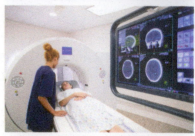

Products created by space research

GROUP 4: Human Relations

- Space exploration has promoted cooperation among different countries. Russia, Japan, the European Union, China, and the United States all work together on most projects. Sixty percent of American scientific projects are done with scientists from other countries, and all the human space flights are done in partnership with other countries.

- The International Space Station was constructed with the cooperation of many nations. Today, scientists from many countries live together on the station and do research.

- Satellite technology has brought people closer together because we can communicate more easily over long distances. International business is also easier because of global banking and communications systems.

- Countries may compete with each other to be the first to do something in space, just as the United States and the Soviet Union competed to put the first person in space. Competition can create negative relationships between the countries.

- Countries use satellite technology to gather information about other countries and their own people. They use the information to make political or military decisions.

- Other: _____

_____

UNIT 8: FINAL SPEAKING TASK

Part A

Topic A: Global CO_2 Emissions

CO_2 Emissions Over Time

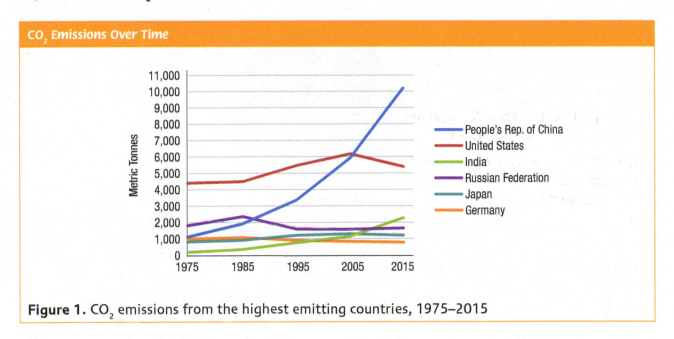

Figure 1. CO_2 emissions from the highest emitting countries, 1975–2015

Per Person CO_2

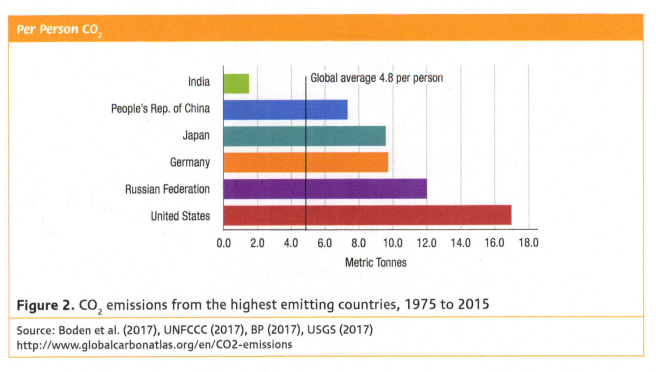

Figure 2. CO_2 emissions from the highest emitting countries, 1975 to 2015

Source: Boden et al. (2017), UNFCCC (2017), BP (2017), USGS (2017)
http://www.globalcarbonatlas.org/en/CO2-emissions

Topic B: Vehicle Use Worldwide

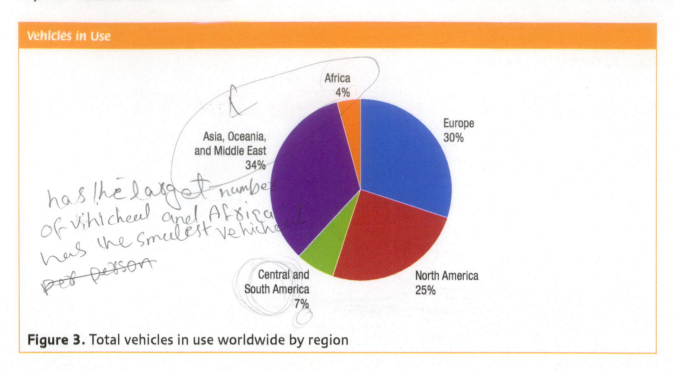

has the largest number of vihicheel and Africa has the smulest vehicheel per person

Figure 3. Total vehicles in use worldwide by region

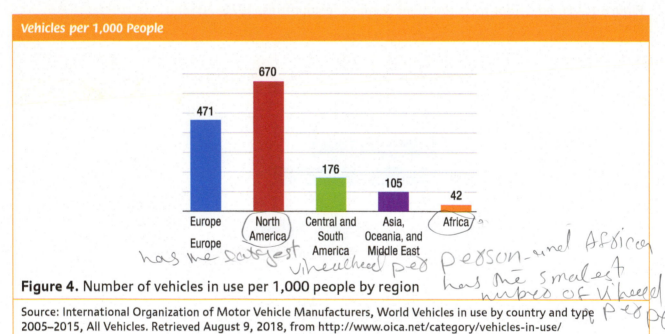

has the batgest vihewheel per person and Africa has the smulest nubres of vihecel per pesson

Figure 4. Number of vehicles in use per 1,000 people by region

Source: International Organization of Motor Vehicle Manufacturers, World Vehicles in use by country and type 2005–2015, All Vehicles. Retrieved August 9, 2018, from http://www.oica.net/category/vehicles-in-use/

Topic C: Natural Disasters and Global Temperature

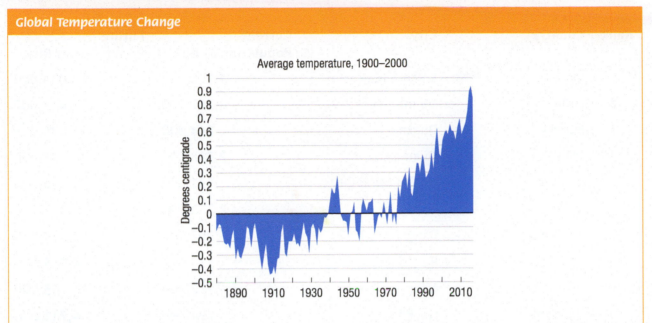

Figure 5. Average global temperature change since 1880, compared to the average for the twentieth century

Source: NOAA National Centers for Environmental information, Climate at a Glance: Global Time Series, published July 2018, retrieved on August 9, 2018, from https://www.ncdc.noaa.gov/cag/

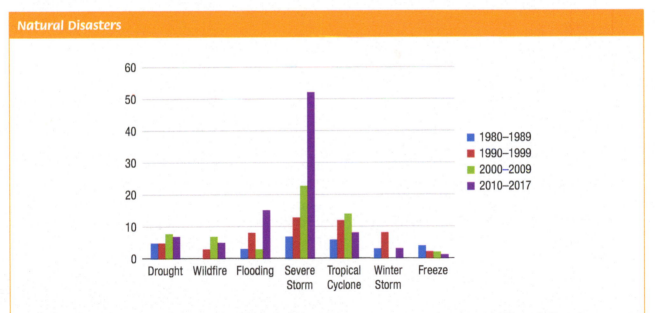

Figure 6. Number of weather and climate disasters causing more than one billion dollars in damage in the United States, 1980–2017

Source: NOAA National Centers for Environmental Information (NCEI) U.S. Billion-Dollar Weather and Climate Disasters (2018), retrieved on August 9, 2018, from https://www.ncdc.noaa.gov/billions/

Topic D: Sea Level Rise

Rank	Country	City	Current Population at Risk	Future Population at Risk
			Populations at Risk from Sea Rise	
1	India	Kolkata (Calcutta)	1,929,000	14,014,000
2	India	Mumbai (Bombay)	2,787,000	11,418,000
3	Bangladesh	Dhaka	844,000	11,135,000
4	China	Guangzhou	2,718,000	10,333,000
5	Vietnam	Ho Chi Minh City	1,931,000	9,216,000
6	China	Shanghai	2,353,000	5,451,000
7	Thailand	Bangkok	907,000	5,138,000
8	Myanmar	Rangoon	510,000	4,965,000
9	USA	Miami	2,003	4,795,000
10	Vietnam	Hai Phòng	794,000	4,711,000
11	Egypt	Alexandria	1,330	4,375,000
12	China	Tianjin	956,000	3,790,000
13	Bangladesh	Khulna	441,000	3,641,000
14	China	Ningbo	299,000	3,305,000
15	Nigeria	Lagos	357,000	3,229,000
16	Côte d'Ivoire	Abidjan	519,000	3,110,000
17	USA	New York-Newark	1,540,000	2,931,000
18	Bangladesh	Chittagong	255,000	2,866,000
19	Japan	Tokyo	1,110,000	2,521,000
20	Indonesia	Jakarta	513,000	2,248,000

Table 1. Population (number of people) in cities at risk from sea rise now and in the future

Source: Hanson, S., R. Nicholls, N. Ranger, S. Hallegatte, J. Corfee-Morlot, C. Herweijer, and J. Chateau (2011), A global ranking of port cities with high exposure to climate extremes, *Climate Change,* 104(1), 89–111, doi:10.1007/s10584-010-9977-4.

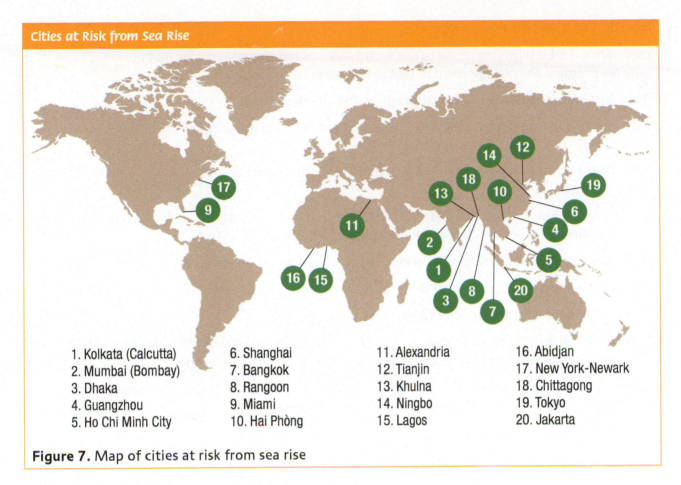

Cities at Risk from Sea Rise

1. Kolkata (Calcutta)
2. Mumbai (Bombay)
3. Dhaka
4. Guangzhou
5. Ho Chi Minh City
6. Shanghai
7. Bangkok
8. Rangoon
9. Miami
10. Hai Phòng
11. Alexandria
12. Tianjin
13. Khulna
14. Ningbo
15. Lagos
16. Abidjan
17. New York-Newark
18. Chittagong
19. Tokyo
20. Jakarta

Figure 7. Map of cities at risk from sea rise

Part B

Topic A: Global CO_2 Emissions

From 1975 to 2015, global CO_2 emission more than doubled, from 16,840 to 36,019 metric tonnes per year. CO_2 emissions come from industry, transportation, farming, and land use, making electricity and heat and other sources. Just six countries produce 60 percent of CO_2 emissions, but the amount of emissions produced by these countries has grown at different rates. In addition to looking at total CO_2 emissions, we can study the amount of emissions per person. The per person CO_2 emissions were 4.8 metric tonnes in 2015.

Data Analysis Questions (Use to prepare for the seminar)

a. Look at Figure 1 on page 195. Which countries have increased CO_2 emissions over time? Which have decreased or stayed the same? Which country has had the biggest change in emissions?

b. Look at Figure 2 on page 195. What is the average worldwide CO_2 emissions per person? Which countries have per person CO_2 emissions that are higher or lower than the average?

c. Look at Figures 1 and 2. Which countries have high total emissions but lower per person emissions? Which lower total emissions and higher per person emissions?

Seminar Discussion Questions (Ask during the seminar)

a. The six countries in Figures 1 and 2 emit the most CO_2. Why do some countries have high per person emissions but lower total emissions, while other countries have low per person emissions and higher total emissions? What is the cause of these differences?

b. What do governments and individuals have to do to reduce total CO_2 emissions?

c. Your question: _____

Topic B: Vehicles Use Worldwide

There are over 1.2 billion vehicles in use worldwide, including cars, trucks, and busses. These vehicles produce about 14 percent of global CO_2 emissions.

Data Analysis Questions (Use to prepare for the seminar)

a. Look at Figure 3 on page 196. Which regions have the largest and smallest number of total vehicles?

b. Look at Figure 4 on page 196. Which regions have the largest and smallest number vehicles per person?

  • Compare Figures 3 and 4. Compare the data on the total number of vehicles and the number of vehicles per person. How do you explain the differences?

  • Compare the data for Europe, North America, and Asia, Oceania, and the Middle East.

  • Compare the data for Central & South America and Asia, Oceania, and the Middle East.

Seminar Discussion Questions (Ask during the seminar)

a. Why are there differences in the number of cars in different regions? Why is there a difference in the number of cars per person? *maybe lake cars not efford by*

b. Reducing the number of cars can help reduce CO_2 emissions. What do governments and individuals have to do to reduce the number of cars on the road? *bike*

c. Your question: _____

Topic C: Natural Disasters and Global Temperature

Global warming causes changes in the weather and climate, which lead to changes in the number and type of natural disasters each year.

Temperature records have been collected since the mid-1800s, allowing scientists to track changes in the average global temperature. To determine global temperature, scientists measure the temperature of the air above land and the ocean and calculate an average temperature for the year.

Scientists also study the number of droughts, wildfires, floods, storms, and freezes to measure the effects of climate change. One way to measure the effect of a natural disaster is the look at the amount of damage caused by the disaster. For example, the United States has had 233 weather and climate disasters since 1980 with overall damages / costs of more than $1 billion each, for a total cost of $1.5 trillion.

Data Analysis Questions (Use to prepare for the seminar)

a. Look at Figure 5 on page 197. How has the average temperature changed over time? How has it changed in the decades since 1980?

b. Look at Figure 6 on page 197. What types of weather and climate disasters have increased most in the decades since 1980? What types of disasters have decreased or stayed about the same?

c. Look at Figures 5 and 6. What is the relationship between average temperature and the number of natural disasters?

Seminar Discussion Questions (Ask during the seminar)

a. Think of a weather or climate disaster that you have heard about or experienced. When and where did the disaster happen? What were the effects?

b. The impact of natural disasters is increasing around the world. What do governments and individuals have to do to protect themselves from the effects of natural disasters?

c. Your question: _____

Topic D: Sea Level Rise

The global sea level has risen over the past century, and the speed of sea rise has increased in recent decades. Sea rise is caused by warming ocean temperatures (since water expands as it warms) and melting land ice in glaciers and ice sheets. Scientists predict that by 2100, the sea level may rise 0.2 to 2.0 meters (0.66 to 6.6 feet).

Data Analysis Questions (Use to prepare for the seminar)

a. Look at Table 1 on page 198. Look at the columns showing current and future populations that are at risk. Which three cities will have the biggest change?

b. Look at Table 1 on page 198 and Figure 7 on page 199. What countries and regions will be most affected by sea rise?

c. Why are the cities in Table 1 more at risk from sea rise than other cities in the world?

Seminar Discussion Questions (Ask during the seminar)

a. What will happen to people who live in the cities affected by sea rise? How will it affect people who live in other cities that are not affected by sea rise?

b. Sea rise will affect many people around the world. What do governments and individuals have to do to protect against the effects of sea rise?

c. Your question: _____

EXPAND VOCABULARY

UNIT 1
Multi-word Units
be (one's) own worst enemy
blow (one's) chance
easier said than done
have what it takes
set (one's) heart on
throw (one) for a loop

UNIT 2
Multi-word Units
clean out
put away
rip off
turn out
watch out for

UNIT 3
Vocabulary
astronaut
atmosphere
commercial
gravity
mission
surface

UNIT 4
Multi-word Units
Buy now and save!
Everything MUST go!
Fantastic bargain!
HOT DEALS!
Smart buy!
Time is running out!

UNIT 5
Multi-word Units
get out of hand
get the lowdown
get your hands dirty
play it by ear
play second fiddle
play your cards right

UNIT 6
Vocabulary
locals

Multi-word Units
find a compromise
get off the beaten path
have an impact
in the long run
way of life

UNIT 7
Vocabulary
arrest
convict (v.)
detain
sentence (v.)
try

UNIT 8
Vocabulary
consume AWL
density
emit
energy efficiency
generate AWL
transportation AWL

ACADEMIC WORD LIST VOCABULARY `AWL`

Words with an * are target vocabulary in the unit. The remainder of the words appear in context in the reading texts.

accumulate

achieve*

adult

affect (v.)*

appreciate

area

author

aware

benefit (n.)

challenge* (n.)

challenging (adj.)

comment (n.)

commit*

communication

community*

computer

confirm*

consume*

consumer

consumption*

context*

controversy*

cooperate*

cooperation

coordination

corporate*

create

creation

cultural

culture

definitely

deny

design

despite

detector

economic

energy

ensure*

environment*

environmental

expert

expose*

facilitator*

feature (n.)

file (v.)

final

financial

focus (v.)

format* (n.)

founder

generate*

generation*

goal*

grade (n.)

identify

identity

image

impact (n.)

imply

individual (adj.)

individual (n.)

injure

innovation*

instance

instructions

instructor

item

job

license

maintenance

major* (n.)

motivate

motivation*

negative

network (n.)

normal

obviously

option

outcome*

partner

percent

period

perspective*

physical

pose

positive

predict

predictable

process* (n.)

professional

promote*

purchase (v.)

purchase* (n.)

quote (v.)

range (n.)

relax

removal

require

research (n.)

resource*

reveal

role

schedule (n.)

shift* (n.)

significant

similar

source (n.)

strategy*

stress (n.)

survey (n.)

symbol

technology*

temporary

tension*

topic

tradition*

transition* (n.)

transport* (v.)

transportation*

ultimately*

unique

vision

volunteer* (v.)

GRAMMAR BOOK REFERENCES

NorthStar: Listening and Speaking Level 3, Fifth Edition	*Focus on Grammar, Level 3*, Fifth Edition	*Azar's Basic English Grammar*, Fourth Edition
Unit 1 Reflexive and Reciprocal Pronouns	**Unit 27** Reflexive and Reciprocal Pronouns	**Chapter 6** Nouns and Pronouns: 6-13
Unit 2 Modals of Advice	**Unit 16** Advice: *Should, Ought to, Had better*	**Chapter 7** Modal Auxiliaries: 7-7, 7-8
Unit 3 Present Perfect and Simple Past	**Unit 11** Present Perfect and Simple Past	**Chapter 4** Present Perfect and Past Perfect: 4-2, 4-5
Unit 4 Superlative Adjectives	**Unit 21** Adjectives: Superlatives	**Chapter 9** Comparisons: 9-10
Unit 5 Gerunds	**Unit 23** Gerunds: Subject and Object	**Chapter 13** Gerunds and Infinitives: 13-1, 13-2, 13-5, 13-7
Unit 6 *Will* and *If* clauses	**Unit 6** Future	**Chapter 3** Future Time: 3-6
Unit 7 *And, But, So,* and *Because*		**Chapter 8** Connecting Ideas: 8-1, 8-2, 8-3, 8-4, 8-6
Unit 8 Modals of Necessity	**Unit 29** Necessity: *Have (got) to, Must, Don't have to, Must not, Can't*	**Chapter 7** Modal Auxiliaries: 7-9, 7-10

AUDIO SCRIPT

UNIT 1: A Test of Endurance

Listening One, Page 5, Preview

JAY BATCHEN: . . . I mean, you're sleeping in a tent every night, there are sandstorms, you're sharing the tent with eight other people. It's not fully enclosed, so you have wind and sand and people snoring and rustling next to you. You're sleeping on rocks.

TIM BOURQUIN: Well, you know Jay, it doesn't sound like a whole lot of fun; so, you know, in the night, you're not getting a lot of sleep. What is in it for you? What does the race do for you personally?

Page 5, Listen

TIM BOURQUIN: Thank you for joining us at EnduranceRadio.com. We've got another great interview for you today. We're going to be speaking with Jay Batchen. He was the first American to finish the Marathon des Sables. We're going to hear about that and his background in ultrarunning and a little bit about his background in endurance sports in general. So, Jay, thanks very much for joining us. I appreciate you taking the time to talk to us on the phone.

JAY BATCHEN: Thank you, Tim. It's my pleasure.

TIM BOURQUIN: So, talk about the Marathon des Sables. How did you get into that?

JAY BATCHEN: It's funny how I did get into the Marathon des Sables. I was introduced to it while working for the Discovery Channel. I filmed the event in 1999, which is actually the year my wife, Lisa Smith-Batchen, won the event. And that's how I ended up in Morocco and ended up learning about the event myself.

TIM BOURQUIN: So, did you know Lisa before that event, or you met her there?

JAY BATCHEN: Met her there.

TIM BOURQUIN: OK, so you ended up marrying the winner of the race that you were filming.

JAY BATCHEN: Yep.

TIM BOURQUIN: Oh, very good. So, talk about that race. How did that start? How long is it? Where is it? That sort of thing, for our listeners that may not know.

JAY BATCHEN: Sure. The race is . . . it takes place in the Sahara Desert in southern Morocco, just outside of the Atlas Mountains. And the course is different every year. For instance, this year, it was a 154-mile course, and the year I ran it, in 2000, it was about 148 that year, so . . .

TIM BOURQUIN: Wow.

JAY BATCHEN: . . . it just changes year to year, and obviously the terrain will change as well, since the course does.

TIM BOURQUIN: Now, is this a stage race, or is it just start and go till you finish?

JAY BATCHEN: No, this particular race is a stage race, and the format is fairly, fairly similar each year in that the first three stages are all around 20 miles, give or take, and then the fourth stage is a 50-mile-long stage. Then that's followed by a full marathon. And the last day basically makes up the difference, just gets you back into a town, and it's a little shorter. Gives everyone a chance to get across the finish line and get back to the small town where we rendezvous and clean up for a nice night of awards and festivities.

TIM BOURQUIN: If you're able to stay standing at that point, I guess.

JAY BATCHEN: Definitely. And what's unique about this race is that you do have to carry all of your food, extra clothing, and things like that for the entire event. You are given a ration of water each day at checkpoints roughly about 6 to 8 miles in length. I mean, you're sleeping in a tent every night, there are sandstorms, you're sharing the tent with eight other people. It's not fully enclosed, so you have wind and sand and people snoring and rustling next to you. You're sleeping on rocks.

TIM BOURQUIN: Well, you know Jay, it doesn't sound like a whole lot of fun; so, you know, in the night, you're not getting a lot of sleep.

What is in it for you? What does the race do for you personally?

JAY BATCHEN: That's a good question, and it's a question that many people ask. And what I tell them is that this race is more than a race. It's a life experience. And what I mean by that is you're sharing a tent with eight other people, and you're going through the same highs and lows every day. It might not be at the same time, but you're running in the same heat, you're running in the same wind, you're sleeping in the same sandstorms on the cold nights, and for me it's about meeting the other people that are running this event and sharing stories with them and sharing the experience with them. And it's so hard to describe to someone who hasn't been there and run the event. So, for me, it's completing the distance and knowing that I can do it, feeling that I can do it; but it's meeting the people from all over the world, from all walks of life, and just sharing it with them that makes it special.

Page 8, Make Inferences

Excerpt One

JAY BATCHEN: . . . the format is fairly, fairly similar each year in that the first three stages are all around 20 miles, give or take, and then the fourth stage is a 50-mile-long stage. Then that's followed by a full marathon. And the last day basically makes up the difference, just gets you back into a town, and it's a little shorter. Gives everyone a chance to get across the finish line and get back to the small town where we rendezvous and clean up for a nice night of awards and festivities.

TIM BOURQUIN: If you're able to stay standing at that point, I guess.

JAY BATCHEN: Definitely.

Excerpt Two

JAY BATCHEN: I mean, you're sleeping in a tent every night, there are sandstorms, you're sharing the tent with eight other people. It's not fully enclosed, so you have wind and sand and people snoring and rustling next to you. You're sleeping on rocks.

TIM BOURQUIN: Well, you know Jay, it doesn't sound like a whole lot of fun; so, you know, in the night, you're not getting a lot of sleep.

Page 10, Note-Taking

Excerpt One

JAY BATCHEN: Definitely. And what's unique about this race is that you do have to carry all of your food, extra clothing, and things like that for the entire event. You are given a ration of water each day at checkpoints roughly about 6 to 8 miles in length. I mean, you're sleeping in a tent every night, there are sandstorms, you're sharing the tent with eight other people. It's not fully enclosed, so you have wind and sand and people snoring and rustling next to you. You're sleeping on rocks.

Excerpt Two

TIM BOURQUIN: What is in it for you? What does the race do for you personally?

JAY BATCHEN: That's a good question, and it's a question that many people ask. And what I tell them is that this race is more than a race. It's a life experience. And what I mean by that is you're sharing a tent with eight other people, and you're going through the same highs and lows every day. It might not be at the same time, but you're running in the same heat, you're running in the same wind, you're sleeping in the same sandstorms on the cold nights, and for me it's about meeting the other people that are running this event and sharing stories with them and sharing the experience with them. And it's so hard to describe to someone who hasn't been there and run the event. So, for me, it's completing the distance and knowing that I can do it, feeling that I can do it; but it's meeting the people from all over the world, from all walks of life, and just sharing it with them that makes it special.

Listening Two, page 11, Comprehension

PROFESSOR: So last time, when we were discussing the growth of endurance sports, a question came up about the motivation for getting into these sports. Why would anyone want to go through so much physical pain and stress? What's in it for them? Well, looking at the research, there are a couple points that seem especially important.

One of these is the personality of endurance athletes. As a group, these people tend to be high achievers— you know, people who set high goals for themselves, both in sports and in life in general. They like difficult challenges, and they aren't happy with goals that are easy to achieve. So, endurance sports fits right into this type of personality. These sports are very difficult, very extreme—like ultramarathons where people run hundreds of miles, often in extreme heat or cold—but the athletes get a lot of satisfaction from it. And when setting goals, most endurance athletes don't focus on winning the race. Instead, they have personal goals, like maybe just finishing the race is enough, or finishing with a better time than before. So, it's really more about the athletes challenging themselves, doing their personal best, and always pushing to do better. Another source of motivation is the relationship between the athletes. In general, endurance athletes don't see the other athletes in a race as opponents or people they're trying to beat. Instead, they see them as partners—partners in this unique adventure, doing something that no one else is doing. They share the highs and lows of the race, the pain and the pleasure, and they feel that they are in the experience together. And the athletes report this as a life-changing experience . . . an emotional high that keeps them wanting to come back for more. So this, this strong emotional experience is a big part of the motivation.

Page 12, Listening Skill

Exercise One

PROFESSOR: Why would anyone want to go through so much physical pain and stress? What's in it for them? Well, looking at the research, there are a couple points that seem especially important.

Page 12, Listening Skill

Exercise Two

1. **PROFESSOR:** Well, looking at the research, there are a couple points that seem

especially important. One of these is the personality of endurance athletes.

2. **PROFESSOR:** And when setting goals, most endurance athletes don't focus on winning the race. Instead, they have personal goals, like maybe just finishing the race is enough. . . .

3. **PROFESSOR:** So, it's really more about the athletes challenging themselves, doing their personal best, and always pushing to do better. Another source of motivation is the relationship between the athletes.

4. **PROFESSOR:** And the athletes report this as a life-changing experience . . . an emotional high that keeps them wanting to come back for more. So this, this strong emotional experience is a big part of the motivation.

UNIT 2: Avoiding Identity Theft

Listening One, page 30, Preview

LILY: So, by the end of the week, I was feeling totally helpless. And, like a total victim. What do I do now? I have $30,000 worth of credit card bills in my name, with my address, and I felt really exposed. Somebody knows who I am, where I live, what my phone number is, and I'm helpless to stop this.

Page 30, Listen

ANNOUNCER: Lily's wallet was stolen at a restaurant. The thief used her personal information to open credit cards in her name. But she had no idea she was the victim of identity theft. Then one day, she was home working on her computer when she got a call from a department store. In this story, Lily describes what happened next.

LILY: So, I was at the computer, and the phone rang. I got this phone call, and she said, "Well, we have here that you've bought a diamond ring, so I'm just confirming the purchase because it's quite a bit of money." And I said, "Well, what is it?" And she said, "It's a $5,000 diamond ring." And I said, "No, I haven't left the house today, so I wouldn't have bought a diamond ring, and anyway, I don't go to that store, I don't go to your store anymore." And so, she said, "Well, somebody who has your name has purchased a diamond ring for $5,000." And I said, "Five thousand dollars! A diamond ring! Well, that's not me. I didn't buy it, and I don't authorize the purchase of this diamond ring, OK? So, we have a problem."

And she said, "We don't have a problem; I think, I hate to tell you this, you have a problem." And I said, "What are you talking about?" She said, "I hate to break the news to you, but I think that you have been a victim of identity theft." And I said, "A victim of what?" And she said, "Identity theft." And she said, "Well, when you get this bill . . ." And I said, "Excuse me? I'm going to get a bill for this?" She says, "Oh, yes. When you get the bill, you need to file a complaint." And I said, "Oh, boy." So, I did that, I filed the complaint. And then, it just went from bad to worse.

On Monday, I got home from work and I checked my mail, and there was a bill from another department store and another department store. On Tuesday, there were two more bills from two other department stores. On Wednesday, there were three bills from three consumer electronics stores. On Thursday, there were four bills from a jewelry store, a clothing store, another department store. . . . By Friday, I had accumulated close to 38 or 39 bills. And I was up to probably close to $30,000 worth of charges, if not more. So, by the end of the week, I was feeling totally helpless. And, like a total victim. What do I do now? I have $30,000 worth of credit card bills in my name, with my address, and I felt really exposed. Somebody knows who I am, where I live, what my phone number is, and I'm helpless to stop this.

So, what did I do? Every night, I had to deal with these bills. And what you have to do, is you have to make copies of the police report, etcetera, that, you know, my wallet was stolen. You have to describe in detail what they had purchased, and you have to write a letter to every single one of these stores that charged me, explaining what

had happened. And you hope that they will not keep the charges there for you.

It took about, I would say, close to four months before the whole thing died away, and just a lot of time and a lot of worry. I worried a lot.

And the paranoia hasn't left, I mean, I'm still really conscious and nervous about receipts I have. I always rip them up into many tiny little pieces. And, the other thing that is really scary is how easy it is to open up credit cards. Shocking! You can go into any store, and you can just give them your name, your address, you don't need any proof of identification, and you can open up a credit card at that particular store. They don't really check who you are. How many clerks really look at the back of your credit card and check your signature? Not many.

There's all sorts of ways that your identity can be stolen. So, I think everybody should be paranoid.

Page 35, Note-Taking Skill

Excerpt One

So, what did I do? Every night, I had to deal with these bills. And what you have to do, is you have to make copies of the police report, etcetera, that, you know, my wallet was stolen. You have to describe in detail what they had purchased, and you have to write a letter to every single one of these stores that charged me, explaining what had happened. And you hope that they will not keep the charges there for you.

Excerpt Two

How does phishing work?

Criminals pretend to work for real companies. They send e-mail messages to thousands of people. They trick people into going to a fraudulent web site (which looks like a real site) and giving out their personal information. Then the thieves use the information to commit identity theft.

Excerpt Three

Keep yourself safe from phishing

- Be careful about e-mail messages and websites that ask for personal information. Don't give out information that a thief could use as proof of identification, such as a driver's license or passport number.

- If you think you have been a victim of phishing, deal with it right away by calling your bank and the police. Don't wait until you start getting bills.

Listening Two, page 36, Comprehension

Public Service Announcement 1

COMPANY: American Bank VISA. May I help you?

VICTIM: Yes, I'm calling about my credit card bill. There's a charge for $4,000 that I know I didn't make . . .

ANNOUNCER: Think you're safe from identity theft? Think again. Every minute, nineteen people in the United States have their identities stolen. However, there are things that you can do to reduce your risk. First: Get a locked mailbox. Don't let a thief steal your mail and use it to steal your identity. Second: Be careful when someone asks you for personal information. Don't give out information over the phone, by mail, or on the internet unless you know who you're dealing with. To see more tips on avoiding identity theft, visit the Identity Theft Helpline . . .

Public Service Announcement 2

ANNOUNCER: Hear that sound? That's the sound of a crime being committed. Every day, criminals find personal information from papers that we throw away. It doesn't take much—a name, an address, an ID number—and the thief has all he needs to commit identity theft.

Hear that sound? That's the sound of someone protecting herself from becoming a victim of identity theft. It only takes a minute to shred papers with personal information, but it can save you years of stress and worry.

Identity theft is the number one crime in the United States, with 10 million cases reported this year. Don't become the next victim. To find out how you can stay safe, call the Identity Theft Helpline at . . .

Page 36, Listening Skill

Exercise One

ANNOUNCER: Think you're safe from identity theft? Think again. Every minute, nineteen people in the United States have their identities stolen.

Page 37, Listening Skill

Exercise Two

Public Service Announcement 2

ANNOUNCER: Hear that sound? That's the sound of a crime being committed. Every day, criminals find personal information from papers that we throw away. It doesn't take much—a name, an address, an ID number—and the thief has all he needs to commit identity theft.

Hear that sound? That's the sound of someone protecting herself from becoming a victim of identity theft. It only takes a minute to shred papers with personal information, but it can save you years of stress and worry.

Identity theft is the number one crime in the United States, with 10 million cases reported this year. Don't become the next victim. To find out how you can stay safe, call the Identity Theft Helpline at . . .

UNIT 3: Why Explore Space?

Listening One, page 51, Preview

REPORTER: When NASA announced in 2011 that an old weather satellite—a six-ton piece of space junk, the size of a bus—was falling back to earth, people worried. Scientists knew when it would fall, but not where. As it turned out, it came down harmlessly in the Pacific Ocean. But this made us wonder: How much space junk is up there? And are we in danger?

Page 52, Listen

REPORTER: When NASA announced in 2011 that an old weather satellite—a six-ton piece of space junk, the size of a bus—was falling back to earth, people worried. Scientists knew when it would fall, but not where. As it turned out, it came down harmlessly in the Pacific Ocean. But this made us wonder: How much space junk is up there? And are we in danger?

MICHAELA JOHNSON: Well, we call it orbital debris, not space junk.

REPORTER: That's Michaela Johnson, a scientist who studies debris in space.

MICHAELA JOHNSON: Most of it's created when satellites collide or explode. Two recent events created one-third of the debris now in space: In 2007, an old Chinese satellite exploded. And in 2009, an old Russian satellite hit an active American satellite.

REPORTER: NASA tracks 21,000 large fragments—fragments more than 10 centimeters in width, or the size a large apple. But there are 500,000 smaller fragments—the size of a grape—that we can't track. And the number of tiny particles, less than 1 centimeter, could be in the hundreds of millions. All these fragments orbit the earth in a giant debris cloud. We're looking at a map of the debris on a computer screen.

MICHAELA JOHNSON: So, this is the earth. And you see here, each dot is a piece of debris larger than 10 centimeters.

REPORTER: So far, no one has been injured or killed by space debris falling to Earth.

MICHAELA JOHNSON: Most of it burns up long before it reaches the ground. But on average, one piece of space debris falls to Earth each day—usually in the ocean or a place where no people live.

REPORTER: A bigger problem is the fragments in Earth's orbit. These fragments are dangerous because they travel incredibly fast, about 8 kilometers per second.

MICHAELA JOHNSON: That's eight times faster than a speeding bullet.

REPORTER: At that speed, even small fragments can do serious damage to a spacecraft. And with each collision, more debris is created, increasing the chances of another collision. The problem will only get worse unless we can stop the creation of more space debris. And with over 1,000 working satellites in orbit, we may all feel the effects.

MICHAELA JOHNSON: Our communication satellites, our weather satellites, our navigation satellites are all in danger.

REPORTER: That means our phone calls, TV signals, weather reports, and GPS map systems.

MICHAELA JOHNSON: And it's not just a U.S. problem, it's an international problem. Every country that sends a spacecraft or satellite into space—we're all part of the problem. So, the international community needs to cooperate. We have to stop creating new debris and to clean up the debris that's already there.

REPORTER: There is some progress. Space agencies from twelve countries have formed an organization, the Inter-Agency Space Debris Coordination Committee, to find a solution. But until then, we'll keep an eye on the sky. Just in case.

Page 54, Make Inferences

Excerpt One

REPORTER: NASA tracks 21,000 large fragments—fragments more than 10 centimeters in width, or the size a large apple. But there are 500,000 smaller fragments—the size of a grape—that we can't track. And the number of tiny particles, less than 1 centimeter, could be in the hundreds of millions. All these fragments orbit the earth in a giant debris cloud.

Excerpt Two

REPORTER: So far, no one has been injured or killed by space debris falling to Earth.

MICHAELA JOHNSON: Most of it burns up long before it reaches the ground. But on average, one piece of space debris falls to Earth each day—usually in the ocean or a place where no people live.

Excerpt Three

REPORTER: A bigger problem is the fragments in Earth's orbit. These fragments are dangerous because they travel incredibly fast, about 8 kilometers per second.

MICHAELA JOHNSON: That's eight times faster than a speeding bullet.

REPORTER: At that speed, even small fragments can do serious damage to a spacecraft. And with each collision, more debris is created, increasing the chances of another collision.

Page 57, Note-Taking Skill

Exercise One

a. solution
b. innovation
c. product
d. example
e. benefit
f. international
g. communication network
h. answer
i. perspective

Page 57, Note-Taking Skill

Exercise Two

An Ecuadorian communication satellite was hit by pieces of an old spacecraft about 1,500 kilometers (930 miles) above the southeastern coast of Africa. The satellite, called Pegaso, was sent into space in 2011. It was Ecuador's first satellite to orbit Earth.

Scientists knew the satellite would pass near the aging spacecraft, which was sent up in 1985 by the Soviet Union. The old rocket broke into fragments and is now surrounded by a cloud of debris

Listening Two, page 58, Comprehension

INTERVIEWER: One criticism of the space program is the cost. The U.S. government is spending over 18 billion dollars on space exploration. Is it worth the price?

SCIENTIST: Space exploration has a lot of benefits. One is innovation. The research for the space program has led to all kinds of innovations.

INTERVIEWER: Can you tell us about some of those?

SCIENTIST: Think about it: to get into space we had to solve all kinds of problems, problems we never had on Earth, that required new ideas and solutions. And these innovations didn't just stay in space. Hundreds of new products have been created from this research— things we use on Earth every day. Let me give you some

examples—water filters, used to clean water, and smoke detectors, to protect your house from fire. They were both developed for use in space.

INTERVIEWER: You've talked about other benefits, ones that can't be measured in dollars and cents. Could you describe some of those?

SCIENTIST: Well, space exploration now requires a great deal of international cooperation. For example, the International Space Station. Five different space agencies worked together to build and run the station. It has brought together international flight crews from fifteen nations. The training and research, the supplies and communication networks: they're all international efforts. This cooperation promotes positive relationships between nations.

INTERVIEWER: There are other, more personal benefits as well.

SCIENTIST: Right. Since the beginning of time, we've had a great curiosity about the world around us. We've always wanted to learn more, to see more. This curiosity has led us to explore every corner of Earth. But we've only just begun in space! There is so much more that we need to find out. And it doesn't just give us answers; it gives perspective. Seeing Earth from space—a small blue planet floating in a giant black sky—we see how precious it is. And that's a perspective we should never forget.

Page 59, Listening Skill

Exercise One

INTERVIEWER: One criticism of the space program is the cost. The U.S. government is spending over 18 billion dollars on space exploration. Is it worth the price?

Page 59, Listening Skill

Exercise Two

Excerpt One

SCIENTIST: For example, the International Space Station. Five different space agencies worked together to build and run the station. It has brought together international flight crews from fifteen nations. The training and research, the supplies and communication networks, they're all international efforts. This cooperation promotes positive relationships between nations.

SCIENTIST: Right. Since the beginning of time, we've had a great curiosity about the world around us. We've always wanted to learn more, to see more. This curiosity has led us to explore every corner of Earth. But we've only just begun in space! There is so much more that we need to find out. And it doesn't just give us answers—it gives perspective. Seeing Earth from space—a small blue planet floating in a giant black sky—we see how precious it is.

UNIT 4: Words That Persuade

Listening One, page 76, Preview

LECTURER: The corporate world loves euphemism. A friend of mine got a letter from his employer that said the company was having a "workforce reduction" because of "changes in the market environment." What they really mean is that a bunch of people are going to be fired because the company is in financial trouble. So why didn't they say that directly?

Page 76, Listen

LECTURER: The corporate world loves euphemism. A friend of mine got a letter from his employer that said the company was having a "workforce reduction" because of "changes in the market environment." What they really mean is that a bunch of people are going to be fired because the company is in financial trouble. So why didn't they say that directly?

Well, it was an attempt to put a happy face on a bad situation. Instead of talking about people getting fired from their jobs, the company used a euphemism to make it sound better—"workforce reduction."

We love to rename things to make them sound better. Who wants to be a garbage collector? Garbage has a negative connotation—dirty, smelly garbage. So now we don't have garbage collectors anymore. No, instead, we have "sanitation workers." Sanitation is the removal of dirt to protect public health. That's a much better connotation, focusing on cleanliness rather than dirt.

Sometimes we make ourselves look better with euphemisms. Unemployed? Out of a job? That doesn't sound good in a job interview. But don't worry, you can say you are "between jobs," implying that it is only a temporary period of unemployment. Or better yet, that you "are going through a career transition." That sounds like you made a choice to be unemployed and find a better career.

But, in other contexts, our euphemisms change. With friends, you might say something else. Have you heard the term "funemployed?" That's how my friend explains his current situation—he's out of a job, but now has the time to do fun things during the work week. "Funemployed"— sounds great, right?

And we're always inventing new euphemisms. Why? Well, most have a short shelf life. They become less effective over time. Euphemisms are created to make an idea sound more positive. But, over time, they can take on a negative connotation, just like the original word! The term "downsizing" is an example. In the 1980s— when we first heard the term "downsizing"—it was a new way to describe a company that was firing people: a company coming "down in size." However, over the years, it's become just as bad—just like saying "we're firing people." The connotation is the same now! So, it's been replaced, too, with new euphemisms like "workforce reduction."

If I could give the corporate world one piece of advice, I'd tell them "Don't overdo it with euphemisms— because, with excessive use, euphemism slides into doublespeak." "Doublespeak" is language that goes beyond making something sound better. "Doublespeak" is deceptive language used to hide the truth. There's a well-known example—you can find it on the internet—of a corporate letter that uses twenty-nine different euphemisms for firing people. Twenty-nine— in one page! That's too much—people get angry at this kind of doublespeak. They want to be told the truth, not hear euphemisms that hide the truth.

So, listen to the euphemisms around you, and learn to use them wisely. Thank you.

Page 78, Make Inferences

Excerpt One

LECTURER: Have you heard the term "funemployed?" That's how my friend explains his current situation— he's out of a job, but now has the time to do fun things during the work week.

Excerpt Two

LECTURER: In the 1980s—when we first heard the term "downsizing"—it was a new way to describe a company that was firing people: a company coming "down in size." However, over the years, it's become just as bad—just like saying "we're firing people." The connotation is the same now!

Excerpt Three

LECTURER: There's a well-known example— you can find it on the internet—of a corporate letter that uses twenty-nine different euphemisms for firing people. Twenty-nine—in one page! That's too much—people get angry at this kind of doublespeak. They want to be told the truth, not hear euphemisms that hide the truth.

Page 81, Note-Taking Skill

Well, it was an attempt to put a happy face on a bad situation. Instead of talking about people getting fired from their jobs, the company used a euphemism to make it sound better— "workforce reduction."

We love to rename things to make them sound better. Who wants to be a garbage collector? Garbage has a negative connotation—dirty, smelly garbage. So now we don't have garbage collectors anymore. No, instead, we have "sanitation workers." Sanitation is the removal of dirt to protect public health. That's a much better connotation, focusing on cleanliness rather than dirt.

Sometimes we make ourselves look better with euphemisms. Unemployed? Out of a job? That doesn't sound good in a job interview. But don't worry, you can say you are "between jobs," implying that it is only a temporary period of unemployment. Or better yet, that you "are going through a career transition." That sounds like you made a choice to be unemployed and find a better career.

Listening Two, page 81, Comprehension

REAL ESTATE AGENT: So, let me tell you a little about this place. It's really great. It's got two bedrooms, and it's right in your price range. Let's go on in. . . .

CLIENT: OK!

REAL ESTATE AGENT: This is the living room. It has some really great features. Look at the nice wood floors and the big windows.

CLIENT: It seems awfully . . . small . . . Where'd my sofa go?

REAL ESTATE AGENT: Yes, it's cozy, but I think you can work with it. I'd definitely put the sofa over here along this wall, and that would open up the space.

CLIENT: There's a lot of noise coming from the street. . . .

REAL ESTATE AGENT: Yes, it's a vibrant neighborhood, lots of shops and restaurants, and very convenient to transportation . . . the subway's right down the block.

CLIENT: OK.

REAL ESTATE AGENT: Can we move on to the kitchen?

CLIENT: Sure.

REAL ESTATE AGENT: Now, this kitchen has all new appliances: new stove, new dishwasher, new fridge.

CLIENT: I love the appliances. They're great. But it's kinda small, too. Not much room to move around.

REAL ESTATE AGENT: Well, it's a compact kitchen. It's very well-organized.

CLIENT: Those cabinets are sorta old fashioned.

REAL ESTATE AGENT: Isn't that a great vintage look? That's really coming back in style.

CLIENT: I guess . . .

REAL ESTATE AGENT: And out here is the backyard . . .

CLIENT: Nice . . . but not much of a garden. No grass or anything.

REAL ESTATE AGENT: Well, it's very low maintenance. You don't have to worry about mowing the grass. Add some nice planters, some flowers, it'll look great! . . . Ready to go upstairs and see the bedrooms?

CLIENT: Actually, I don't need to see any more. It's got some nice features, but it's just not gonna work for me.

REAL ESTATE AGENT: OK, no problem! I've got lots of other places to show you.

Page 82, Listening Skill

Exercise One

So, let me tell you a little about this place. It's really great.

Page 82, Listening Skill

Exercise Two

Excerpt One

This is the living room. It has some really great features.

Excerpt Two

It seems awfully small.

Excerpt Three

I'd definitely put the sofa over here along this wall, and that would open up the space.

Excerpt Four

I love the appliances. They're great. But it's kinda small, too.

Page 91, Speaking Skill

Ad 1

Tired of paying too much for a pair of stylish jeans? Well quality doesn't have to come at a price. Rico jeans give you the fit you want at a price you can afford. Rico jeans. Fabulous fit, incredible comfort! For the best jeans at the best price, Rico has it all!

Ad 2

Tired of paying too much for a pair of stylish jeans? Well quality doesn't have to come at a price. Rico jeans give you the fit you want at a price you can afford. Rico jeans. Fabulous fit, incredible comfort! For the best jeans at the best price, Rico has it all!

UNIT 5: Follow Your Passion

Listening One, page 99, Preview

JULIE: . . . My dad is the first person that ever told me to follow your passion, and, make, you know, make money off of it. And I've always, you know, I know that's a huge phrase right now, you hear that all the time, but I heard that from my dad a long time ago.

SIMON: And I never fought so much with my parents than during this time. And I remember my parents tried everything, you know: They played good cop, bad cop. They tried bribing me. They tried saying, "We're your parents, and you're going to do this."

Page 100, Listen

HOST: Erik Michaelson talked with two professionals to find out how their parents influenced their career choices. Julie Hession is a cookbook writer and the founder of a company that makes breakfast cereal.

ERIK: What role has your family played in shaping your career aspirations?

JULIE: I have a very supportive family. My dad is the first person that ever told me to follow your passion, and, make, you know, make money off of it. And I've always, you know, I know that's a huge phrase right now, you hear that all the time, but I heard that from my dad a long time ago.

ERIK: After majoring in hotel and restaurant management in college, what made you decide to shift away from that in your career?

JULIE: Well, the fact that, about three months into my first job out of college, I decided that I hated hotel and restaurant management, that was my first clue. And it was interesting because, you know, when you're an undergrad, and you're taking four years in this, in this curriculum, and all you're learning about is, you know, hotel restaurant management, hotel restaurant law, hotel restaurant marketing. . . . So, I kind of had tunnel vision, and I was thinking, well this is what I've chosen to do, I'm tied to it. This is going to be my life. And I got my first job with Wyndham Hotels. They don't tell you where they're going to put you when they hire you. . . . So, anyway, I got the job with Wyndham. They put me in Annapolis, Maryland, which I had, you know, great city, but I had no friends there. You didn't really make a lot of friends working in this small hotel in the city, and I was just . . . I was so unhappy, I know, I wasn't happy at work, I wasn't happy with what I was doing, and this was an instance where my dad came down to Annapolis. He drove down to Annapolis, took me to lunch. And he said, "You know, this isn't right for you. But I think you need to figure out what you want to do, and make a change, and figure out how you're going to get there." So that was, like, such an ah-ha moment for me, that I could do something else than my major! I didn't have to do my major! So that was huge, because then I started just kind of looking around, and, I think, kind of opening my mind a little bit.

Host: Simon Sinek is an author and public speaker who studied in England and now teaches leaders and organizations how to inspire people.

Erik: Where has your family been most supportive in your career development?

Simon: When I graduated college, I went to law school. And after not quite a year of law school, I realized that I didn't want to be a lawyer. And so, I decided that I was going to drop out of law school. And I never fought so much with my parents than during this time. And I remember my parents tried everything, you know: They played good cop, bad cop. They tried bribing me. They tried saying, "We're your parents, and you're going to do this." They tried being my friend, like, "Look, just get your law degree, then you can do anything you want." You know, I mean, every strategy that exists, they tried, right? And at the time, I wanted to go into marketing, right? I was . . . I wanted to go into, to join the ad world, right? And my dad was in England on a business trip, about the time that I had to re-enroll, and he sits down with me and he says, "So?" And I remember it, I remember sitting in our friend's house, and he says to me, "So?" And I said, "I didn't re-enroll." And the first words out of his mouth were, "Right. Let's get you into advertising then." My parents were 100 percent against me until the decision was made, and then after that point, they were 100 percent supportive. And never, ever, ever raised it ever again. They literally never mentioned it again. And so, I have to say, my, my, I've been very lucky in my life, which is my parents will give advice, my parents will give strong advice, my parents will try and push and move, you know, where they would like their children to go, but ultimately once the kids have made the decision, they're 100 percent supportive. And so, I've been very lucky.

Page 101, Make Inferences

Excerpt One

Julie: So, I kind of had tunnel vision, and I was thinking, well this is what I've chosen to do, I'm tied to it. This is going to be my life.

Excerpt Two

Julie: And he said, "You know, this isn't right for you. But I think you need to figure out what you want to do, and make a change, and figure out how you're going to get there." So, that was, like, such an ah-ha moment for me, that I could do something else than my major! I didn't have to do my major!

Excerpt Three

Simon: My dad was in England on a business trip, about the time that I had to re-enroll, and he sits down with me and he says, "So?" And I remember it, I remember sitting in our friend's house, and he says to me, "So?"

Page 104, Note-Taking Skill

Excerpt One

. . . when you're an undergrad, and you're taking four years in this, in this curriculum, and all you're learning about is, you know, hotel restaurant management, hotel restaurant law, hotel restaurant marketing . . .

Excerpt Two

They tried bribing me. They tried saying, "We're your parents, and you're going to do this." They tried being my friend . . .

Excerpt Three

So, I kind of had tunnel vision, and I was thinking, well this I what I've chosen to do, I'm tied to it. This is going to be my life.

Excerpt Four

And I have to say, my, my I've been very lucky in life, which is my parents will give advice, my parents will give strong advice, my parents will try to push and move, you know, where they would like their children to go, but ultimately once the kids have made the decision, they're 100 percent supportive.

Listening Two, page 105, Comprehension

JEREMY BREZDEN: Just out of college—with a degree in biology—I got a job as a research assistant in a biotech company. Now, this was a "good job"—the pay was good, and I had the chance to move up—but after a while, I realized that I didn't want to get up in the morning and go to work. I had to figure out what my real passion was. And that's what I want to talk to you about today: finding your passion.

So first, I want you to ask yourself, "What am I good at?" Think about skills that come easily to you, like maybe you're very artistic. Or, maybe you're good at building things. Also, think about areas where other people think you're an expert. In my case, I've always loved science. And in high school, my friends always asked me for help with their science homework.

The next thing is to think about all the things you like to do. Do you love making dinner for your friends? What were your favorite classes in school? What do you do in your free time? Me, I've always liked helping people. Starting in college, I volunteered for the Red Cross, helping people in disasters or after fires. I get a lot of satisfaction from that.

My final suggestion is to make a list of the things that are important to you. What kind of environment do you want to work in? Do you want to work with your hands? Do you want a job where you can travel? As a research assistant, I mostly worked alone. But when I thought about it, I realized that I really like working with people.

So, I went through this process. I looked at my scientific skills, my desire to help people, and my love of working with people, and decided that nursing was the perfect career for me. I quit my job and went back to school, and now I'm a nurse at Children's Hospital. And guess what? I love it. I took a chance, and it paid off. And that's how I found my passion in life. Thank you.

Page 106, Listening Skill

Exercise Two

A: What are you doing after college?

B: I'm going to look for a job. But there's a problem. I'm a business major, but I want to be a teacher. I should have gotten a teaching certificate. Do you think I could get a teaching job?

A: I think you should try. There's no rule that says you have to get a job that matches your major.

B: You're right. I've got to think about this some more.

Page 115, Speaking Skill

Exercise One

1. What kind of job would be good for a person who hates predictable schedules?
2. When I was six years old, I remember telling my mom that I already knew what I wanted to do when I grew up. . . .
3. A recent survey from Forbes magazine revealed that people who work from home are more likely to be satisfied with their jobs.

4. Famous painter Vincent van Gogh once said, "I would rather die of passion than of boredom."

5. When I was in high school, I went on a school trip to a wind farm that produced renewable energy. It was amazing to see the big windmills up close and to talk with the people who worked there. . . .

6. "Never work just for money or power. They won't save your soul or help you sleep at night." These are the wise words of author and activist Marian Wright Edelman.

UNIT 6: Culture and Commerce

Listening One, page 121, Preview

REPORTER: Each year around 10,000 tourists visit three small villages along the Thai / Myanmar border to see the famous long-necked women. The attraction is a tradition that requires women to stretch their necks by wearing brass coils. Originally from the Padaung tribe, the women and their families came from Myanmar to Thailand in the 1980s to escape poverty and war. Their new lives are very different from their lives as farmers in Myanmar. Now they make a living talking with tourists, posing for pictures, and selling handmade souvenirs.

Page 122, Listen

RADIO ANNOUNCER: Critics call it "a human zoo." Tour companies consider it a tourist attraction. Whichever the case, the long-necked women of Padaung have become an important source of money for several small villages on the border of Thailand and Myanmar. Reporter Mike Danforth has this report.

TOUR LEADER: Welcome to Nai Soi. Please buy your ticket here.

REPORTER: Each year around 10,000 tourists visit three small villages along the Thai / Myanmar border to see the famous long-necked women. The attraction is a tradition that requires women to stretch their necks by wearing brass coils. Originally from the Padaung tribe, the women and their families came from Myanmar to Thailand in the 1980s to escape poverty and war. Their new lives are very different from their lives as farmers in Myanmar. Now they make a living talking with tourists, posing for pictures, and selling handmade souvenirs.

When a Padaung girl turns five, a thick coil of brass is wrapped around her neck. Throughout her life, more coils are added until her neck carries up to twenty-five brass rings, weighing up to 22 pounds. The coils push up her chin and press down her collarbone, making her neck longer. Pa Peiy, a young woman with twenty neck rings, describes her early years of neck stretching:

PA PEIY: At first it was painful, but now it's OK. Now sleeping, eating, working . . . everything is OK, but I cannot take it off . . . so this is my life.

REPORTER: It truly is her life. Pa Peiy's neck is now so weak that if she takes off the coils, her head will fall forward, and she'll stop breathing. Despite the discomfort, Padaung women in Thailand continue to wear the coils even though the tradition has almost disappeared in Myanmar. Why? Because there's money in it. Ma Nang, a graceful woman with twenty-four neck rings explains:

MA NANG: In Myanmar, I worked hard growing food. Now I sit, and tourists take pictures. In one month, I get $70 to $80. It's easy, and it's good money for my family. Sometimes I'm tired of tourists always looking . . . but it's good money.

REPORTER: Each year, as the long-necked women have become more and more popular, the controversy about them has increased. In an outdoor restaurant near Nai Soi, tourists discuss whether or not to visit the village. Sandra, a Canadian woman, feels that it's fine to visit.

SANDRA: I don't really see a problem. I mean this is their tradition . . . and so if I go, it's like I'm helping them to preserve it. Spending my money is also helping them. You know, they make a living from tourism, so they need us.

REPORTER: Fredrick, from Germany, feels differently.

FREDRICK: Actually, I don't see that we're preserving tradition at all. This tradition has died in Myanmar already. These women are just hurting their bodies to entertain us. It's like paying to go see animals in a zoo. It's degrading.

REPORTER: For now, the future of the long-necked women is easy to predict. As long as there are tourists who will pay to see them, they will continue to wrap their daughters' necks. The controversy continues, with one side seeing the villages as examples of how tourism can save dying traditions, and others criticizing it as harmful and degrading to the Padaung women.

Page 124, Make Inferences

Excerpt One

REPORTER: Originally from the Padaung tribe, the women and their families came from Myanmar to Thailand in the 1980s to escape poverty and war. Their new lives are very different from their lives as farmers in Myanmar. Now they make a living talking with tourists, posing for pictures, and selling handmade souvenirs.

Excerpt Two

FREDRICK: These women are just hurting their bodies to entertain us. It's like paying to go see animals in a zoo. It's degrading.

Page 126, Note-Taking Skill

Exercise One

REPORTER: Each year, as the long-necked women have become more and more popular, the controversy about them has increased. In an outdoor restaurant near Nai Soi, tourists discuss whether or not to visit the village. Sandra, a Canadian woman, feels that it's fine to visit.

SANDRA: I don't really see a problem. I mean this is their tradition . . . and so if I go, it's like I'm helping them to preserve it. Spending my money is also helping them. You know, they make a living from tourism, so they need us.

REPORTER: Fredrick, from Germany, feels differently.

FREDRICK: Actually, I don't see that we're preserving tradition at all. This tradition has died in Myanmar already. These women are just hurting their bodies to entertain us. It's like paying to go see animals in a zoo. It's degrading.

Listening Two, Page 127, Comprehension

MAYOR: OK. We're here today to talk about tourism in our community. Let's start with the first item on our agenda—identifying some of the problems caused by the increasing number of tourists we get every year.

WOMAN 1: Well, for one, the traffic is just terrible in the summer! In winter, it takes me about 15 minutes to drive into town. But in the summer, it can be 45 minutes or more. It's ridiculous!

MAN 1: I agree, traffic gets bad, but in my mind, the biggest problem is housing. The cost of buying or renting a home here is way too high! Yeah! It's just too expensive on a regular salary. Too many homes are sold as vacation homes for rich people. And that leaves nothing for the working people who live here. I mean, I own a seafood restaurant, OK? And I've got a waitress who's living in her car right now because she can't afford any other place to live. We've got to do something about that!

WOMAN 2: Can I say something? OK, I know it's difficult to have all these tourists around during the summer, but I, for one, am very happy to have them. I run a souvenir shop, and I do about 80 percent of my business for the year in the summer. And I'm not the only one. Tourists are the lifeblood of our community. Without them, I wouldn't be able to make a living. We've got to keep them coming.

MAN 2: Of course, we need the tourists, no one's denying that. But I'm a business owner, too, and one problem I see is that we depend on the weather so much. When it rains, tourists don't come, huh? This season has been really difficult for my business 'cause of that. With all this rain last month, I lost a lot of money because people weren't coming in the door. I'd like to see us develop where we don't depend on the weather so much.

MAYOR: OK, before we move on, I'd like to address one of the comments made here . . .

Page 128, Listening Skill

Exercise One

MAN 1: I agree, traffic gets bad, but in my mind, the biggest problem is housing. The cost of buying or renting a home here is way too high.

Page 128, Listening Skill

Exercise Two
Excerpt One

WOMAN 2: OK, I know it's difficult to have all these tourists around during the summer, but I, for one, am very happy to have them.

Excerpt Two

MAN 2: But I'm a business owner, too, and one problem I see is that we depend on the weather so much.

Excerpt Three

MAN 2: I'd like to see us develop where we don't depend on the weather so much.

UNIT 7: Restorative Justice

Listening One, page 145, Preview

FACILITATOR: It can be a quite scary experience for the victim and the offender. You can feel the tension in the air. The victim might get angry, or annoyed, or cry at some point, and the offender has to see and feel that. The offender can get upset, too.

Page 145, Listen

INTERVIEWER: So, to begin, what is the goal of restorative justice?

FACILITATOR: Well, it's about communication. Restorative justice brings together victims and offenders affected by crime, so that the harm caused by the crime can be repaired. The idea is that by coming together, victims and offenders can begin to understand each other better and come to some sort of resolution.

INTERVIEWER: And the victims, why do they participate?

FACILITATOR: For some victims, just knowing the offender was caught and went through the criminal justice system is enough. But for others, it's not enough. They're frustrated. They want answers to their questions. They want the chance to tell the offender how they feel. So, some victims want to meet with the offender personally. It's an opportunity to fill that need. It can be very powerful.

What's important to remember is that restorative justice is about taking the lead from the victim, letting the victim decide what to do. We want to ensure that the process is absolutely safe and helpful for the victim.

INTERVIEWER: Now, you're a restorative justice facilitator. What is your role in the process?

FACILITATOR: The facilitator has a very important role. We don't just throw people in a room together and say: "Talk!" We prepare everyone for the meeting. We find a safe space for the meeting to take place, sometimes in the community, or in prison, if the offender is incarcerated. And it's important that the victim knows they don't have to do anything they don't want to— they don't have to shake hands or answer the offender's questions, and they can leave the meeting anytime. So, it really is about the facilitator actively managing the meeting, making sure the victim can talk, the offender listens, and ensuring that the victim's needs are met.

INTERVIEWER: I'm curious about the offenders. How are offenders selected to participate?

FACILITATOR: We don't go forward with every case. We have to look at the motivation and why people want to participate, both the offender and the victim.

If the offender agrees to meet the victim, that's a big step. To do this, first they have to take responsibility for the crime. So that means maybe they have pleaded guilty or made restitution in some other way.

Often, for the offender, they don't know the victim. It may be someone's name on a piece of paper or someone they saw in court. So, restorative justice is a way for the offender to make some good, to make up for the harm done. Sometimes they're feeling remorse for their crime, so this is a powerful way for them to move on.

INTERVIEWER: So now, can you tell me about the meeting between the victim and offender? What happens during the restorative justice conference?

FACILITATOR: When the meeting actually happens, there can be a lot of emotion. It can be a scary experience for the victim and the offender. You can feel the tension in the air. The victim might get angry, or annoyed, or cry at some point, and the offender has to see and feel that—that's part of the process. The offender can get upset, too. And that's why the facilitator is there, to help the participants express their emotions in a safe way, a way that leads to a positive outcome . . . some kind of resolution for the victim and the offender.

INTERVIEWER: What kind of outcomes?

FACILITATOR: One thing I can say is that the meetings can be life-changing. We see that all the time. Sometimes the offender apologizes right away. Sometimes there are tears when the victim finally gets answers. Sometimes there is forgiveness. Sometimes the two people continue to communicate after the process is over.

Often the victims feel a lot of relief and like they can move on from the bad experience they had. And for the offenders, it can change their life as well. It's all about seeing their victims and the hurt they caused, maybe for the first time, and trying to make some good out of it.

Page 147, Make Inferences

Excerpt One

FACILITATOR: The facilitator has a very important role. We don't just throw people in a room together and say: "Talk!" We prepare everyone for the meeting.

Excerpt Two

FACILITATOR: Often, for the offender, they don't know the victim. It may be someone's name on a piece of paper or someone they saw in court. So, restorative justice is a way for the offender to make some good, to make up for the harm done.

Excerpt Three

FACILITATOR: The victim might get angry, or annoyed, or cry at some point, and the offender has to see and feel that—that's part of the process. The offender can get upset, too. And that's why the facilitator is there, to help the participants express their emotions in a safe way.

Listening Two, page 151, Comprehension

DEREK: When he first came in, I didn't know how to react. I was afraid I'd lose it. The anger and emotion had built up for so long.

Then the facilitator invited me to talk. At first, I didn't know what to say, but then it all came pouring out. How my wife died and I kept her wedding ring to remember her, and how upset I was when it was stolen, like he stole a part of me. And how I didn't feel safe in my own house anymore.

It felt good to get it all out. It was emotional. And Marcus seemed so . . . so shocked that I was upset. Really surprised. But I'll say this: He listened to all of it. He sat there quietly and just listened. And then he apologized, and I could see his remorse . . . that he really meant it.

After I left, I felt a huge weight off my shoulders. I realized that I can move on. I don't have to be afraid anymore. Seeing how young he was, seeing his remorse . . . In my heart, I started to forgive him. He was just a kid who made some bad choices.

MARCUS: I was nervous about the meeting. I wasn't sure what to expect. When I saw him first, he looked real serious, and, like, mad. Part of me wanted to run out of the room . . .

It was hard to listen to him talk about it. I never thought about the people who lived in the house. To me, it was, like, I really needed the money, and they live in a nice neighborhood, so I figured they wouldn't miss it. I felt like I wasn't hurting anyone.

And he looked so sad when he talked about his wife and the ring. I told him I was sorry. I didn't realize what it meant to him.

I'm glad I got to say, "I'm sorry." I know I broke the law and hurt someone, and I can't change the past, but I feel like now I want to be better, be a better person. I'm gonna try, anyway.

Page 152, Listening Skill

Exercise Two

1. **DEREK:** At first, I didn't know what to say.
2. **MARCUS:** I never thought about the people who lived in the house.
3. **MARCUS:** I felt like I wasn't hurting anyone.
4. **DEREK:** I realized that I can move on.
5. **MARCUS:** . . . but I feel like now I want to be better, be a better person.

Page 161, Pronunciation

Exercise One

MAN 1 AND MAN 2: There are many ways to punish criminals. Restorative justice is one way, and it can be very effective in many situations.

UNIT 8: Reducing Your Carbon Footprint

Listening One, page 172, Preview

JULIA: My name is Julia Peters, and I live in Portland, Oregon. It's important for me to live with a small personal carbon footprint because I realize that there are lots of people sharing this earth, and lots of people that will come after us. It's my responsibility to protect it and make it better, to live as small as I can, so that it doesn't affect future generations. . . .

Page 172, Listen

JULIA: Hey, come on in! Welcome to my house! My name is Julia Peters, and I live in Portland, Oregon. It's important for me to live with a small personal carbon footprint because I realize that there are lots of people sharing this earth, and lots of people that will come after us. It's my responsibility to protect it and make it better, to live as small as I can, so that it doesn't affect future generations, their ability to live well and healthily on the planet.

We're in my house today, which is a small house, but we try to do the most with what we have. Our yard is almost all used for growing food. . . . So, you have to make your way through the jungle here. . . . Here in the backyard, you can see, it's not much of a yard. There's not much grass. We've taken out most of the grass to put in raised beds so that we can grow more of our own food. Right now, with it being spring, early summer, we have a lot of things that we grew from seeds inside the house, but if you were here in August and September, hopefully this would be really full, with lots of tomatoes, basil plants, squash, all kinds of things.

We try to grow as much of our own food as we can because it reduces our carbon footprint. If we grow it on our own property, we don't have to go to the store and get it, and then the store buys it from someplace. For the average American, food on your plate has traveled 1,500 miles. That, obviously, is a huge environmental impact, when your food gets transported from so far away.

We also have chickens, as a way to reduce our impact. We eat mostly vegetarian. A lot of our protein comes from beans, but also from eggs. We have six chickens. "Hi, girls!" . . . They lay eggs, and in the summertime, they lay more, so right now we get about four eggs a day.

Another thing that we try to do on-site is to create our own energy. We have solar panels on our roof, and in the summertime, they produce about enough energy to power our house. Obviously, energy that doesn't come from our solar panels, we have to get from an energy company. But a lot of power in the United States comes from coal, and coal has a huge environmental impact. If we don't reduce our coal consumption, the average temperature of the earth will go up by one to two degrees, so it's a really critical time to think about how we get our power.

Our house is a small house. It has three small bedrooms, and we have four people living here. And that's another way we try to reduce our footprint, is by dense living. If I were going to live in this house by myself,

I would still use energy for the lights, to heat it, to run the refrigerator. By having four people, we are collectively using almost the same amount of energy, but it's split by four people, instead of each person living in their own apartment or house. By sharing more, by living together and sharing resources, that's another way we try to reduce our footprint and limit what we use.

For some people to say that small, personal efforts are just a drop in the bucket, that they don't really have an effect, I can understand that, that makes sense. That how does one person out of 6 billion have an impact. And I think there are a few things about that to remember, is that the more people that do it, it's not just one drop, it's a lot of drops, and that can make a change.

Page 175, Make Inferences

Excerpt One

JULIA: We try to grow as much of our own food as we can because it reduces our carbon footprint. If we grow it on our own property, we don't have to go to the store and get it, and then the store buys it from some place. For the average American, food on your plate has traveled 1,500 miles.

Excerpt Two

JULIA: Our house is a small house. It has three small bedrooms, and we have four people living here. And that's another way we try to reduce our footprint, is by dense living. If I were going to live in this house by myself, I would still use energy for the lights, to heat it, to run the refrigerator. By having four people, we are collectively using almost the same amount of energy, but it's split by four people, instead of each person living in their own apartment or house.

Page 177, Note-Taking Skill

Exercise One

Excerpt One

If we don't reduce our coal consumption, the average temperature of the earth will go up by one to two degrees . . .

Excerpt Two

By having four people, we are collectively using almost the same amount of energy, but it's split by four people, instead of each person living in their own apartment or house.

Excerpt Three

. . . the more people that do it, it's not just one drop, it's a lot of drops, and that can make a change.

Page 177, Note-Taking Skill

Exercise Two

Excerpt One

Your personal carbon footprint is the amount of carbon dioxide (CO_2) that you put into the air when you drive a car, fly in an airplane, or use electricity made by burning coal or gas.

Excerpt Two

CO_2 and other greenhouse gases have a serious impact on the environment. They make Earth warmer, causing climate change.

Excerpt Three

Even the food you eat affects your personal carbon footprint. A diet that includes a lot of meat creates a bigger footprint, while the footprint of a vegetarian diet is smaller.

Listening Two, Page 178, Comprehension

SPEAKER: We are here today because we want to stop global warming. Like me, you're trying hard to reduce your own personal carbon footprint. And these small, individual changes do have an impact, do help lower our carbon emissions.

But it's not enough. It's not enough for individuals to change. We need governments to change. We need industry to change. We need big changes if we want to stop global warming from destroying our planet.

One-third . . . one-third of our global carbon emissions—35 percent—comes from producing electricity. We need government and industry to work together to lower these emissions. To develop new, cleaner technology to heat our homes, power our factories, and to keep the lights on.

Another 20 percent—20 percent!—of our emissions comes from transportation. We need government and industry to work together to build more energy-efficient cars and trucks. To build more public transportation. Good quality public transportation that will let us get rid of our cars and the pollution they produce forever!

Another 20 percent of all emissions comes from industry—our factories and businesses. Putting tons upon tons of carbon into the air —our air—every single minute. It's time to say enough! We need these businesses to lower their own personal carbon footprints!

So, my message to you today is: Keep trying to reduce your personal carbon footprint. But also stand up, stand up and demand . . . demand that government and industry do their part. Because that is what will really make a difference!

Page 179, Listening Skill

Exercise One

SPEAKER: But also stand up, stand up and demand . . . demand that government and industry do their part.

Page 179, Listening Skill

Exercise Two

Excerpt One

SPEAKER: We need government and industry to work together to lower these emissions. To develop new, cleaner technology to heat our homes, power our factories, and to keep the lights on.

Excerpt Two

SPEAKER: We need government and industry to work together to build more energy-efficient cars and trucks. To build more public transportation.

THE PHONETIC ALPHABET

Consonant Symbols			
/b/	be	/t/	to
/d/	do	/v/	van
/f/	father	/w/	will
/g/	get	/y/	yes
/h/	he	/z/	zoo, busy
/k/	keep, can	/θ/	thanks
/l/	let	/ð/	then
/m/	may	/ʃ/	she
/n/	no	/ʒ/	vision, Asia
/p/	pen	/tʃ/	child
/r/	rain	/dʒ/	join
/s/	so, circle	/ŋ/	long

Vowel Symbols			
/ɑ/	far, hot	/iy/	we, mean, feet
/ɛ/	met, said	/ey/	day, late, rain
/ɔ/	tall, bought	/ow/	go, low, coat
/ə/	son, under	/uw/	too, blue
/æ/	cat	/ay/	time, buy
/ɪ/	ship	/aw/	house, now
/ʊ/	good, could, put	/oy/	boy, coin

CREDITS

VIDEO CREDITS

Unit 1: Pearson Education
Unit 2: NBC Universal Archives
Unit 3: ABC News Internet Ventures
Unit 4: Insight Media, Inc.
Unit 5: ABC News Internet Ventures
Unit 6: Pearson Education
Unit 7: AFP/BO Clips
Unit 8: ABC News Internet Ventures.

TEXT AND AUDIO CREDITS

Unit 1

Pages 5, 8, 205–207, classroom audio, and MyEnglishLab "Focused Listening": Listening One Ultrarunner Jay Batchen: Ultrarunner Jay Batchen talks about his experience as an ultramarathon runner. Courtesy of Tim Bourquin.

Unit 2

Page 30, classroom audio, and MyEnglishLab "Focused Listening": Listening One Lily's Story: Background music from Scheming Weasel (slower version) by Kevin MacLeod (incompetech.com). Licensed under Creative Commons: By Attribution 3.0 License http:// creativecommons.org/licenses/by/3.0/

Unit 5

Pages 99, 101, 214–215, classroom audio, and MyEnglishLab "Focused Listening": Listening One Changing Career Paths: "When to Pursue a Career That Is Not Your College Major" and "How Parents Influence Career Aspirations" interviews with Julie Hession from the "Capture Your Flag" Career Documentary Interview Series. Copyright © Capture Your Flag LLC. Reproduced with permission.
Pages 99, 214–215, and classroom audio: "Getting Parent Support for a Career Change Decision" an interview with Simon Sinek from the "Capture Your Flag" Career Documentary Interview Series. Copyright © Capture Your Flag LLC. Reproduced with permission.

Unit 7

Page 149, classroom audio, and MyEnglishLab "Focused Listening": Listening Two Derek and Marcus: Background music "Take a Step" by Mocha Music/Shutterstock.

Unit 8

Pages 172, 175, 221–222, classroom audio, and MyEnglishLab "Focused Listening": Listening One Living Small: Julia Peters describes her life. Used with permission from Julia Brown.
Page 197: Figure 5 and Figure 6 from NOAA National Centers for Environmental information, Climate at a Glance: Global Time Series, published July 2018, retrieved on August 9, 2018 from https://www.ncdc.noaa.gov/cag/df
Page 198: Table 1: Hanson, S., Nicholls, R., Ranger, N. et al. (2011). A global ranking of port cities with high exposure to climate extremes, Climate Change, 104(1), 89–111, doi:10.1007/s10584-010-9977-4. Figure 6, p. 99. Used with permission from Susan Hanson.

PHOTO CREDITS

Cover

Kochneva Tetyana/Shutterstock (main); Youimages/ Shutterstock (top).

Frontmatter

Page vi: Klemen K. Misic/Shutterstock; vii (p. 4 runners): Pierre Verdy/AFP/Getty Images; vii (p. 4 background): Vixit/Shutterstock; vii (p. 9 top): SAMPERS Erik/Hemis.fr/ Alamy Stock Photo; vii (p. 9 bicyclists): Debra Anderson/ Shutterstock; vii (p. 9 swimmers): Ammentorp/123RF; vii (p. 9 runners): Robert Daly/Caiaimage/Getty Images; viii (MyLab screenshot, swimmer): Maridav/Shutterstock; ix (p. 14–15): Pavel Burchenko/Shutterstock; ix (photo on cell phone) : Klemen K. Misic/Shutterstock; x (p. 20): Ryan DeBerardinis/Shutterstock; x (p.22 (A)): Ronnie Kaufman/ Corbis/Getty Images; x (p.22 (B)):Tim Macpherson/Cultura/ Getty Images; x (p.22 (C)): Yiorgos GR/Shutterstock; x (p.22 (D)): Bob Thomas/Bob Thomas Sports Photography/ Getty Images; xi: Pikoso.kz/Shutterstock; xiv (Unit 1 opener): Klemen K. Misic/Shutterstock; xiv (Unit 2 opener): Sergey Nivens/Shutterstock; xv (Unit 3 opener): Vadim Sadovski/Shutterstock; xv (Unit 4 opener): Party people studio/Shutterstock; xvi (Unit 5 opener): LightField Studios/Shutterstock; xvi (Unit 6 opener): Paweenlum/ Shutterstock; xvii (Unit 7 opener): Photographee.eu/ Shutterstock; xvii (Unit 8 opener): Shutterstock.

Unit 1

Pages 2–3: Klemen K. Misic/Shutterstock; 4: Pierre Verdy/ AFP/Getty Images; 4 (background): Vixit/Shutterstock; 9 (top): SAMPERS Erik/Hemis.fr/Alamy Stock Photo; 9 (bicyclists): Debra Anderson/Shutterstock; 9 (swimmers): Ammentorp/123RF; 9 (runners): Robert Daly/Caiaimage/ Getty Images; 14–15: Pavel Burchenko/Shutterstock; 16: Maridav/Shutterstock; 18: Juice Images/Getty Images; 20: Ryan DeBerardinis/Shutterstock; 22 (A): Ronnie Kaufman/ Corbis/Getty Images; 22 (B): Tim Macpherson/Cultura/ Getty Images; 22 (C): Yiorgos GR/Shutterstock; 22 (D): Bob Thomas/Bob Thomas Sports Photography/Getty Images; 24: Pikoso.kz/Shutterstock.

Unit 2

Pages 26–27: Sergey Nivens/Shutterstock; 28: Jemastock/123RF; 28 (background): Bestfoto77/ Shutterstock; 29: Sata Production/Shutterstock; 30: Lucky Business/Shutterstock; 33: Weerapat kiatdumrong/123RF; 34: MIXA/Getty Images; 38: Brian Jackson/123RF; 41: Shutterstock.

Unit 3

Pages 48–49: Vadim Sadovski/Shutterstock; 50 (satellite): Douglas Pulsipher/Alamy Stock Photo; 50 (background): Alexey Filatov/Shutterstock; 51 (left): NASA; 51 (right): Science Source/Getty Images; 55: Dotted Yeti/Shutterstock; 56 (telescope): photoHare/ Shutterstock; 56 (space station): Nikonaft/Shutterstock; 61: Visdia/Shutterstock; 63: Gorodenkoff/Shutterstock; 64 (top): Lazyllama/Shutterstock; 64 (bottom): Benchart/ Shutterstock; 67 (left): Rawpixel.com/Shutterstock; 67 (right): Shutterstock; 70: SergeyDV/Shutterstock.

Unit 4

Pages 72–73: Party people studio/Shutterstock; 74: Rob Hainer/Shutterstock; 79: Rawpixel.com/Shutterstock; 80: Artashes/Shutterstock; 84: Maria Avvakumova/Shutterstock; 89 (room 1): Foamfoto/Shutterstock; 89 (room 2): Artazum/Shutterstock; 89 (room 3): Pics721/Shutterstock; 89 (room 4): B Brown/Shutterstock; 92 (car): CoolR/Shutterstock; 92 (lipstick): Yellow Cat/Shutterstock; 92 (woman with mouthwash): Jedimaster/123RF; 92 (man with chocolate): Zurijeta/Shutterstock; 92 (sunglasses): Nor Gal/Shutterstock; 92 (jogging feet): Paul Maguire/Shutterstock.

Unit 5

Pages 96–97: LightField Studios/Shutterstock; 99 (Julie Hession): Neilson Barnard/Getty Images; 99 (Simon Sinek): Nancy Kaszerman/ZUMA Press, Inc./Alamy Stock Photo; 102: Pixelheadphoto digitalskillet/Shutterstock; 103 (speaker and audience): Django/E+/Getty Images; 103 (close up of speaker): Django/E+/Getty Images; 105 (left): Michael Ventura/Alamy Stock Photo; 105 (right): RTimages/Shutterstock; 108: Ximagination/123RF; 112: Shutterstock.

Unit 6

Pages 118–119: Paweenlum/Shutterstock; 120 (background): Jaran Jenrai/123RF; 120 (bottom): Juniors Bildarchiv/F300/Alamy Stock Photo; 125: Olga Yarovenko/Shutterstock; 129: Steve Bruckmann/Shutterstock; 131: Sborisov/123RF; 133: Lucky-photographer/Shutterstock; 135: Tekkol/Shutterstock; 136–137: Virojt Changyencham/Shutterstock; 140: Byelikova Oksana/Shutterstock.

Unit 7

Pages 142–143: Photographee.eu/Shutterstock; 144 (top): Pattanaphong khaunkaew/123RF; 144 (bottom): BlurryMe/Shutterstock; 148: Freedomz/Shutterstock; 149 (older man): Sergii Mostovyi/123RF; 149 (younger man): Eric Audras/ONOKY/Getty Images; 155 (background): Only_kim/Shutterstock; 156: George Rudy/Shutterstock; 157: Pineapple studio/Shutterstock; 159: Antoniodiaz/Shutterstock; 160: Westend61/Getty Images; 161 (left): Amenic181/Shutterstock; 161 (right): Andrey_Popov/Shutterstock; 166: Shutterstock.

Unit 8

Pages 168–169: Shutterstock; 170 (solar panels on house): Manfredxy/Shutterstock; 170 (raised garden beds): Pilens/123RF; 170 (bulldozer and logs): Pedro Antonio Salaverría Calahorra / Alamy Stock Photo; 170 (background): Avigator Fortuner/Shutterstock; 172: Courtesy of Julia Peters; 173: Chinnna/123RF; 174: Daxiao Productions/Shutterstock; 176: Marin Tomas/Moment/Getty Images; 178:Valery Rizzo/Shutterstock; 181: Kenny Tong/Shutterstock; 182–183: Bubble_TeStock/Shutterstock.

Student Activities

Page 193 (top): Maryna Pleshkun/123RF; 193 (bottom): Harvepino/Shutterstock; 194 (sunglasses): Akatiev Andrey/123RF; 194 (CT scanner): Juice Images/Getty Images; 194 (airbag): Caspar Benson/fStop Images GmbH/Alamy Stock Photo; 194 (cosmonauts): NASA Photo/Alamy Stock Photo.

ILLUSTRATION CREDITS

ElectraGraphics, Paul Hampson, Dusan Petriçic

NOTES

NOTES

NOTES

NOTES

NOTES

NOTES

NOTES

NOTES

NOTES

NOTES

NOTES

NOTES